TravelAbility

TravelAbility

A GUIDE FOR PHYSICALLY DISABLED TRAVELERS IN THE UNITED STATES

Lois Reamy

Foreword by Arthur S. Abramson, M.D.
Photographs by Todd Weinstein

MACMILLAN PUBLISHING CO., INC.
New York

COLLIER MACMILLAN PUBLISHERS
London

Macmillan Publishing Co., Inc.
866 Third Avenue, New York, N.Y. 10022
Collier Macmillan Canada, Ltd.

The author has carefully researched this book, giving attention to the reliability and availability of the products and services mentioned. However, inclusion here of products and services does not imply endorsement thereof.

Because of the nature of the travel industry, change is imminent. On the subject of rates alone, travel products are likely to carry the line, "*Rates are subject to change.*" So too in this book: prices that were correct at press time could rise or fall, and they are given herein only as an indication of what you might expect to pay.

This book is not intended as a substitute for medical advice of physicians. The reader should regularly consult a physician in matters relating to his or her health and particularly in respect of any symptoms which may require diagnosis or medical attention.

Reader response is welcome.

Library of Congress Cataloging in Publication Data
Reamy, Lois.
TravelAbility.
Includes index.
1. United States—Description and travel—1960- —Guide-books. 2. Physically handicapped—United States—Recreation. I. Title.
E158.R39 917.3'04'926 78-13569
ISBN 0-02-601170-0

FIRST PRINTING 1978

Printed in the United States of America

To the readers and to my parents,
Alexander and Helen Muse Major Reamy.

CONTENTS

PART III Where to Go and Where to Stay

PART IV Getting Ready to Go

FOREWORD

It is pleasant to think about, participate in, and write about travel. Having done the thinking and participating in large measure, I am grateful to the author for giving me this opportunity for a small measure of writing.

Before preaching about my favorite hobby, I should establish my bona fides. The travel bug hit me over thirty years ago after I began using a wheelchair as my sole means of locomotion. I must admit that just prior to that time the army gave me a first taste of movement in the United States and overseas. I have since never sat still. I have been to every part of the Western Hemisphere from Alaska to Chile, from Nova Scotia to Brazil. In addition, I have been to every part of the world except Africa and intend to go there next year. I have traveled by train, by ship, by automobile, and by airplane. It was all done without walking a single step. It was fulfilling and, as a rule, not difficult. However, I would be less than candid if I said that the process was entirely free of problems. An uneventful life eventually must become dull for anyone. Traveling is never dull and always eventful. It is especially eventful for the disabled and a constant challenge to their problem-solving abilities, without which the disabled can never feel whole. It is a finishing school or a school of higher education for such abilities. One feels more whole after a trip because successful accomplishment is self-satisfying.

I had mentioned that there were problems. The first that comes to mind is the inability to see and do everything. The world is not entirely free of architectural barriers, whether man-made or fashioned by nature. My own view is that even the nondisabled do not see everything and that there is enough to see that is available. That is true almost everywhere. A ridiculous example is that I cannot climb Mount Everest, but neither can anyone else (with very rare exceptions). Fortunately, all of us can experience it. Acceptance of the inability to do everything is not in the nature of the Hindu concept of "divine resignation" but rather in keeping with the Bantu saying that "enough is as good as feast." After all, you experience nothing by staying at home for fear that there are a few things out of reach while traveling.

A related problem is the matter of attitude. There is more than a subtle distinction between being firm about your rights and being demanding and less than polite. It is not surprising that people who are extremely anxious to help get turned off under those circumstances. As this is true in response to the ablebodied so it is equally true for the disabled, but the disabled can afford it less. Travel provides not only places to go and things to see but also an association with people. In my experience, the overwhelming majority of people want to help, and it is with such unsolicited help that I have gotten places and seen things that would have been out of my reach. For instance, I visited the magnificent Escorial, near Madrid, the great palace of Philip II of Spain, the man responsible for the Spanish Armada. The architectural barriers were formidable and forbidding. Were it not for a guard who had lost an arm in the Spanish Civil War I would have admired only the exterior. Not only did he haul my chair up numerous flights of stairs, but he recruited many other willing hands. That has been my experience everywhere. Patience, warmth, and politeness pays off, and the world can be your oyster.

Most residual problems seem to be with questions of health and elimination. I have tried to answer these questions in the medical chapter of this book, but it is by no means comprehensive since not all possible questions were posed to me. There is no doubt about the wisdom of seeing one's physician prior to traveling nor about obtaining information from organizations whose interests are appropriate to your condition. These organizations have been listed. But every question cannot be answered. For instance, the problem of getting to a bathroom on an airplane when one is nonambulant. There are second best ways of handling this problem and some have been mentioned. Nevertheless, the first best way will eventually depend upon the good-will and cooperation of the airlines. Why can't a lightweight, folding, easily stored wheelchair be part of the equipment for any flight which carries an individual with such need? If this were done, the nonambulatory traveler could use any aisle seat and not be confined to the crowded approaches to the toilet. Such a traveler would not have to restrict fluids or think of other tricks to avoid elimination.

I have tried to paint a picture of the joys of traveling but have not hesitated to point out some of the problems. How can we know that we are having pleasure unless we can contrast it to some pain? Everyone has problems, but they lend spice to life.

—Arthur S. Abramson, M.D.

ACKNOWLEDGMENTS

First I wish to acknowledge the stars of this book, who are featured in the picture stories on these pages: Bob and June Arzt, Luceille Candeletti of the Travelers III agency in Fort Lee, New Jersey, Teri Feinstein, Rosemarie Kasper, Dorothy Ravior, Julius A. Shaw, and Janis Wilson. All permitted us to photograph them with the hope that others could learn by their example that travel is possible.

I am most grateful for the help and support of Bernard W. Albert of the Moss Rehabilitation Hospital in Philadelphia, William A. Blodgett, Al Chioda, Charles Contois of Handi-Cab of the Pacific, Charles Corn, Neil Hartbarger, Ray Dargan, Bonnie Gellman, Dr. C. C. Gullett, who is the medical director of TWA, James Hanifin, Al Hayes, Betty Hoffman of Wings on Wheels, Barbara Jacobson and Sharon Schleich of Flying Wheels Tours (FWT), Buddy Jennsen, Carol Munter, Beth Rashbaum, Joyce Seid, Jim Stone, William Sweigart, and Ronnie Trabman.

Also, Arnold Light, James Seix, and Murray Vidockler of the Society for the Advancement of Travel for the Handicapped (SATH); and the readers of *Paraplegia News* and *Accent* magazines and the SATH and FWT newsletters, who contributed travel tips, experiences, and information.

It is impossible to mention every one of the hundreds of persons who have contributed to the insight, research, and production of this book. They include personal friends and representatives of associations, federations, foundations, societies, state and federal government agencies, and suppliers of travel services. They include a full complement of editors, proofreaders, book designers, typesetters, and printers. I thank you here collectively.

Very special thanks go to the two men who share the byline and whose invaluable contributions make this the book that it is: Dr. Arthur S. Abramson, chairman of rehabilitation medicine at Albert Einstein College of Medicine, who wrote me in June 1977, "Being a wheelchair traveler myself, I have had very few problems in my extensive travels throughout the country. That may be because I adapt to constraints by my willingness to accept less than the whole thing. There is enough left for anyone's enjoyment. . . . If your book will increase the vistas of the handicapped, it would be worthwhile." Thank you for your interest and encouragement as well as for the experience and knowledge that are evident in the Foreword and the medical chapter.

Todd Weinstein, whose fine photographs enhance this book. Thank you for the human concern that initially attracted you to this project and ultimately made the long, hard photography sessions a pleasure. And for being supportive when my research and arrangements seemed an impossible task.

INTRODUCTION

You may be toying cautiously with the idea of flying to Maine or Oregon to visit your daughter and grandchildren, or signing up impulsively for a wilderness survival course. You may feel only a vague need to get away—enjoy a change of air—or have a very concrete itinerary all mapped out. Whatever your motive, you have the travel bug or you would not be reading this book.

The fact that you have a temporary or long-term physical disability does not mean that you do not have the ability to travel, for if you are able to get around by cane, crutches, wheelchair, or with uncertain steps plus a strong arm to lean on, you probably can travel.

To mobility and the inclination to travel, add the right frame of mind, financial means, leisure time, and know-how, and you have TravelAbility.

This book is about that know-how.

Do you know how to find a hotel with barrier-free rooms?

How to figure out what your trip will cost?

How to get selective information about almost any place in the United States?

How to find the most accommodating airline?

How to find a companion, medical aide, or nurse to accompany you as an attendant or traveling companion?

How to choose a travel agent, or even that there are agents who specialize in bookings for disabled clients?

How to get great travel bargains by choosing from the options offered on a typical tour package (versus a tour designed for handicapped groups or expensive independent arrangements)?

Whom to call in an emergency? How to find a doctor away from home? How not to lose your medicine or luggage?

This book answers these and other questions. It is based on the theory that many disabled persons have never traveled because they did not know it was possible. This is, therefore, a primer, setting forth a methodology that can be applied to any travel within the United States. Picture stories of actual travelers checking in at an airport, boarding a plane, claiming their luggage, taking a bus or train, renting a car, cruising, or checking into a hotel allow you to project yourself into similar situations.

Some of you may be well traveled—you already know the ropes of tipping and packing—but perhaps you are planning your first trip since having suffered a stroke or broken a leg. You can catch up here on the special services and facilities available to anyone with limited mobility.

Heretofore, while travel was possible, it was difficult. Disabled travelers were—and in some cases, still are—pioneers in this last frontier of travel. Only within the past two or three years have facilities and services been provided for disabled travelers to any extent. Improvements are due partly to recent state and federal legislation, partly to civic awareness, and partly to the demands of the disabled communities. The turnaround has taken place, and while there is a long way to go, consider just this one point as a sign of progress: a 1966 issue of a hotel industry magazine reported that the United States in that year had 60 barrier-free hotel *rooms* (in 28 states). Today, there are more than 2,000 *locations* (some with two or more wheelchair units) listed by the major hotel and motel chains alone. Many, many small chains and independents also have accessible rooms. (A tax incentive of up to $25,000 often encourages hoteliers to modify their properties.)

In order to provide a detailed approach to travel, this book is limited to the United States, with only an occasional international reference and an appendix of international sources.

While some other places (Scandinavian countries, England, and the Netherlands, among others) have made notable strides toward a barrier-free society—either architecturally or attitudinally or both—disabled foreigners visiting here have also commented on positive efforts in America. In a survey made in Sweden in 1977 by a commission concerned with handicapped travelers, one wheelchair traveler emphasized the excellent and considerate service he had received on domestic flights within the United States.

The U.S airlines are working toward better accommodation, but some individuals and the Civil Aeronautics Board say they are not moving fast enough. Keep in mind that in many European countries if your appearance even suggests a disability you may be asked for a permit or doctor's certificate (usually required by U.S. carriers only for medically related conditions) and may be required to use an ambulance for getting to and onto the plane. Disabled travelers on some foreign airlines are asked to sign a waiver of rights, declaring that they will not hold the airline liable in the event of an accident. Both U.S. and European carriers are trying to standardize procedures that will make interline air travel more uniform. Some European lines, which require disabled persons to have a permit, are discussing a standardized permit that would be honored by them all.

A major problem in air travel is the design of the standard aircraft, with aisles too narrow and lavatories too small to accommodate wheelchairs.

"You would think that *they* could make accessible airplanes if they could send men to the moon," I happened to remark to a friend.

"Somehow," said my friend, "that seemed easier."

Ripping out whole rows of seats and enlarging lavatories on a plane is not as easy as turning your garage into a family room, but we are assured by several airlines as well as by aircraft manufacturers that barrier-free features will be a reality with the next generation of aircraft that comes along in the mid-eighties, if those features are not introduced before.

The one single thing that will bring the greatest response from the various segments of the travel industry—the hotels, motels, airlines, attractions, and the like—is demand. And only you can make it happen by traveling. By so doing you will effect improvements through the simple law of supply and demand. At the present time, disabled travelers are not taking full advantage of industry efforts, but perhaps that is because they do not know what facilities exist. Amtrak has estimated that only about 3,500 handicapped passengers traveled by train in 1977, although last year special cars were added to accommodate them. Holiday Inns, which is working toward a goal of one wheelchair unit per 100 rooms, has mentioned that while the demand is small, the company likes to have such units available. The marketing vice president at one of the airlines says that only 400,000 of its 34 million annual passengers (or one per 85) are disabled. Yet at least 20 million, or one of every 10, Americans are physically disabled (the figure swells to 36 million when you include persons who are blind, deaf, mentally retarded, or have other impairments).

While the travel industry continues to get its act together through such efforts as those of the airlines to standardize procedures and the noteworthy collection and dissemination of information by the Society for the Advancement of Travel for the Handicapped (SATH), an industry-level clearinghouse, one of the greatest obstacles to travel is at the local level. How are you going to get from the airport into town? Are the sidewalks at your destination properly ramped? Are the museums and those atmospheric little restaurants accessible?

Many architectural and attitudinal barriers do exist. One could write a book about what is not possible, but why? This book deals with the possible. A spokesman for the Mystic Seaport in Connecticut, where about one-half of the maritime museum buildings are wheelchair accessible, has observed that "the degree of accessibility often depends on the attitude of handicapped individuals, some of whom will let no barrier stop them."

If travel within the United States is not duck soup, it can go smoothly if you plan your strategy in advance. Once you've practiced the ins and outs of travel in this country, you may want to consider going abroad. Or if your heart is set on a foreign trip for starters, you might consider taking a group tour or going with a friend or relative who is an experienced traveler. But for most inexperienced travelers, it will probably be advisable to start your traveling in this country.

The United States probably offers the world's greatest range of vacation possibilities to ablebodied and disabled travelers alike. Somewhere it is always winter. Somewhere it is always summer. You can enjoy sunny beaches in January or glacier-viewing in June. Our cities have museums galore. You can hole up at a nearby state park or go all out at a distant luxury resort. You can sample Creole or Cajun cuisine in New Orleans, Chinese in San Francisco or New York, and the famous Maine lobster all along the salty New England coast. The Grand Canyon, the New York skyline at dusk, the volcanoes of Hawaii and the Golden Gate Bridge are world famous. People travel from far and wide just to view them. "See America First" may be a cliché, but it's not such a bad idea.

Your vacation need not cost more—or much more—than anyone else's. You may not need expensive independent arrangements. It's likely that you, too, can mainstream by picking and choosing among the bargain package tours and matching their hotel options to a list of accessible hotels. An airline may recommend that you'll be more comfortable flying first-class (and well you might), but you can always say no. If you can't travel alone, consider that a companion can accompany you free on interstate Greyhound and Trailways trips. Your hotel choice from grand to modest can pretty much be determined by your preferences and budget. Several tour operators specialize in independent and group arrangements for handicapped travelers at prices somewhat above the average tour price: you pay extra for the extras—vans with lifts for sightseeing, for example, or a medically trained escort—and that's pretty much the same everywhere.

When Hal O'Leary, director of the Winter Park (Colorado) Handicap Skiing Program, called to tell me about their summer activities, such as float trips on the Colorado River and camping at Devil's Thumb Ranch, it was a breakthrough in my research. Prior to that I had felt that at best the possibilities were limited, but that day I realized that if float trips, camping, and mountaineering, as well as rugged winter sports, were possible, then almost anything is. I subsequently heard about wilderness survival courses conducted by the renowned Outward Bound School, horseback riding, and other possible impossible dreams.

In my research, I have traveled more than 14,000 miles, making one trip by each major mode of transportation with a person in a wheelchair. These are all persons who lead independent lives—drive their own cars, hold responsible jobs, run their own homes—but who, with two exceptions, are unable to take so much as one step alone.

Every trip had been carefully worked out. In the case of the two longer trips, Bob and June had methodically planned their own Hawaiian vacation, and Dot's cruise had been arranged by Flying Wheels Tours. Except for the car trip, there were no mix-ups to speak of. In that instance, although a two-door car with hand controls had been ordered, when we arrived at the car rental station, a four-door LTD with hand controls was waiting. No two-door car was available for a switch, and if a photographer and I had not been along to assist with the chair, Julius could not have used the car.

Other problems were only minor and were corrected on the spot. For example, while the hotel room assigned to Bob and June in Hawaii was barrier-free, it was a long haul to/from the elevator in the 1,900-room Sheraton-Waikiki; but before the bellman even left their room they were assigned a more conveniently located one.

Travel is increasingly difficult as the degree of disablement increases. And yet a quadriplegic friend of mine, a disabled veteran who uses a powered chair and travels with the aide who normally cares for him, successfully made two trips from New York to California, as well as trips from New York to Las Vegas and from New York to Hawaii, within one nine-month period in 1977. Prior to that, he had not even attempted to travel for many years. Now he is talking about a world tour.

Start watching at airports, hotels, theaters, and other public places for the International Symbol of Access, a stylized wheelchair identifying paths, corridors, doorways, lavatories, elevators, parking lots, switches, drinking fountains, telephones, and ramps that comply with the barrier-free specifications established in 1969 by the International Committee on Technical Aids, Housing, and Transportation of Rehabilitation International. The symbol tells you at a glance that this facility is wheelchair accessible. When located at ramp side you'll know that the grade is no greater than one inch in twelve, for example; affixed to a door you'll know that it clears at twenty-eight inches.

The wheelchair is frequently mentioned herein as a measure of accessibility, for if a wheelchair can gain entrance, there can be few or no architectural obstacles of the kind which might also hinder persons relying on canes, crutches, walkers, or who walk with difficulty. At times, however, distance can be your greatest obstacle, especially if walking is a problem. Ambulatory persons should remember to inquire in advance about the distances at airline terminals, for example, and if the corridors are too long, to request a wheelchair.

While this book was researched primarily for physically disabled persons—those with locomotion problems—whenever information surfaced that might be useful to blind, deaf, or mentally retarded individuals, I have included it.

Many blind persons do not consider themselves disabled, but rather inconvenienced. Some who are disabled maintain that they are not handicapped; others consider themselves handicapped but not disabled. The Canadians often use the word disadvantaged, but in the United States that has economic and social connotations. Americans tend to make the words handicapped and disabled into nouns: *the* disabled, *the* handicapped. The British, on the other hand, as Lady Hamilton of the Disabled Living Foundation has pointed out to me, insist that *handicapped* and *disabled* be used only as adjectives—I agree—thus stressing a person's being, not his capability. Even so, the British often use *invalid* interchangeably with *handicapped.*

A word which disabled persons sometimes use is *nondisabled.* As a writer, I see it as hopelessly clumsy, but at the same time I recognize that to the persons who coined it, being disabled is the norm, and it is appropriate to use negatives to convey deviance from that norm. My own choice of language for this book is somewhat more conventional than that.

Rather than constantly repeat "persons with limited mobility," I use the words *disabled* and *handicapped* interchangeably here, with apologies to those who object to either word.

Everybody has his own definition of the word *handicapped.* The Federal Aviation Administration uses it to describe anyone who might need assistance in evacuating an airplane in an emergency. The Department of Health, Education and Welfare generally uses it to describe anyone with a physical or mental impairment which substantially limits one or more major life activities.

When I use the word I am thinking here primarily of those of you with limited physical mobility who need special arrangements when you travel. This book is for you.

Happy landing.

"I'll give you some folders on Knott's Berry Farm and one or two other places, and you can decide what you'd like to do," a travel agent tells her client (page 18).

PART I

TRIP PLANNING

1

HOW GOOD A TRAVELER ARE YOU?

People travel to meet new people, gain new experiences, see different places and things, and even to try new foods. Traveling is a break in routine. This break enables you to see yourself in new situations, thus gaining a different slant on life's possibilities and your own potential. In fact, someone has called travel the ultimate recreation (i.e., re-creation). It allows you to stretch the range of your imagination through experience. TV, books, and movies do that up to a point, but at best they only present someone else's impressions of the volcano, the Grand Canyon, or a museum exhibition. There is no substitute for the real thing.

Although you are visiting new places, *you* are the constant in the situation, and of course your physical and emotional needs and preferences remain the same wherever you are. This book is designed to help you make travel plans that put *you* in the picture.

Everyone needs to feel at home away from home. Some people do it by taking a few familiar photographs along to put on the bedside table. You can do it by making the kinds of arrangements that make you feel comfortable and secure. For example, if you don't like being alone—not even at home—then do not plan to travel alone. You will feel happier with family or friends or on a group tour. If you need a bathroom door wide enough for your wheelchair to clear, do not assume that the hotel door will be wide enough. Find out for sure from the management.

Travel, according to the census bureau definition, is a trip of at least 100 miles from home. But travel really has more to do with your intent than with distance. You hardly think of a drive of 150 miles to keep a doctor's appointment as travel, and yet you would consider a shorter trip for a week at a resort as vacation travel.

You are ready to travel when you feel the itch to break your routine and place yourself in a new setting—in a word, to expand your horizons.

But what makes a successful traveler?

First and foremost, a successful traveler must have a basic trust in his or her own ability to deal with new and changing circumstances. He must be flexible. Bear in mind that nothing is foolproof. No matter how carefully you plot and plan, something can always go wrong. Many factors are outside your control. The more complicated your trip, the more segmented your journey, the more times you change planes and check into and out of hotels, the greater the chance that adjustments will have to be made.

There are six qualities which we believe a successful traveler should have or strive for: physical stamina, flexibility, affability, sense of humor, patience and resourcefulness. In fact, these are qualities that stand you in good stead in your everyday life. This exercise is designed to show you whether you possess these qualities in good measure, to help you think about yourself as a voyager/traveler. If you'd like to evaluate yourself, decide how you would react in the situations described below.

POOR	FAIR	GREAT	
___	___	___	Physical Stamina. No situation described—only you and your doctor can determine what degree of travel you are physically up to. (See Medical Questions and Answers in Part IV.)
___	___	___	Flexibility—ability to adapt or adjust to new situations and unexpected changes.

POOR FAIR GREAT

Situation 1: You are visiting your son and daughter-in-law, whose routine is totally different from yours. For example, they have dinner at six o'clock in order to put their young children to bed at eight. You never eat before eight at home. (There is no reason why you must eat at eight, it is not built into a medication timetable or anything. Just habit.) Do you start eating a light lunch so you'll be ready for an early dinner? Or do you insist upon sticking to your own schedule?

Situation 2: Because of dicey weather, all flights from Boston are cancelled on the day you were to leave on vacation. Do you take it as a bad omen and cancel the trip? Or do you call your travel agent and/or hotel (and other ground services that you have booked) and advise them of the delay?

___ ___ ___ Affability—an ease and interest in dealing with people, especially new acquaintances.

Situation 1: As you are tooling down the street on your new scooter-type chair, a man with a limp says to you, "That looks like a fine machine." Do you say, "Thank you, sir," and push right along? Or do you tell him that it's new but that it has already changed your life in terms of mobility, and let the conversation proceed from there?

Situation 2: Your office has a cafeteria where you usually have lunch. Do you generally eat alone or have you gotten to know your co-workers, with whom you enjoy small talk over lunch?

___ ___ ___ Sense of Humor—not your joke-telling talents, but your ability to laugh at yourself and at life instead of feeling awkward, ignorant, or embarrassed.

POOR FAIR GREAT

Situation 1: The most accessible seats in the theater for a play you are attending happen to be the box seats. And that's where the usher seats you. Do you feel that everyone must be looking at you and try to disappear into the woodwork? Or do you feel quietly amused as well as delighted with your great vantage point?

Situation 2: Your wheelchair is damaged in flight. The airline offers to lend you theirs to use on your weekend vacation in San Francisco while yours is being repaired. So you wheel around in a chair with "Property of Air X" stenciled all over it. Wise guys keep calling, "Stop, thief," and "Hey, stew," and the like. Do you exchange pleasantries with them and keep rolling on? Or do you feel self-conscious?

___ ___ ___ Patience—the ability to accept unavoidable delays and not be demanding or ruffled over situations that are out of your control.

Situation: On a trip from Washington to New York, your train halts halfway between Washington and Baltimore, where there is a power failure. You sit and sit and sit while a diesel locomotive is dispatched from Washington to tow the train. Meanwhile, you are afraid that the New York hotel where you have a reservation will not hold your room. Would you throw a large-scale tantrum? Drink yourself silly in the club car? Sit quietly and simmer? Or ask the conductor if Amtrak could notify your hotel of your late arrival?

___ ___ ___ Resourcefulness—your ability, on your own, to find more than one way to solve a problem.

> *Situation:* You cannot take your motorized chair in a conventional taxi. What if the ambulette you have engaged to meet you at the airport is not there and you can't reach the company by phone? Do you panic and immediately envision a lifetime spent in the airport, or does your mind turn to the possible alternatives, such as asking the airline Special Service desk if it can help arrange transportation to your hotel, or calling the hotel and telling them your predicament to see if they can send a car or van, or calling a local limo service whose number your travel agent has given you as a backup?
>
> This exercise, in fact, is a good technique to practice before you leave home. Determine in advance how you might deal with any problem you can envision. List everything that could go wrong on a sheet of paper headed "What if . . ."
>
> What if I lose my medicine? I can (1) pack the most important or hard-to-find medicines in my hand luggage to reduce the risk, (2) take a copy of the prescription from my doctor (which I can have rewritten by a doctor licensed in the state I am visiting), so that I can have it filled at a drugstore, or (3) I can always phone my doctor and have him telephone the prescription to a local doctor, whom I may consult.
>
> What if I lose my airline ticket? What if the people in my tour group turned out to be a bunch of turkeys? What if I miss a flight? What if I hate my hotel? What if my car breaks down? What if my traveler's checks are lost or stolen? What if I run out of money?

There's nothing like being prepared, having ready solutions to problems before they arise. If you are not an experienced traveler, and especially if you are anxiety-prone, before your trip, make up a list of realistic problems and work out the answers with your friends, family, and travel agent. Do not do this exercise until you have read this book, which offers solutions as well as ways to avoid certain problems in the first place. Prevention is still the best cure.

VACATION PREFERENCES

Now that you have some idea of how good a traveler you are, and keeping your personality type, stamina, and budget in mind, start thinking about the best vacation for you—a visit to a nearby friend, a car trip or a cruise, a few days in a city or a resort. Once you have determined what kinds of holidays best suit you, consider your likes and dislikes. Take this preference test.

Do I like my vacations to be:

1. *Structured or unstructured?*

By structured we mean with a timetable of events, such as you would find on many guided tours. Unstructured, of course, means that you fill in the fine points in your own schedule as you go along. If a daily routine makes you comfortable at home, you are probably the structured type. Note that some vacations, such as a cruise, can be either. A cruise can be structured, complete with a social director and an agenda that begins with yoga or exercise on deck at sunup and goes through a day hour by hour: two o'clock art lecture, three o'clock bingo, four o'clock tea and a fashion show. It can also be unstructured, if you prefer to disregard the fun and games and spend your time sleeping late, sunning on deck, and playing bridge with friends.

2. *Solitary or convivial?*

Again a cruise offers either possibility. You decide. Even on a cruise ship with more than a thousand passengers it is possible to find your own, alone place in the sun or a quiet deck where you can contemplate the sunset while most passengers are living it up at the happy hour inside.

3. *Serene or hustle and bustle?*

This obviously has to do with the setting. If your idea of a great vacation is to sit on a riverbank and watch the boats glide by you might make out very well with a cottage at a state park, but you wouldn't enjoy a swinging weekend in Vegas. If the last thing you want on vacation is peace and quiet, then go to Las Vegas or San Juan or a big city.

4. *Familiar or different?*
Some vacation possibilities offer either. A resort in Hawaii would rate as different (unless you lived there, or course). If you live in Virginia, The Homestead resort in the Virginia mountains might seem pleasantly familiar.

5. *Solo or in company?*
If you'd really rather be on your own, you might be uncomfortable on a group tour, where everyone is sociable. But you would make out very well on a driving trip, a self-guided tour, or even a cruise where, even if sociability is a virtue, it is not an entrance requirement.

As a potential traveler, *you* have choices. You have a right to plan your vacation to order. This book contains information to help you do that. It is up to you to put yourself in the picture. If you have never traveled and want to check out your hunches about your strengths and preferences, you might make some test runs. Plan an overnight stay in a nearby city or resort. If you have never flown and would be flying on your ultimate vacation, make a short plane trip. If you've never traveled alone and think you might like it, try it first on a short solo excursion.

A WORD TO THE WISE

No matter how great their intentions are, the people serving you in the travel industry (from your own travel agent to the airline personnel, Amtrak red cap, hotel staff, or tour guides) are serving a very large audience, and they cannot be expected to know all of your needs. Only you know what makes you comfortable, and if you are going to be a successful traveler—even though you have all the other necessary traits—you must make your needs known firmly and politely. Be willing to ask questions and to request help when necessary. Be pleasant and straightforward about your special needs. That will not only help make your trip successful but will smooth the way for other travelers who come after you.

2

WHY PLAN A TRIP?

Could you imagine starting off on a long car trip with no road map, only a vague idea of where you were going, and not even a remote idea of how much gas was in your tank or how much money was in your pocket?

Probably not. Yet every year millions of vacationers set forth with only the foggiest notion of where they are going, what they will do there, what their hotel will be like, where it is situated in terms of the attractions, what amenities it offers, or even how much the trip will cost. These same vacationers often travel with a great deal of unnecessary anxiety, and they certainly cannot avail themselves of all that the place has to offer. Trip planning is essential to the success of any trip. Don't go anywhere without it. You'll arrive at your destination ready to relax and have a good time, free from last-minute details and fear of the unknown.

Trip planning involves deciding when, where, how, and with whom you wish to travel; selecting and working with a travel agent; choosing between an organized tour and independent travel; setting up itineraries; and determining trip costs.

Planning is one of the most enjoyable stages of a vacation. Once you get involved in your trip you can begin to project yourself into a new setting—being met by your grandchildren at an airport halfway across the continent, soaking up the sun on the Florida Gulf Coast, or whatever.

For anyone with a mobility problem, trip planning is super essential. The limited facilities for the disabled demand that you plan ahead or risk compromising your dream vacation or, in an extreme case, not going at all.

Case in point: Hertz, Avis, and National have only a few cars with hand controls at given locations. If you do not reserve early you may not get one.

Case in point: A cruise ship that accommodates wheelchairs may have only a limited number of staterooms that do, and those are often reserved well in advance.

Case in point: Some of the most attractive hotels are often hard to book. One woman who uses a wheelchair is taking her young nephews to Disney World in several months and has already reserved rooms. Careful reconnaissance revealed that one of the hotels right on the grounds, the Polynesian Village, is connected with the Magic Kingdom by monorail, while the Contemporary Hotel there is not. Therefore, although many hotels and motels in the Disney World/Orlando area are wheelchair-proof, this woman has her heart set on the Polynesian, and has wisely done enough pretrip planning to ensure she gets what best suits her.

Trip planning begins with an idea as rudimentary as the need to get away for a few days, or as precise as wanting to visit your brother in Atlanta or see the New England countryside at the height of the fall foliage season.

Talk over your idea with friends or family. Who wants to go along? Get brochures from commercial companies, tourist offices, and travel agencies. Bone up. How much can you spend, when can you go, and how long can you stay? Consult a travel agent unless you have decided on a simple trip like going to a nearby state park or driving upstate to visit friends.

The time allowance for preplanning varies. You can probably work out a trip from Chicago to California in two or three weeks if it is not at a peak travel season, such as Thanksgiving or Christmas, and has no unusual features. On the other hand, one travel agent asked a quadriplegic who wants to tour the outer reaches of South America to allow at least a year to arrange it.

Careful advance planning:

• Alleviates anxieties about the unknown (Who will meet me? What if I run out of money? Suppose my room is inaccessible?).

• Allows for a contingency plan. You should have the phone number of a backup limousine service, for example, and you should know in advance what's available in the way of sightseeing tours by bus or taxi, should driving a rental car in a strange city not work out.

• Assures you of a place to sleep. Even if you are moseying across country in your own car with no set itinerary, be sure to take the directories of hotels and motels with accessible rooms along and call ahead for your next night's accommodation. The same woman who has booked the Polynesian Village months in advance recounts a driving adventure to Grand Canyon country she had with an ablebodied woman and a disabled man. Upon leaving the canyon they chose a route that showed not a single motel in the directories they had been relying on. Within hours they were driving into the night with no motels in sight. They finally hit Page, Arizona, but everything was full up. These unsinkable travelers had read that strangers in distress sometimes got to sleep in the local jail, so they turned themselves in. The police put the man up at a monastery and the two women at a hospital. It makes a good story, but the weary travelers were tired and hungry and not without some unquiet moments.

Careful planning also:

• Enables you to "have it in writing." Get a confirmation letter stating that your hotel or cruise ship is barrier-free, that a special diet can be served, that oxygen is available, or whatever. This reinforces any future complaint for promises not delivered on. One wheelchair passenger carried a letter assuring him that he could go ashore at Bermuda. When the ship anchored—rather than docked—there and an officer told him he'd have to stay on board, the passenger asked to see the captain, presented the letter, and was sent ashore with dispatch by launch.

• Helps you get more out of your vacation. Talk to people who have been there. Read. Study maps. *Know Before You Go* could well be your motto. For once you arrive you must come to grips quickly with a brand-new place. The more you know about it the more comfortable you will be staying there and the more the local population will respond to you and help you.

• Lets you advise the railway, airline, busline in advance that you will be traveling and will need assistance getting down to the tracks and onto the train, or boarding the bus or plane.

• Gives you time to work with a professional highway route planning service, such as those offered by auto clubs and oil companies, for mapping the best car trip.

Schedule your pretrip agenda to include a doctor's visit if advisable, and an overhaul of car, wheelchair, respirator, or other equipment you rely on. Buy spare parts, get your tickets, letters of confirmation, and traveler's checks in order before the last minute. Secure your house and let friends and family know how to reach you.

THE TRAVEL AGENT

A Day in the Life of a Travel Agent

If you have never consulted a travel agent, you might imagine yourself in Rosemarie's place in the typical session that follows.

Scene: A travel agency in New Jersey. Rosemarie (R), *a new client, has just entered in her wheelchair. Luceille* (L), *the travel agent, greets her.*

L: How did you hear about us?

R: From a disabled friend who has used your agency.

L: Good.

R: Have you arranged many trips for handicapped persons?

L: Quite a few, including cruises, and trips to California and Florida. We aren't afraid to work with the disabled traveler, and we like to do as much as we can to help everyone see the world.

R: I'm glad you've arranged trips to California because I'm planning a trip to L.A. I have friends out there.

L: Would you like to go to Disneyland?

R: Yes. I'd like to make that our headquarters.

L. Okay. Fine. Ever been before?

R: Never.

L: Could you stay at least a week?

R: Yes. As a matter of fact, I had in mind about a week and I'd be going on a Saturday.

L: Fine. If you can stay at least a week, there are better airfares. [Consults the *Official Airline Guide* of fares and schedules.] We have a Freedom Fare now, which you have to purchase in advance. On it you have to stay at least a week and not more than thirty days. And then we have one called the Tour Basing Fare at approximately the same cost—maybe a dollar or so difference—but to qualify you must prepay a certain amount of your hotel arrangements as well as at least sixty-five dollars of either car rental or sightseeing. The saving is small and in your case it might be better *not* to prepay but to take the Freedom Fare in case the hotel doesn't work out for you and you want to move to another hotel, or your friends say, "No, we really want you to come and stay with us," or you decide, "I've seen enough of Disneyland. Now I want to go somewhere else in California." I leave it up to you, however.

R: The Freedom Fare sounds fine.

L: On that fare if you were going to make any changes or revisions it would have to be done two weeks prior to your outgoing flight and prior to your return. Now which airport do you prefer?

R: Newark.

L: I'm sure you'd much rather have a nonstop flight.

R: Definitely.

L: Can you leave any time of day?

R: Not really. I'd like to go by noon at the latest, but yet not too early in the morning.

L: Well, we have an American Airlines flight at 12 noon that gets into L.A. at 2:29 Los Angeles time. A five-and-a-half-hour flight. Lunch is served on board. Now, that's going out on a Saturday. What about coming home?

R: I'd better plan on a Sunday.

L: Fine. You'd be staying the one week the Freedom Fare requires plus one day. The American flight from L.A. leaves at 1:30 in the afternoon and gets you into Newark at 9:32.

R: I don't know any disabled persons who've flown that particular airline. United and TWA seem to have the names. Do you know if American serves disabled individuals?

L: First of all, we'll call them and tell them you're disabled. We'll also check on whether or not there's room for you on the flight, because sometimes airlines limit the number of disabled persons permitted on one flight.

R: Well, I'll be traveling with my mother.

L: Okay. Offhand I would say yes for American. Perhaps they haven't done as much publicizing as some of the other carriers but that doesn't mean they haven't transported disabled passengers or aren't willing to do so. I'll double-check and make sure. We do know that United and TWA are very interested in helping you to travel, but so are other carriers. I'll call my sales rep at American and tell him what you require.

R: As I said, I'll be traveling with my mother. She's a senior citizen so she really won't be able to offer that much help. One thing we'll need is special skycap [porter] help with the luggage. Can the airline arrange that?

L: Yes. They can put the request in their computer when we make your reservation. I can also ask them to Telex L.A. so that their people out there know you need assistance with your luggage. To back it up, I'll also tell the sales office.

R: Of course I need to have the wheelchair arranged. And I will need to have help getting in and out of the airplane seat.

L: Are you willing to have your wheelchair put in the baggage compartment and use the airline's?

R: Some airlines I've flown on have insisted on it. But I would really prefer entering the plane in my own chair if possible.

L: All right, we'll try. If it's not possible I'll let you know. American will probably want to preboard you and get you all settled in your seat before the other passengers board.

R: What type of airplane is it?

L: That'll be a DC-10. Have you ever flown on one? No? It's like a short, fat version of the Boeing 747. It has two aisles and seating on the sides where there are two seats abreast. I think you and your mother will like that. In fact, we'll request a seating assignment for you. Would you rather be in the smoking or nonsmoking section?

R: Nonsmoking.

L: I'll request a seat for you right from the beginning.

R. We've usually found that one of the front rows is best.

L: We'll try. Most of the time the airlines will not put you on an exit row, but many times they'll give you a bulkhead seat [the front row of any section of the aircraft]. Let's leave it up to American and see what comes back in the computer. Then we'll look on their seating chart to see if those seats are okay with you. I want to remind you that all luggage and your wheelchair must have baggage tags with the name the same way it's written on your airline ticket. You and your mother are each allowed two standard suitcases, and your chair goes free. Where would you like to stay?

R: At Disneyland if possible.

L: Let's try one of the major hotel or motel chains. [She takes a motel directory from the shelf.] Now out there Motel X has a number of locations close to Disneyland. We'll find one with the wheelchair symbol, and then I'll telephone and get the rates. Would you prefer a twin-bed room or two double beds?

R: Two double beds.

L: When we request the room we'll also guarantee a late arrival. Your flight does get in at 2:30 but if the plane should be a little bit late or if the transfer to the motel should be a little bit longer than you anticipated or you should stop off to see your friends first thing . . . we'll just guarantee a late arrival in the name of our agency.

R: We'd like a motel with an adjacent restaurant. This helps in bad weather and it's great for breakfast.

L: Good idea. We'll call and request a room that can accommodate a wheelchair, preferably ground floor, and then we'll back it up with a letter. I'd feel better having it in writing, and I will request a written reply so that we all understand each other.

R: Good. We'd like a motel in walking distance of Disneyland.

L: (Laughing.) A short walk?

R: My mother is pretty good at walking but I'd like something within a couple of blocks.

L: [Consulting the motel directory.] It says that this motel is located right next door to Disneyland and offers free transportation to the theme park every half-hour. We'd better find out just what kind of transportation that is and if it would be convenient for you. Now they say they're located right next door, but let's make sure they aren't too far away from the front entrance because "right next door" could mean one side of Disneyland while the entrance is on the other side.

R: Is the motel air-conditioned?

L: Let's see. Yes.

R: Good. I don't have a tremendous tolerance for hot weather.

L: The rates are listed so let's see what's available.

R: I wouldn't want to go much higher than thirty or thirty-five dollars a day.

L: It's good you tell me. We need to know your budget. This way we don't waste your time or other people's by trying to get accommodations and not having them right. For about thirty-four dollars a night you can probably get just what you want. We will always give you our own voucher [the agency coupon guaranteeing payment] when you travel.

R: Does the Los Angeles airport have jetways [telescoping corridors connecting the terminal with the airplane]?

L: Yes. Now the ground transportation and the transfer from airport to hotel are the areas that will take time to work out. You say you have friends in L.A.?

R: Yes. But I don't have a commitment from them yet as far as transportation is concerned. They may meet us and take us around some, but I'd like a backup.

L: There are a few transportation services we can try. I'll call the Gray Line because they have sightseeing as well as airport transfers. And then we have a friend who is a TWA pilot and happens to be on the L.A. route at this time. I'll ask him to check around. Perhaps there's an ambulette or taxi company I'm not aware of that works with disabled individuals. There are also wholesalers and tour operators who work with disabled groups, and maybe they can give us a line on someone who offers the service we're looking for. Now, do you mind transferring from your chair to a conventional taxi?

R: Not if I have to. I'll also need transportation such as taxis to go from one point in L.A. to another. I want to sightsee, and again I—

L: You don't drive? Neither of you?

R: We wouldn't want to in a strange city. Besides visiting friends and Disneyland, I'd like to see Knott's Berry Farm and take the Universal City Studio Tour and—

L: I do know that an accessibility guide to Los Angeles and the attractions is published by the Junior League. I don't know if you have time to write for a copy, but perhaps you could call when you arrive and pick it up. [See state listings in Part III, Section 3 of this book.] I'll give you some folders on Knott's Berry Farm and one or two other places, and you can decide what you'd like to do, and we'll see if any of the organized sightseeing tours are accessible.

R: Ground transportation is always the biggest problem.

L: That's true. But it's improving. Now how much time do you want to spend in Disneyland?

R: Two or three days.

L: Well, you can purchase ticket books for one- or two-day admissions that include a number of attractions, but I suggest you wait until you're out there, because, first off, you might decide that you aren't interested in certain attractions, and second, some might not be accessible to you. You can always purchase your admission to Disneyland itself and to single attractions as they come along. The price is the same whether you buy the books here or there. It's just a convenience to buy them here. It would be too bad to pay for something you couldn't use.

R: That's a good idea. I've been to Disney World in Florida and found a number of features that weren't possible unless you had someone to carry you. I'd still recommend Disney World for disabled persons, however. I loved it. But we did come home with quite a few unused tickets.

L: Would you give me a note on Disney World when you have time? Also on your California trip when you return? This could help me plan trips for others.

R: Sure. How soon can you arrange this trip? I'd like to go as soon as possible.

L: I can book your flights and motel right now, but if I have a minimum of two weeks I can get the confirmation I want in writing.

R: That's fair enough. What is your agency fee?

L: We have none.

R: No fee?

L: No fee. There is no service charge. We work on commissions paid by the airlines, hotels, and sightseeing companies. If you were to make all the reservations, all the long distance calls, and write a number of checks, you would still pay the same price as if you used an agent, and we do all the work for you.

R: That's very interesting. I wasn't aware of it.

L: Most people aren't. They just assume there's a fee. Consequently many people are afraid to come to a travel agency because they think it's going to cost them, when, in fact, most of the time we can save you money because we know the latest money-saving fares. We also save you time. We write the airline tickets right here. As a matter of fact, I'd be more than happy to mail the tickets to you and you can send us the check. If you want to use a credit card you can.

R: I was wondering about that.

L: We have no choice over which credit cards an airline will accept, but almost all airlines take all the major credit cards, and so do the major hotel chains, although I must say that most hotels want the deposit by check. If you were buying a prepackaged tour and paying in advance, then you could use a credit card. I can give you a quick approximation now of what the trip will cost. If we use the Freedom Fare, it is at this point [June 1977] 350 dollars per person round trip, tax included. And if we can hold the motel at 34 dollars a night I would say that the airfare for you and your mother and two nights' deposit at the hotel would be . . . ohhh . . . 768 dollars. Now because you are on a Freedom Fare you have to purchase your tickets in advance, and there would be a cancellation penalty. I'm wondering about insurance, especially for your wheelchair, as well as your baggage. You might consider insurance. First, you could check your homeowner's policy to see if it covers your chair and the articles you would be carrying with you. I'll give you a brochure on trip cancellation insurance to look over and see whether or not you want insurance. It's up to you. I'll also check to see if there's a cancellation penalty, should you have to cancel the motel at the last minute. Sometimes—especially in a busy season—the hotel or motel will want one night's deposit as a cancellation penalty. If any kind of cancellation penalty is involved, we often suggest you take only enough insurance to cover what you would stand to lose, but not be overinsured. There's plenty of time on that because we write the insurance policies right here.

R: Good.

L: The airlines usually ask disabled passengers to check in about an hour before departure on a domestic flight. Take into account any possible traffic jams. On a weekend you might run into a lot of people going "down the shore," but even so, it's better to be at the airport a little early for the check-in and get everything squared away and be relaxed for your trip. American will probably want to preboard you and load your chair into the hold. It'd be a good idea for you to ask the stewardess —maybe a half hour or so out of Los Angeles—to remind the captain when he is in contact with the tower to let their ground personnel know that you will be requiring assistance with your baggage and that your wheelchair should be unloaded first thing and waiting for you planeside. It never hurts to remind people. We'll call the reservations desk the day before you leave and make sure all requests are in. And we'll call the sales office and remind them to have everything in order and to notify the station manager in L.A. of your arrival.

R: Should I call the airline the day before my return to check on our flight?

L: It's always a good idea. It might make you feel more at ease. It couldn't do any harm to leave a phone number where they could reach you if there were a time change or a route change or even an equipment change that might mean you would need a different seat assignment or that you would need to use their wheelchair instead of your own, or whatever. Here's my business card and another phone number where I can be reached and where my associate Helen can be reached. If at any time you should need us or need an answer to a question and you think we can be of help, call us, and call us collect.

R: Thank you. You've been extremely helpful and I'm certainly looking forward to the trip.

ROSEMARIE EVALUATES THE CALIFORNIA TRIP

In general, the trip was smooth and thoroughly enjoyable. The one or two rough spots could not have been foreseen easily or avoided. The American Airlines flights were wonderful, and the crew was very competent and thoughtful in serving me. I was permitted to board in my own chair, which was quickly unloaded upon arrival. There was no skycap waiting in California, however, so we had a lengthy wait at the airport. A lovely stewardess from our plane waited with us until the skycap arrived. When I telephoned from L.A. to confirm my return flight, we were not listed, but American got us on without difficulty. So it's important to confirm your return flight. Our friends picked us up and returned us to the airport, so we didn't need limousine service. I had checked prices beforehand, however, and learned that taxis from the airport to the hotel would be much lower than the limo. Yellow Cab was very reliable, and we used it for much of our sightseeing when our friends couldn't go. We also used Gray Line Sightseeing (limo) for a couple of longer trips and found the driver and car delightful. We had a shock when we arrived at the motel after the long journey and found—despite Luceille's best efforts—that the entrance to our room was inaccessible. It was at the end of the motel, next to a heap of rubbish, and access was by means of a very steep ramp. *No one* pushing a wheelchair could have maneuvered the grade. Ironically enough, the one room that was designated as the "wheelchair room" was the least accessible one in the entire motel. They switched us to a standard room, which was quite fine. (And when Luceille wrote to them later to point this out, enclosing a photo of that ramp that I had taken, they sent us a check to cover any inconvenience.) The motel was within walking distance of Disneyland and also had a restaurant. We couldn't use its bus service to Disneyland so we strolled over. Besides Disneyland, we visited the Farmer's Market (delightful and accessible), the lovely Mission of San Juan Capistrano (generally accessible, with the exception of a couple of buildings and the uneven brick walkways), San Diego Zoo (which I found very difficult to see from a wheelchair without a strong man to push, and whose sightseeing train, I understand, is not accessible), and Knott's Berry Farm (also quite accessible). Of course, many areas of Disneyland are not accessible, but visitors are provided with accessibility information, and there's still a great deal to see and do. In general, I would definitely recommend L.A. to handicapped travelers. It's so large and has so much to offer one must be able to decide what interests him or her. Without independent transportation, however, handicapped tourists must be prepared to pay for taxi or limo service, since there is no other practical way to get around, and it's a big place. I did not, by the way, check out our insurance policy or take out any special trip cancellation insurance. [The latter would have been advisable. See discussion of such insurance under General Information in Part IV.]

—Rosemarie K.

YOU AND YOUR TRAVEL AGENT

The conversation above illustrates a number of points in a good agent/client relationship, which is implicitly one of mutual trust. A client must know that the agent designing his or her trip is responsible and experienced. Rosemarie—there on a friend's recommendation—also asked, "Have you arranged many trips for handicapped persons?" and was reassured by Luceille's reply. A travel agent, in turn, wants a client to level on when and where and for how long he wants to travel and how much he plans to spend for the trip. You must let the agent know the extent of your disability and the amount of assistance you may need and any special requirements (diet, close proximity to a medical center, a hotel room without a platform bed or whatever).

As travel prospects increase, it becomes more and more important for any traveler planning anything more complicated than a short car trip to find and work with a good travel agent. This is especially true if you need precision planning. In the one area of air travel alone, consider the following: An agent can help you select, from any number of airlines flying between the same cities, the best for you in terms of flight times, whether or not the flight is nonstop or direct (and if not, the best connection), and the type of aircraft, in regard to comfort in boarding and seating (e.g., Luceille thought Rosemarie would like the two-abreast seating on the DC-10, with the spaciousness a wide-bodied airplane can afford). To have found the best flight for herself,

Rosemarie would have had to call the three airlines flying from Newark to L.A., because a call to any one would not necessarily provide information on its competition. Luceille was impartial and found a suitable flight by referring to her *Official Airline Guide* (often called the *OAG*), which is one of about fifteen standard reference books an agent uses for booking U.S. travel alone.

It takes a professional to keep up with this huge industry—travel—already accounting for more than $100 billion worth of business annually in the United States and expected to be the country's number one industry by the year 2000.

A travel agent is a specialist who sells travel. What can he do for you? He can:

- Give unbiased advice on the best flight, cruise, car rental, or whatever, and book your reservations.
- Provide firsthand knowledge of many destinations, or know where to get the best information for places he has never visited.
- Lend the clout of his agency to an individual booking that could result in special consideration for you during a peak period.
- Supply travel tips. For example, Luceille reminded Rosemarie to identify her baggage and wheelchair, to allow for potential traffic jams, and not to buy the Disneyland ticket book in advance.

A travel agency provides:

- Routine services, as well as a reasonable amount of customized planning, at no charge to the client. There is usually no fee, because the retail travel agent earns commissions (usually 8 to 10 percent) from the supplier (airline, hotel, car rental company, and the like). Where a complicated domestic tour is made to order, however, a slight markup—no more than 10 percent—is sometimes charged. Some travel "counselors" who specialize in personalized planning do charge a fee, but such agents are rare. If in doubt, ask. Also note that an agent may bill you for some long distance calls or cables required in making your reservations. Most major travel suppliers have toll-free numbers, however, or authorize travel agents to call collect. But if an agent should call long distance to arrange an airport pickup for you through a small ambulette company, do not be surprised to be billed for the call.

• Folders and recommendations on a wide range of money-saving prepackaged tours for everything from sports specials to city or resort holidays. More than three thousand such packages to U.S. destinations alone are now available, on which you can make substantial savings. On a Hawaiian package discussed in this book, one traveler alone saved $244 by taking a package rather than by booking the exact airline and hotel accommodations individually. Some packages and charter flights are available only through travel agents.

• The luxury of making a single office visit or phone call to outline your proposed trip and letting an agent do the rest. Some agents even deliver your tickets and vouchers. Trips can be arranged entirely by phone, but if possible, it's good to meet in person initially.

• Trip insurance and advice on when you need it. On a charter flight, for example, insurance is vital, since you stand to lose the airfare if you miss either the outgoing or return flight. With scheduled flights at regular fares you can simply reschedule and take a later flight at no penalty. Check the index for a full discussion of trip cancellation insurance.

• Better chances of being reimbursed for any services not delivered.

It pays an agent to be reliable. First of all, he relies on recommendations from satisfied customers for new business. He also tries to keep satisfied customers coming back. Most agents go all out to sell reliable products, for in lawsuits involving packaged tours where the wholesale agent who packaged the tour is at fault, the retail agent who sold it has been held liable as the only direct link with the consumer.

You will most likely deal with the retail agent, the guy in the agency down the street. Another type of agent is the wholesale agent, who is also referred to as a wholesaler or tour operator. He rarely works directly with the public (although some agents are both wholesale and retail). He produces packaged tours.

Your travel agent has this operator's brochures in his rack. The operator buys huge blocks of hotel and airline space at net prices, adds his own markup, and still offers you a price advantage on a vacation. There are also the so-called "travel promoters," who sell trips but who are not approved by the International Air Transport Association (IATA) or the Air Traffic Conference (ATC) and thus may operate under no published code of ethics.

Travel agencies come in different sizes and shapes, ranging from the "supermarkets"—often at midtown locations—that deal primarily in packaged tours and do little customized work, to the more personalized agencies, such as the one Rosemarie visited.

How to find the best agent for you?

- Ask friends who use agents.
- Don't be afraid to shop around. Make appointments and stop in if convenient. Don't hesitate to interview the agent. Have preliminary trip discussions to see how you like an agent, but don't be unfair and have him work out a detailed trip that you do not intend to take.
- Find an agent who has been in business for several years.
- Look into the travel agency at a reliable department store.

If you prefer an agent who has already handled disabled clients, ask disabled friends, at rehab centers, and at foundations or associations identified with your particular disability. Attend travel seminars put on by Disabled in Action and other groups and inquire there. Look for an agent who belongs to the Society for the Advancement of Travel for the Handicapped (SATH). *See below.*

One test of an agency's reliability is whether it is a member agency of the American Society of Travel Agents (ASTA). This is not to say that because an agent is not an ASTA member he is not reliable, or that every ASTA member has sterling character. But the agency business is not federally regulated, and the 5,000 plus ASTA agencies have met certain financial, business, and ethical requirements that membership in this trade association implies. They have been in business at least three years and must be approved to issue tickets by at least two carrier conferences, one of which must be the ATC or IATA. Agency affiliation with the Institute of Certified Travel Agents and Association of Retail Travel Agencies also speaks for sound business and ethical codes.

What to do when something goes wrong:

- Report any problems to the agent who arranged your trip.
- If you think your agent is responsible for the problem, file a complaint with the Consumer Affairs Department of ASTA (711 Fifth Avenue, New York, NY 10022), whether or not he is a member. ASTA

can usually get an adjustment from a member. Also see Routine Complaints and Rights in the General Information section in Part IV. You can also check *first* with the Better Business Bureau or ASTA to see if any complaints are registered against an agent you are considering using, or a wholesaler whose package you might buy.

Because of the number of things that can go wrong when you travel, it is particularly important to find and work with a good agent. If there are no travel agents in your town, you can find one by telephone or mail. You might initially track down some agents through some of the sources mentioned above. A few long-distance phone calls are a fair investment in a smoother trip.

HOW TO WORK WITH A TRAVEL AGENT

If you turn up a congenial, reliable travel agent who lacks experience with disabled clients, don't let it be a problem. If the agent is careful and willing, you can work with him by asking questions and filling in with your own knowledge of the subject. Therefore, you must have as much travel methodology under your belt as possible. Even the most conscientious agent can make mistakes. One agent carefully wrote to a hotel in Europe requesting a room on the first floor unless there was a lift, or elevator. But in Europe and on some Caribbean islands the second floor is considered the first floor. So the client arrived with a letter of confirmation for a room that was one flight up, and unreachable. Another agent cabled a hotel in the French West Indies concerning the arrival of a disabled person, or an "invalid." When the client arrived his arrangements had been cancelled. In travel terms, *invalid* is usually read as *not valid*.

Supply your agent with any information you have. Be forceful about what you need for your own maximum and minimum comfort. When he communicates with an airline, ship line, hotel, or whatever, your agent will begin by mentioning your disability. A number of chain hotel directories are now coded for wheelchair-accessible rooms. And the *Official Airline Guide*, which your agent relies on, runs a special quarterly "Trip Planner" issue containing information on airport accessibility. These are standard directories an agent works with. An innovative new tool that is now routinely coded as to wheelchair accessibility is *Intros*, an official source book of U.S. and international travel and reception operators' services. In plain terms, it provides booking information on ground services, such as tours, attractions, motorcoach transfers, and hotels. Intended for agents, it shows at a glance, for example, that the spooky Winchester Mystery House in San Jose, California, or the Enchantment Tours in Santa Fe, New Mexico, are barrier-free. Published quarterly, it is mailed free to a controlled-circulation list of travel executives or is available to agents at $5 from International Reception Operators, 9601 Wilshire Boulevard, Beverly Hills, CA 90210. Other useful sources are mentioned throughout this book.

As for you, the client, do not be afraid to question an agent's recommendations (what does he know about the operator? what about a hotel's cancellation policy? where are the hidden costs in a tour?). Remember that you have the final word; an agent is supposed to work on your behalf. Don't sign anything until you have satisfactory answers to your questions and have read all the fine print.

Finally, remember that a good client gets involved in his own trip, expresses thanks and appreciation for a job well done, reports back on his trip, and pays his bills readily. He is resourceful when mix-ups occur, and he doesn't make unreasonable demands on an agent trying to work in the pioneer field of travel for disabled persons.

TRAVEL AGENCIES/OPERATORS

Some of the most experienced tour operators specializing in group tours for disabled travelers are listed below. Ablebodied companions are welcome on any of their tours, which can be booked through your retail travel agent.

Flying Wheels Tours (FWT)—Offers Hawaii, Caribbean cruises, and a series of U.S. tours by motorcoaches equipped with lifts or ramps through colorful and scenic areas. Also tours of Europe and the Scandinavian countries. Medical assistants accompany each group, and tour rate includes nominal routine needs such as emptying urinal bags and help in and out of bed. Care with dressing, feeding, pushing wheelchairs can also be provided but at an additional cost, and such services must be prearranged. FWT also books independent travel. The seven-year-old company is owned by a quadriplegic. Newsletters, $1/year. Flying Wheels Tours, 143 W. Bridge St., Box 382, Owatonna, MN 55060, 507-451-5005.

Rambling Tours (*RT*)—Annual tours have included Hawaii (on an Orient package). Also Central America and Panama, Europe and the British Isles. RT's limit is three tours a year. A hydraulic lift is used on all motorcoaches. The owners accompany each group. Tour cost includes transfer in and out of bed, cutting food, partial dressing/undressing (tying shoes, zipping, and other finishing touches). Nominal fee for more personal attention. Individual aides can be arranged for those who require extensive help. This company also customizes tours for affinity groups. Eight years experience. Rambling Tours Inc., Box 1304, Hallandale, FL 33009, 305-456-2161.

Wings on Wheels—Tours for the physically disabled, blind, or mentally retarded, in respective groups, to Hawaii and Alaska (cruise), as well as tours within the 48 contiguous states. Also an extensive international program including world tours, South Pacific, several European countries, Great Britain, and more. Wings on Wheels also books independent travel. The owners or their son accompany every group. If you are unable to operate your own chair, you must bring a companion. Eighteen years experience. Wings on Wheels, 19429 44th St. W., Lynnwood, WA 98036, 206-776-1184.

In addition to these three specialists in travel for disabled individuals, there are also national associations, clubs, rehab centers, and other organizations with tours that cater to or will accommodate travelers with mobility or health problems. The professionalism of their arrangements tends to vary, however. If possible, talk with one of their "alumni."

For a list of travel agencies nationwide that belong to the Society for the Advancement of Travel for the Handicapped (SATH), write to SATH at 26 Court St., Brooklyn, NY 11242, 212-858-5483. Agency membership in this organization tells you that it is concerned enough to belong, and that it receives monthly newsletters and other briefings on developments in the field and has an opportunity to attend SATH conventions and meetings.

HOW TO READ A TOUR FOLDER

Most tour folders are purposefully vague in the descriptive portions, so read between the lines. Take special note of any fine print. Read again. Ask questions.

If the hotels are not listed on a tour folder, ask which hotels are used and where they are. Check their locations on a map (usually available from the tourist office or chamber of commerce). If a hotel is not central, you could spend a fortune in taxi fares. Rates are usually based on two persons sharing a room. How much is the single supplement?

A room with a "spectacular ocean view" *implies* that the hotel is on the beach but means that it probably is not. It could be across the street or on the mountainside. Even photographs can lie. Ask.

By whose standards is a first-class hotel first-class? Are the rooms barrier-free? Even companies specializing in handicapped clients have been known to book hotels with inaccessible bathrooms. If in doubt about any features of a hotel, write directly to the manager.

What kind of motorcoaches or limousines are used for sightseeing and transfers to/from the hotels and airports? How steep are the bus steps or are there ramps or lifts? Ask.

Check to see which meals are included, which services are extra and how much you pay, and if gratuities are included in the package price.

How much luggage are you allowed?

Do not compare apples and oranges when cross-examining several tours for the same destination. How many days and nights in a week (5 nights/6 days or 7 nights/8 days)? Which sightseeing attractions are included, which optional? If it is a tour for disabled persons, does an escort or attendant from the tour company go with you *all the way* or simply give you an airport send-off, with a representative of the company meeting you at the other end? If the flight is your major concern, this is important. Does an attendant go along on any optional tour, or must you pay his way as well? What airfare does the package price include? If a Hawaii tour advertises airfare from Los Angeles and return, don't forget to add Hometown-to-L.A. fare when you compare the tour with one originating locally.

Operators tend to print the lowest price—"From $299"—in bold type. Is that only for ground arrangements (a growing trend)? What must you actually pay for the accommodations of your choice? Is $299 the off-off-season rate? Is there a departure date bridging the low and high seasons that could give you the best season at the lowest price?

A guided tour is not always the best buy, especially if it includes features you don't want. If you plan to plop on a sunny terrace, why pay for sightseeing? If you'd rather be in one place, why pay for a progressive tour?

Who is the tour operator? Is he reliable? (Ask your travel agent or American Society of Travel Agents.) Has your agent ever booked a client on this tour, and was he satisfied? What are the cancellation or refund policies? Does the tour have a warranty assuring a refund for any item or service not delivered? Note that operators usually reserve the right to make certain changes of hotel or itinerary.

On a progressive tour, try to avoid one-night stands and hotel changes. This becomes tiresome to the able and disabled alike. How many flights are listed? Every day you pack and unpack, check in and out of hotels, go to and from airports counts as a "travel day."

SHOULD YOU TAKE A GUIDED TOUR?

Yes and no. Yes if you don't want the responsibility of trip logistics, do like the security of a group or of a leader or medical aide, or have never traveled before and think you'd rather start this way. Yes if you figure you can save money by prorating the cost of an ambulette, a medical attendant, or whatever. (Most travel agents and travelers alike agree that travel in some European countries is now so geared to groups at reasonable prices that individual services have become financially out of sight. One travel agent reports that a Paris limousine charged $100 to pick up a party of two at Orly Airport and drive them to their Paris hotel 10 miles away. So for Europe, generally speaking, yes, if you require private transportation and the like.)

No if you really don't like being shepherded around, like to set your own pace, and feel confident about handling your own arrangements. No if you have selected a destination where a guided tour offers no price advantage and you don't require any special attention.

MAINSTREAM?

Why not? If you generally interact with ablebodied persons in everyday life, why not on vacation? Work out your own travel plans, or hook up with a basic package (see Trip Planning and Airlines, Airfares, and Packages in the Hawaii section, Part III). Throw in any special features you need. Hobbyists might look into the wide array of special interest tours and cruises featuring everything from birdwatching to photography and nostalgia film festivals. Inquire from the hundreds of operators who advertise in the newspapers and magazines nationwide. Among those who have indicated that they can take disabled travelers with certain provisions are American Express, on its independent tours and escorted tours if arrangements can be made (800-241-1700); Cartan (800-323-7888); and Travcoa, a wholesale international operator (by writing to Melvin Dultz, Travcoa, 875 N. Michigan Ave., Chicago, IL 60611). Both American Express and Cartan offer national and international tours. Mention the extent of your disability and whether you'll be traveling with a companion. If you require anything extra, you will pay more. On the other hand, if you don't need buses with lifts, medical assistants, and the like, you can probably save money by taking a conventional tour, especially if you are traveling with an ablebodied companion. On an ablebodied tour it may be left for you to contact the scheduled hotels to find out if they are accessible or to check on the altitude or whatever. If you are not ambulatory, you'll need your own companion to hoist you into the motorcoach. Persons with very limited mobility should avoid too many one-night stands on progressive tours. Check itinerary for days "at leisure." Be prepared to sit out any events that might slow down the group (something you wouldn't have to do on tours designed for disabled persons). Some tour operators are quite amenable to wheelchair tourists on regular tours. Others hesitate. Some refuse. Should you need a medical attendant or a lot of personalized aid and have no friend or family to provide it, be unable to leave your chair and require lifts, or just feel more secure on a tour for disabled persons, then mainstreaming may not be for you.

TRIP COSTS

The big cost items are the transportation and hotels. Add them up and put the figure aside.

If you are taking a package tour, look for the hidden costs (gratuities, meals, optional sightseeing).

When estimating trip costs, keep your own life-style in mind. If anything, people tend to upgrade—not downgrade—on vacation. If you are in the habit of before-dinner drinks and nice restaurants, for example, you are not likely to dispense with the ceremonies and head for a fast-food place when you travel.

In most American cities or resorts, you can allow three, five, and ten dollars or under for breakfast, lunch, and dinner respectively, and twenty dollars and up for dinner at fine restaurants.

Study the tourist literature for your destination. Which sightseeing tours will you take? How much are they? How much for nightclubs, taxis, or ambulettes? If you rely on taxi drivers and doormen to help you in and out of your wheelchair, need a waiter to serve you at buffet meals and the like, plan to tip a dollar or so for their assistance over and above the usual gratuities. (For tipping guidelines, check the index or see specific sections, such as Hotels and Motels.)

How much is the taxi fare from the airport to the hotel? Is the airport transfer included in your tour price? Or can you use the airport bus or limo service? How much?

On a cruise, everything is included except the shore excursions, drinks and gratuities.

Add up all expenses other than transportation and hotels. Increase the figure by one-third. Now add in the transportation and hotels and you'll have an estimate of what the trip will cost (shopping not included).

Any rates quoted above are subject to change.

PART II

HOW TO GO

1

CARS

The automobile—when it can get you where you want to go—is the final word in transportation, providing a degree of customized travel not offered by public conveyances. For in addition to the luxury of door-to-door service, driving allows you to establish your own pace, stop when and where you please, and throw your timetable to the winds if you decide to linger a while in the Painted Desert.

The Paralyzed Veterans of America (PVA) has gone so far as to call the automobile the best means of travel for the severely disabled person. "It is safe and comfortable. It is always there. And, when one can afford it, it is always reliable." (PVA acknowledges air travel, if available, as the best and safest means of long-distance travel, however.)

The United States is ideal for a driving holiday. It has excellent highways, a growing number of rest stops for disabled travelers, and a good range of hotels, motels, and restaurants. Every region is endowed with characteristic scenery, often breathtakingly beautiful, as illustrated by the diaphanous wooded mountain vistas seen from the Blue Ridge Parkway running from the Shenandoah Valley of Virginia to the Great Smoky Mountains of Tennessee, or by California Highway 1, which skims the sheer coastal cliffs between Monterey and

San Luis Obispo. (Make the latter a northbound drive; the inside lane hugs the mountains.) These two, always counted among the country's most scenic routes, are just for starters. You could also opt for the impeccable New England villages and covered bridges, the sandy islands along the Outer Banks of North Carolina, the cultivated heartland of America, or the big country of Wyoming and Montana.

If you or someone in your family is easily fatigued or has just recovered from a stroke, consider a series of short car trips spaced out over a season in lieu of one long vacation. One man who suffers from multiple sclerosis has made car trips, with his wife driving, from his home near Albuquerque to the Grand Canyon, to Colorado Springs, where he stayed at the fabled Broadmoor Hotel, and to Sante Fe for the summer opera festival.

Your entire vacation could be the drive itself, or driving might simply be a means to a destination. If you are in the mood for a change of scenery, the car is a great way to go.

TIPS FOR THE ROAD

• Make sure your car is in top condition, and that includes the spare tire.

• Equip the trunk with a pressure can (quick help for a flat tire), a gallon jug of water for radiator leaks, a white rag or handkerchief for a distress signal, a flare, and a first-aid kit.

• If you do not have a CB radio, consider installing one for emergency use. Tune to channel nine (the police band) or nineteen (the truckers' band—they'll let you know where "Smokey" is).

• Never let your gas tank go below half empty. Do *not* carry a jug of gasoline in the trunk.

• Have a sign made noting that this car is operated by a disabled driver and that any proper courtesies would be appreciated. Stick this in your windshield in cities which have parking privileges for the disabled (but where the traffic cops may not recognize your state's HC license, sticker, or other designation).

• Don't overdo it. The American Automobile Association suggests that a driver can comfortably cover about 300 miles a day (highways, health, and driving skills taken into account).

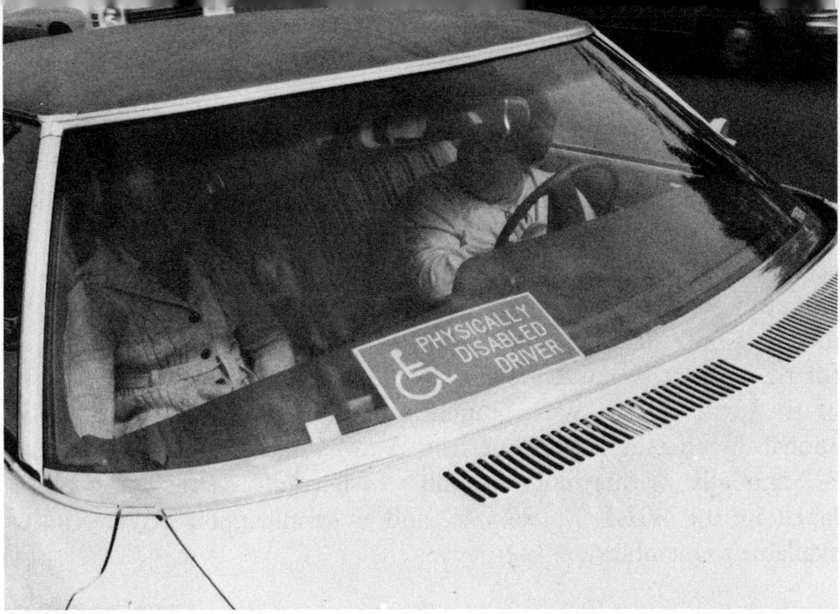

• *Highway Rest Areas for Handicapped Travelers* lists over 800 accessible comfort stations in forty-eight of the fifty states in its new edition. Keep a copy in your glove compartment. It's available free from the President's Committee on Employment of the Handicapped, Washington, D.C. 20210.

ROUTE PLANNING

If you write in advance, the major oil companies, as well as the auto clubs, will plot your trip and send you marked route maps. Mention the places you wish to visit, your travel dates, the kind of vehicle you will be driving, the nature of your disability, and any other pertinent information. The route planners are privy to the latest data on highway construction. They will detour the drivers of RVs around a tunnel that prohibits them (either for clearance or the restricted compressed gas). They also take highway weather conditions into consideration. They'll chart you on the shortest route, the smoothest route, or the most scenic route, as you request.

Oil companies offering free route planning to everyone include: Exxon Touring Service, P.O. Box 307, Florham Park, NJ 07932, which also forwards motel directories identifying barrier-free facilities to disabled drivers who request lodging suggestions; Mobile Travel Service, Box 25, Versailles, KY 40383, whose *Mobil Travel Guides* indicate some accessible establishments; and Texaco Travel Service, 135 East 42nd St., New York, NY 10017, which suggests accessible accommodations when requested as part of the route information.

Automobile clubs offer route planning and other services to paying members only. Disabled drivers are often advised to join such a club for the various benefits, especially the emergency road service. Two of the largest clubs, with branches nationwide, are Allstate, $22.50 annual membership, and American Automobile Association (AAA), $30 annually, with a limited number of barrier-free accommodations listed in the *AAA TourBooks*, and a handicapped driver's guide available to members.

TRIP COSTS

The national average for regular gas is about 63 cents a gallon at press time, and the standard car averages 15 miles to a gallon (somewhat more in highway driving). If you limit yourself to 300 miles a day, you can plan to spend about $14 daily for gasoline and oil. If you get better mileage, figure it out accordingly.

RENTAL CARS

We are dealing here with the so-called Big Three car rental agencies, not because big is necessarily best (although they do have some fine attributes), but because the Hertz, Avis, and National car rental companies all rent cars with hand controls, and at no extra cost.

Almost everything you ever wanted to know about such rentals is spelled out on the table Rental Cars at a Glance.

Other tips are brought out in this picture story of Julius, who rents a car and drives to the country.

HAND CONTROLS

The following hand controls have been tested and approved by the Veterans Administration: Blatnik Precision Controls, Car Hand Controls, Hughes Hand Driving, Kroepke Kontrols, Manufacturing and Production Services (MPS), Mross Control, Nelson Products, Smith's

Hand Control, and Trujillo Industries. Also, Drive-Master, Ferguson Auto Service, Gresham Driving Aids, Handicaps, Inc., Thompson Controls, and Wells-Enberg, provided the models were modified and produced after September 1975 (June 30, 1975, for Gresham; for Wells-Enberg, only those with serial numbers greater than 10,003 and manufactured after March 1, 1976).

If you want to take your own controls on vacation to attach to a car obtained there, check with your hand controls dealer to determine which makes they are compatible with.

Note that while some car rental agencies will let you attach your controls to their cars, it is best to get advance confirmation.

PARKING

Access to America: Update 1977, a compendium of nationwide legislation on matters concerning the disabled, includes parking and driving regulations for cities and states. Available prepaid from Michigan Center for a Barrier Free Environment, 22646 Woodward, Ferndale, MI 48220. $15.

He brings along any custom equipment he needs for driving comfort—in his case, a folding seat. Drivers who use a wheel spinner knob should bring theirs, as the agencies do not furnish them.

Julius takes a cursory glance at the car assigned to him. He had specified a two-door car with bench seats when he reserved. The agency did not have one available and installed the hand controls on a four-door job. (Agencies rarely guarantee a specific car but will try to honor your preference or will substitute a similar or better car.) Julius cannot get his chair into the backseat of this car, but the agency cannot switch cars today. A friend is along to handle the chair, so Julius agrees to take this car. Which brings up a good point: You cannot over-emphasize the importance of a two-door car if that is what you must drive. (National rents only two-door cars with hand controls.)

Picking up the car is easy if you have a major credit card, and difficult without one. (See text below.) The agent will ask to see your driver's license. You sign a simple form. The agent turns the keys over to Julius, along with a copy of the contract. The motorist should keep this contract with him whenever he is driving.

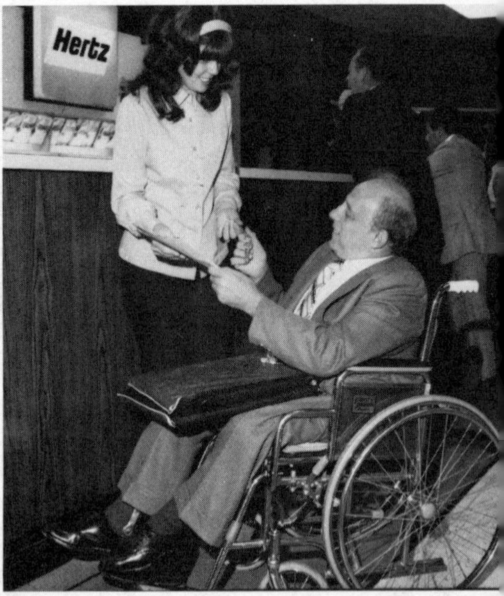

Julius inspects the hand controls. They appear to be in order. In reserving your car, always specify whether you want left- or right-hand controls. (National offers left only.) Emphasize the importance of this. When you are inspecting the car, look for any damage (any scraped paint that could be attributed to you later, for example). Also check the spare tire.

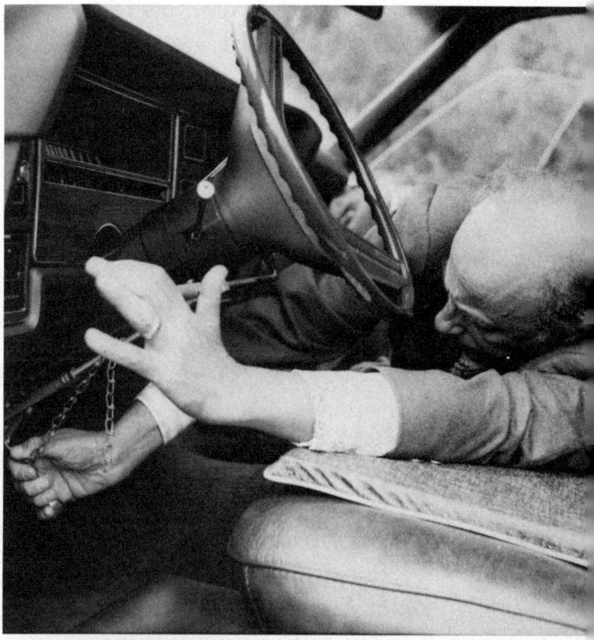

Just rolling along . . .

Still life with snack. In addition to a road map, it is always good to have a thermos of water, some fruit or other snacks, and a copy of the *Highway Rest Areas for Handicapped Travelers* directory.

In this case, the rest stop at Ardsley, New York, was incorrectly listed as accessible. Julius could not use the men's room. Most of the 800 listings may be correct, however. They are usually identified in this manner.

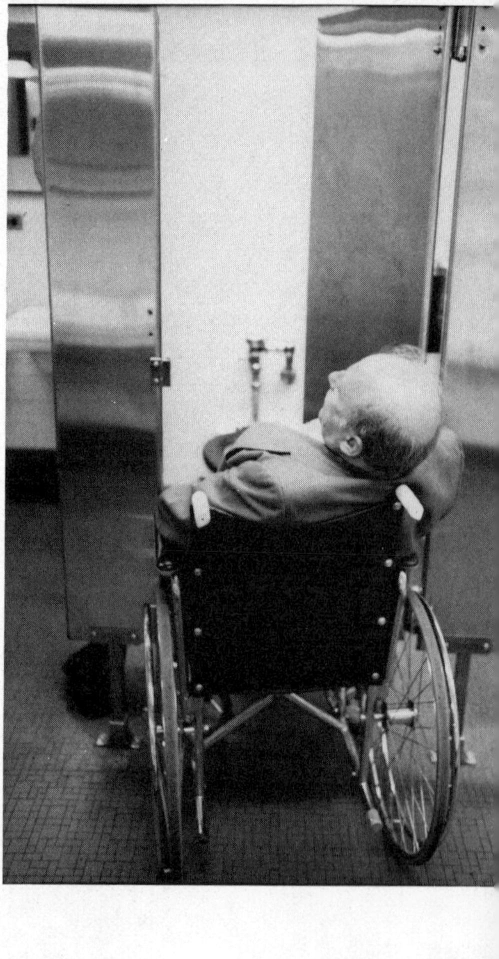

Courtesy New York Thruway Authority

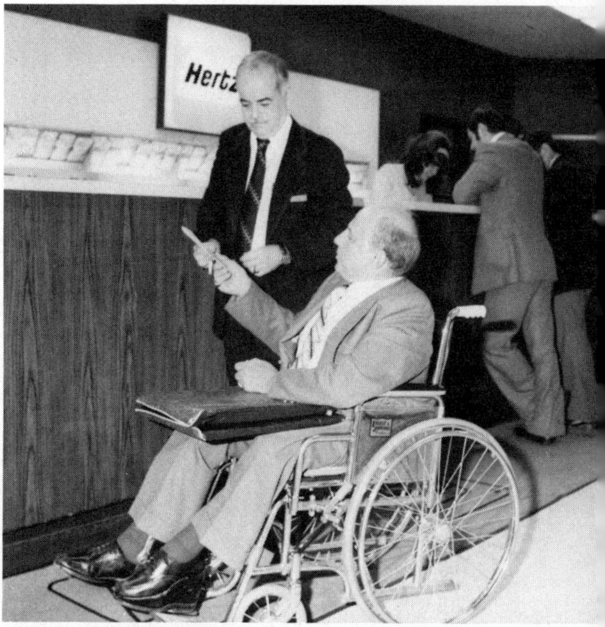

Back to Square 1. Julius returns the car to the station where he rented it. An agent checks the mileage and determines the charges. He also sees that no damage was done. Julius gets a receipt for his records.

If you do not need hand controls, you have a wider range of rental agencies to choose from. If your driving will be limited to a city and its environs, you might find your best deal with a local operator. The better-known agencies, however, have often earned their reputations because they do offer new model cars and have sizeable fleets and can make a substitution should you get a lemon. They also have a large network of stations you can turn to if anything goes wrong, and they will come to your aid in the event of a breakdown.

One man named Les reported that a car rented from a small company broke down in the middle of nowhere, and when he called in, he was told to have the car towed to the nearest garage and to get back to town the best way he could. No reflection on Les, but a few months later he was driving a car rented from one of the "biggies" and it, too, broke down in the country. He called in and was told to wait there and they'd come to his rescue with a replacement car.

The established companies also offer you substantial liability insurance. Over and above this, if you are an infrequent renter, you may be well advised to take the optional $250 collision damage waiver (about $2.00 to $2.50 a day) that pays for minor damage. If you rent frequently, you'd soon pay more than the $250 protection. Whether

Rental Cars at a Glance

Agency	Reservations	Locations	Advance Booking	Additional Deposit Required	Cars Controls Are Applied To	Make of Control	Both Left- and Right-Hand	Car Must Be Returned to Originating Station
Avis	800-331-2112	all major U.S. cities	3 weeks	none	Dodge Monaco, Colt, Sportsman Wagon; Plymouth Volaré, Volaré wagon, Fury, Fury wagon, Gran Fury; Chrysler Le Baron; Ford Granada; Chevrolet Chevette, Malibu, Caprice; Pontiac LeMans	assorted VA-approved makes	yes	no
Hertz	800-654-3131	airports in L.A., San Francisco, Chicago (O'Hare), Boston, Miami, Dallas/Ft. Worth, Atlanta, Washington (National), Detroit (Metro); also midtown NYC	10 days	$25 when renting on cash basis	Chevrolet Caprice, Impala; Pontiac Catalina; Mercury Montego MX, Cougar; Olds Delta 88; Dodge Diplomat, Royal Monaco; Plymouth Gran Fury, Le Baron; Ford Gran Torino, LTD, LTD II	Drive-Master	yes	yes
National	800-328-4567 (in MN 612-830-2345, collect)	Phoenix, L.A., San Francisco, Washington, Miami, Atlanta, Chicago, Detroit, Minn./St. Paul, Houston*	48 hours	none	Chevrolet Monte Carlo and Olds Cutlass (two-door models)	Kroepke	left only	yes

The information herein pertains only to cars with hand controls in domestic locations.

*Also in other cities with reasonable lead time

you buy the optional dollar-a-day personal coverage offered by the companies should depend on how comprehensive your own medical insurance is.

Rental plans and rates vary widely, from agency to agency, from city to city, and even for the same agency within one city. Among the plans usually offered are those with "wet rates" (gas included) and "dry rates" (you buy the gas), daily, weekly, or weekend, and plans with limited or unlimited mileage.

Hertz cites as "representative" its Chicago (O'Hare) rates with cars such as Chevrolet Caprice or Ford LTD at $17.95 a day plus $.24 a mile.

Which of the various plans offered is your best bet?

Let's say that you need a car for a weekend. Should you take a weekend plan at $74.85 with unlimited mileage? Or the daily rate of $17.95 plus $.24 a mile? The answer, of course, lies in the mileage. Thus, if you are going to drive eighty-eight miles or more, the unlimited mileage plan is better.

If you rent from Hertz, Avis, or National, at the time you return the car they will give you the benefit of the lower rate (whether it be daily rate plus mileage or the flat rate).

Their charge cards are called respectively #1, Avis Executive Card, and VIP card. If you hold the Hertz card (or Avis card, provided you request a Wizard number), you can have information on your specific requirements—including the fact that you need a left-side hand control and a two-door car or whatever—stored in their computer memory banks. Thus, whenever you call to reserve a car you need only call the agent's attention to your special requirements without going into detail each time. Do be sure that your requests have registered with him.

A major credit card—not necessarily that of the car company—is almost indispensable when it comes to renting a car. With it the agency knows that your credit rating is acceptable and it can turn a car worth $5,000 to $8,000 over to you in good faith. Without it, they must conduct their own credit check, which could take several days. Without it, spur-of-the-moment rental is often impossible. Without it, once having been cleared, you would have to lay out a great deal of cash security in advance. To rent from Hertz in Los Angeles, for example, you would have to pay in advance the estimated cost of your bill *after* verifying your place of employment and proving you have a listed home telephone. In New York, you would pay as security $75 a day, $150 a weekend, or $250 a week. In New York, to rent from Hertz on a cash basis you would have to be twenty-one years old, whereas cardholders can rent at eighteen. You must always have a valid driver's license. The age requirement usually varies from eighteen to twenty-five, depending on the company, the location, and the rental terms.

FLY/DRIVES

If you want to fly to a city and rent a car there for a minimum of three days, you can often buy a fly/drive package and save money. The package can include accommodations and other elements as well. Your largest saving is on the round-trip airfare which, because you have purchased what the industry calls "ground arrangements," allows you to qualify for a Tour Basing Fare, a saving compared to the regular airfare. Cars offered in conjunction with fly/drive tours usually have unlimited mileage. Buying the package in advance also eliminates the security deposit discussed above, should you not have a credit card acceptable to the car rental company. If you need a car with hand controls, match the city you are flying to with the chart on these pages and see if a company has hand controls there. Then check with your travel agent for the availability of fly/drive packages to that city. Fly/drives must be purchased through either a travel agent or airline. They are not sold by the car companies.

RVs

Recreational vehicles (with compact bed, kitchen, and bath) can be a restful way to travel with a disability. If you are able to walk even a few steps and be lifted or guided into the living quarters, a conventional camper is feasible. If you are confined to your chair, a modified camper is required. At this time, we know of only one company that rents such a camper. That is a New Jersey company that has one Class A Winnebago (twenty-two feet) modified for a paraplegic. It features a hydraulic lift, accessible plumbing, and a lock-in apparatus for a wheelchair passenger next to the driver.

Contact Paul Phillips, Campers of America, 3405 Rt. 33, Neptune, NJ 07753, 201-922-2500.

RVs are not usually available through conventional car rental companies, although Avis does rent a spacious Sportsman Wagon with removable seat. The wagon can seat eight and provides ample room for camping or fishing gear.

Recreational vehicles can sometimes be rented from local dealers. Check the Yellow Pages for dealerships such as Winnebago. Also check the *Buyer's Guide*, a national classified directory of goods and services for the disabled published by *Accent* (see References under General Information), to see if local dealers for Speedy Wagon vans and similar accessible vehicles can rent to you.

Away Motor Home Rentals, one of the largest camper rentals nationwide, has unmodified RVs that rent from $275 a week plus $.10 a mile and $375 a week plus $.12 a mile respectively for minis (Cobra, Lindy, and Super-Mini at twenty to twenty-three feet and sleeping up to six) and Class A (Cobra and Titan, twenty-two to twenty-six feet and sleeping up to eight). Away Motor Homes is at 58 E. Merrick Rd., Valley Stream, NY 11580, 516-825-1119.

On TWA's Camper Fly/Drive program, motor homes that sleep four to six are available out of San Francisco, L.A., Phoenix, and Denver.

The San Diego Hilton provides a package for three nights at the hotel and four nights/five days in an RV, on which you could even drive to Mexico.

HINTS

- Rent early for a holiday season.
- Take careful note of the time your car must be turned in to avoid paying for an additional day.
- See car rental category on the airports accessibility chart (Part II, Section 4).

2

BUSES

The travelers you meet on a bus are the friendliest folks in the world, ever ready to lend you a hand or share their life stories and ham sandwiches with you as the miles roll by.

Along with being possibly the friendliest way to go, the bus comes closest to home, threading its way into tiny villages and past rural post offices, even making occasional highway flag stops. Some travelers choose the bus as the most immediate public transportation. Others choose it for the low promotional fares. Still others, for the eye-level scenery and the feeling that highway travel is the only way you can discover America.

While the bus may lack some of the comforts of planes, trains, and cars, if it is your chosen way to travel, and if you really want to travel, then why not try it?

A woman who signed herself "Grateful" wrote a letter, which appeared in the nationally syndicated Ann Landers column, saying that her handicapped brother had always wanted to see the country and she had decided to take him to California and "show him the time of his life." Since they lived in Pennsylvania the trip meant quite a lot of money, and they were people of modest means. When she went to the Greyhound bus station to purchase the tickets she found out that she could ride free provided she had a letter from her brother's doctor saying that he needed assistance to make the trip. Greyhound calls this their Helping Hand Service. Grateful found several terminals along the way with specially built ramps, restrooms, handrails, water fountains, and even telephone booths low enough for wheelchair users.

Even before the Interstate Commerce Commission (ICC) regulation* adopted in 1977 stated that intercity buses must transport persons with a disability (or blindness) and must provide assistance in boarding the bus and when possible help with luggage, both Greyhound and Trailways, the two principal interstate buslines, had facilitated travel for the disabled by way of the program described by Grateful. Greyhound's plan is the Helping Hand Service. Trailways calls theirs the Good Samaritan.

On these programs anyone who needs assistance to travel by bus may bring along an assistant at no additional fare. To qualify, however, you must present a certificate from your doctor, written on his letterhead, stating that you cannot travel alone.

A sample wording is reprinted here by permission of Greyhound Lines, Inc.

CERTIFICATE OF ELIGIBILITY

Greyhound Lines, Inc., allows an attendant to travel with a disabled person when the person is disabled to the extent of requiring the assistance of an attendant to board, alight, and travel on a bus.

____

is disabled and in my judgment can travel by bus if accompanied by an attendant to assist him or her in boarding, alighting, and traveling on a bus.

The disability is ☐ permanent ☐ temporary.

Date ____________________

Doctor's name ____________________

Address ____________________

____

____

(Signature of Doctor)

* Interstate Commerce Commission rules decided May 20, 1977, and docketed as Ex Parte No. MC-95 *Interstate Transportation of Passengers by Motor Common Carriers.*

A similar wording could be used for Trailways.

Whether you are traveling with a companion or alone, these points will help you map out the smoothest trip.

- When you call for schedule information, ask for the information clerk, and if there are unanswered questions, speak to the terminal manager. Mention that you are disabled and get full information about arrival and departure times.
- If you can be flexible about travel time, mention this. Weekday travel is usually less hassle than weekend.
- Even express buses make stops every few hours and if getting to the restroom at the rear of the bus presents a problem, work out a schedule that allows convenient rest stops.
- Be sure you understand when and where you might have to change buses (and, in some cases, terminals).

It is not obligatory to travel with a Helping Hand or a Good Samaritan, it simply may be pleasanter for you. But if you normally get around independently and wish to go alone, the bus driver and other company personnel (many of whom have had training in assisting the disabled) will help you in and out of the bus, and those friendly bus riders can generally be counted on for an assist.

One woman in a wheelchair took the bus from Los Angeles to Washington to attend the White House Conference on Handicapped Individuals in 1977 and reported that she did not encounter a single problem on the entire trip of more than 2,000 miles. Her only companion was a preschool daughter.

Teri, our "model," who had made a number of solo bus trips as a college student, had not realized at the time that a bus company—if it knew she was coming—would provide assistance. (Greyhound suggests you call their terminal information clerk thirty minutes before leaving home if you wish assistance.) Teri had explored the vast Port Authority bus terminal in New York until she had located a remote freight elevator that she thereafter took down to the gates. Here Teri is making her first trip with special assistance.

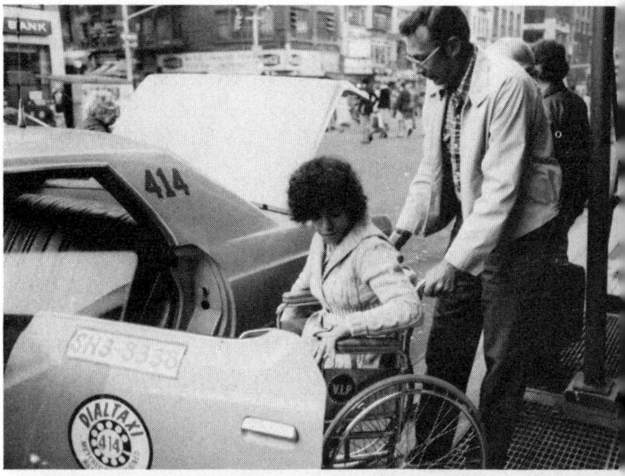

Teri arrives at the station by taxi and meets her friend, or Helping Hand, who is making the trip to Philadelphia with her. She does not need Greyhound personnel to meet her taxi.

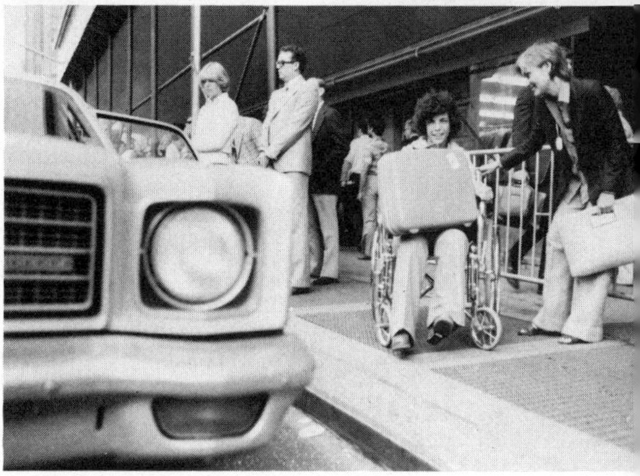

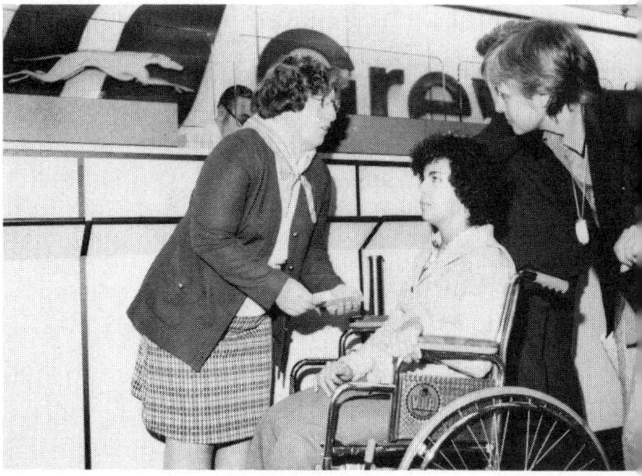

Teri presents a letter from her doctor (see above) that entitles her to travel with an HH on a single ticket. Dorothy, an assistant station manager, is called (she had been expecting Teri, who had informed Greyhound that she was coming).

Time to kill before departure, so Dorothy invites Teri into the Greyhound lounge to wait. The general waiting room of the New York terminal is inaccessible to wheelchairs, as are the restrooms.

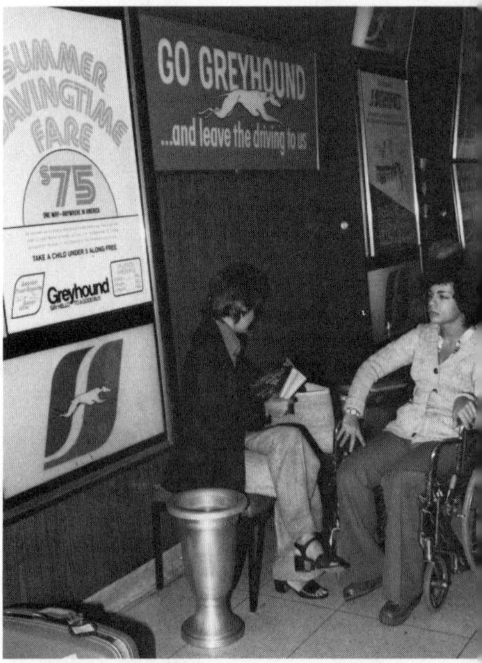

At bus time Dorothy escorts Teri down to the gate. She uses a more convenient elevator than the one Teri had found on her own.

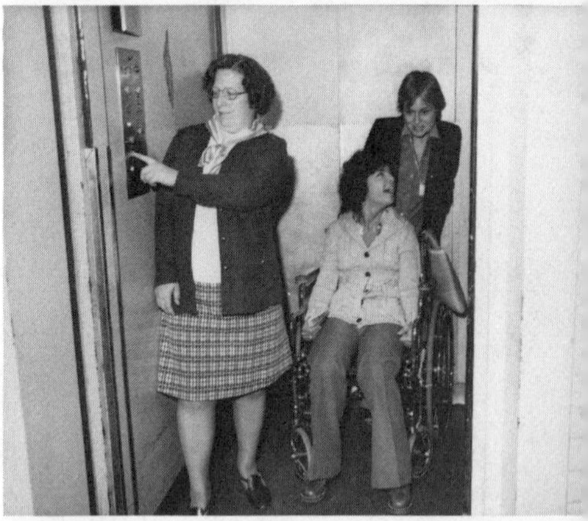

When a bus originates at your station (as this one does), you will be boarded before the other passengers and given a front seat (unless you request the smoking section, which is farther back). The bus driver discusses seat preference with Teri.

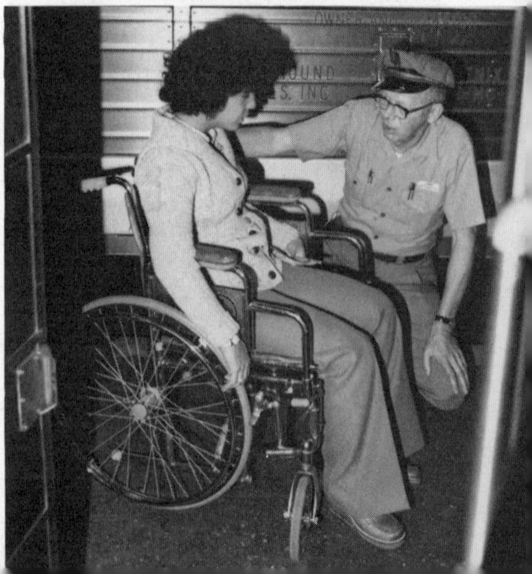

The baggageman puts a baggage tag on Teri's chair and gives her the stub. (Always keep your baggage stub.)

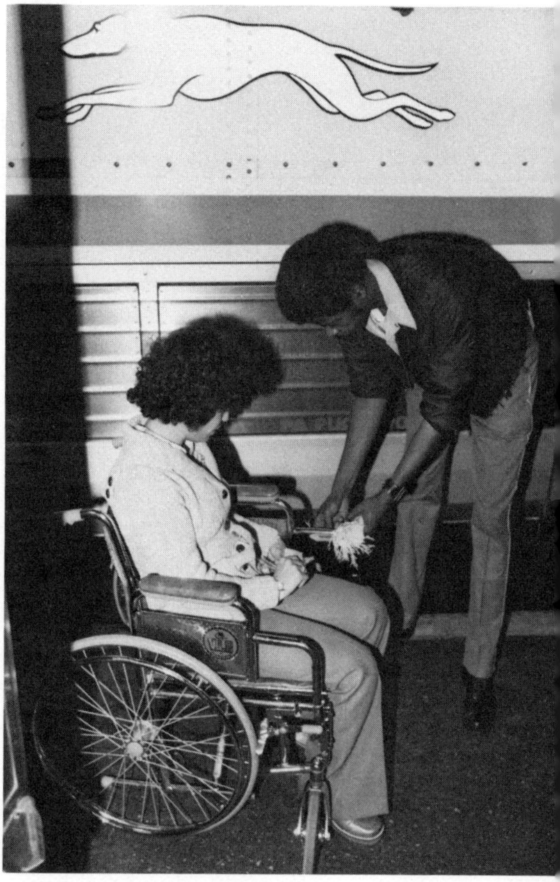

The driver helps Teri onto the bus and into her seat.

And the chair goes down below.

Refreshments en route . . . on a bus ride, especially on a long trip, it's a good idea to take a beverage and some food along. You might hit a rest stop where the restaurant is inaccessible.

Arriving in Philadelphia, the chair is first out. New York has advised its Philly office that Teri is arriving at noon, and a bus-line rep meets her.

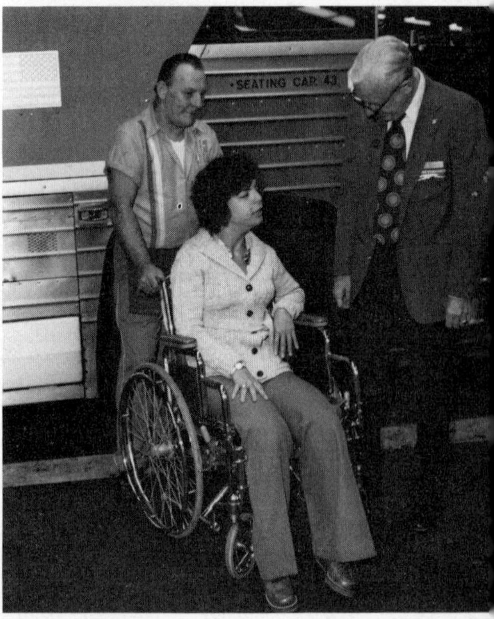

He assigns a porter to take her up to the street. This time it is tricky, but fun. The porter is adept in handling wheelchairs, even on an escalator. A tip of a dollar or so is in order for such personalized service.

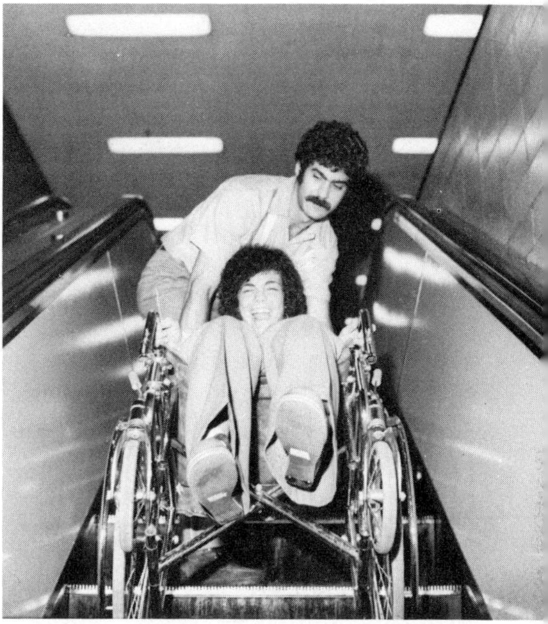

Journey's end. Friends meet Teri at the station.

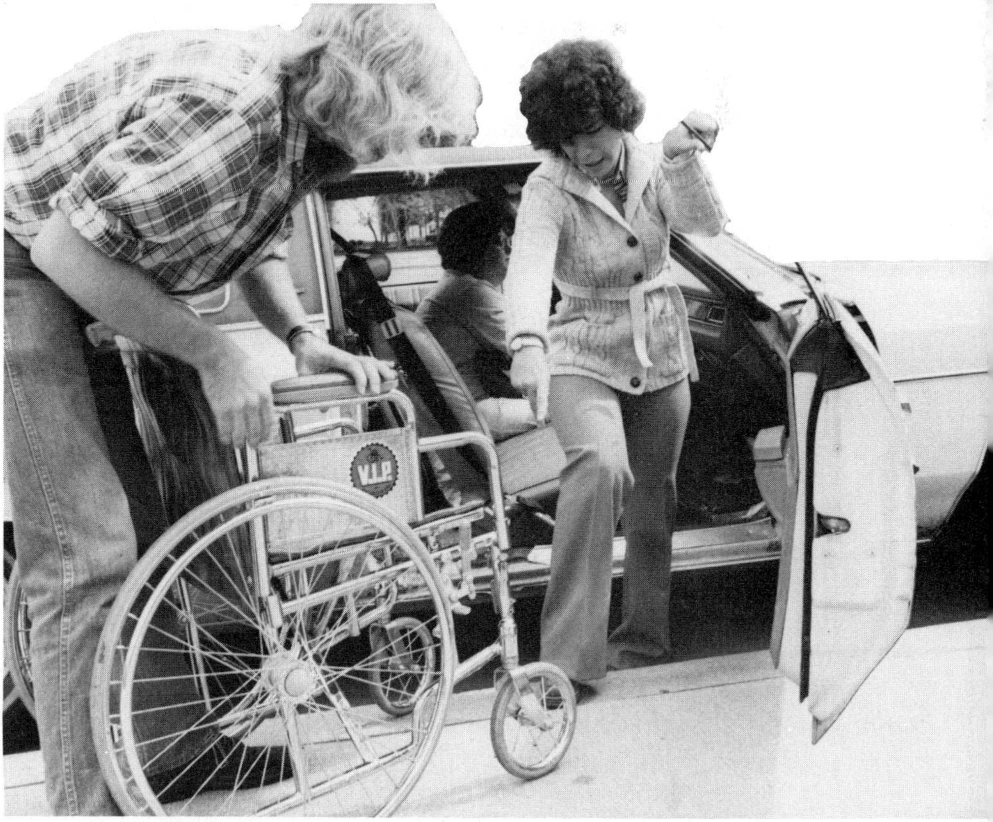

The ICC regulation* concerned with disabled travelers also requires that all stations constructed or renovated after January 1, 1978, be barrier-free. Already many stations are, and in routing you, Greyhound and Trailways will try to build your rest stops around terminals that feature lowered drinking fountaions and telephones, special wide restroom stalls, and ramps. The Greyhound and Trailways facilities at Albuquerque and Denver are among the modified stations. Also, Greyhound terminals in Miami, Reno, Cincinnati, Little Rock, Buffalo, and Albany; and Trailways terminals in Jackson (Mississippi), Chattanooga, San Antonio, Fort Worth, and El Paso. New stations are being added to the list monthly.

THE BASICS

EQUIPMENT

Intercity buses have two-abreast reclining seats that are seventeen inches wide. In general they are climate controlled, have tinted windows, individual reading lamps, and a compact restroom in the rear. (Ambulatory passengers who can easily sit anywhere often try to avoid the very back rows, which always have the traffic to and from the restroom.)

The aisle is only fourteen inches wide and there are at least two steps into a bus. Greyhound's new Americruisers have the first step fifteen inches from the ground. Older model buses may have a steeper step, while some newer ones kneel by an air suspension system that lowers them an additional four inches to facilitate boarding. Thirty kneeling buses are now in Greyhound's fleet on an experimental basis, and other buses could be retrofitted with similar systems.

FARES, PASSES AND TOURS

In addition to their regular fares (compare the regular bus fare of $60.30 Dallas to Chicago with $64 by train and $93 by air), the buslines at times offer a number of special promotional fares.

* Interstate Commerce Commission rules decided May 20, 1977, and docketed as Ex Parte No. MC-95 *Interstate Transportation of Passengers by Motor Common Carriers.*

Both Greyhound and Trailways offer passes at a fixed price for unlimited travel in the United States (except Alaska) and Canada for a given time period. Called Ameripass and Eaglepass respectively, sample rates are $165 for fifteen days, $225 for thirty days, and $325 for sixty days.

To determine whether the pass or straight tickets are your best buy, add up the cost of straight tickets to the places you will visit and see which figure is lower. Note that the Helping Hand and Good Samaritan systems apply to any of the promotional fares or passes, letting two go for the price of one.

Greyhound's escorted tour program, with hundreds of tours featuring national parks, scenic attractions, and special events, can be built around a Helping Hand fare arrangement: the helper rides free, but he or she pays the regular rate for hotels, sightseeing, and meals. Three places or more, depending on space availability, are designated for handicapped travelers and their companions on any tour. Examples of the escorted tour possibilities are as follows: the Black Hills, eight days from Chicago at $396 per person twin room basis, minus $125 HH reduction; and Utah Parks, seven days from Los Angeles at $298 per person twin room basis, minus an HH reduction of $82.38. Check with Greyhound information offices for departure dates and other tour possibilities.

Both Greyhound and Trailways allow guide dogs for blind or deaf passengers to ride free with their masters, and Greyhound offers discount rates to blind persons.

All fares quoted above are subject to change.

OVERNIGHTS

Discounts at Rodeway or Ramada Inns, courtesy car pickups at the terminal, and discounts at some restaurants are offered in conjunction with the Greyhound Ameripass. They are detailed in a folder available from Greyhound. The hotel list includes some very fine ones. Again, check individually for accessibility.

Trailways provides basic information about hotels or motels within walking distance of its terminals, and will probably suggest a Holiday Inn when convenient.

BAGGAGE

One nonmotorized, folding wheelchair, crutches, a walker, or any similar device can be carried free in the baggage compartment. You are allowed three suitcases, but if you are touring by bus, it is advisable to travel light. Loose fitting, wrinkleproof clothes feel best and look best after sitting in a bus all day. Keep with you a small flight bag of things you might need en route, such as medicine, a sweater, folding slippers, or a transistor radio with an earplug attachment. Most major stations have a baggage counter or lockers where you can leave bags overnight. Note that if your bags are not available within thirty minutes of arrival, the carrier must deliver them to your local address at its expense. Liability for loss of or damage to checked baggage is limited, not to exceed $250 per adult ticket.

GRATUITIES

The going rate to tip a red cap is thirty-five to fifty cents per bag, depending on the location (more in the big East Coast cities, for example, than in a small Midwestern town). If a porter pushes your chair and gives special attention, a dollar or two may be offered.

HINTS

- Take a thermos of something to drink and a sandwich, fruit, cheese and crackers, or other light foods when you travel by bus. Not all terminal restaurants are accessible.
- Take a small pillow along for naps—the inflatable kind often used at the beach is handy.
- The new Day Insert Travel Chair is narrow enough to move through a bus aisle. Contact YAD, Route 2, Box 78, Ladson, SC 29456. Also see index.

3

TRAINS

The first thing to know about train travel in America is that it is now possible for you. The concurrent comeback of the railroad and the growing awareness of handicapped and elderly persons have happily resulted in new accessible cars, sixty new or modified barrier-free stations, and a personnel training program that makes even much of the old equipment and many of the antiquated stations negotiable, if not ideal, by aid of manpower.

The second thing to know about train travel is how to go about it. Amtrak, the national railroad passenger corporation, recommends that when you call for a reservation—as much in advance as possible—you discuss fully your disability and requirements and ask yourself and the reservations clerk questions along these lines:

- Will I be able to move unassisted from the street, through the station, to the train platform, and onto the train?
- If not, will someone be on hand to help me?
- Are wheelchairs available at my particular station?
- Do I need to travel with a companion?
- Are the train aisles wide enough for my chair?

• If I have difficulty walking through a moving train, will someone bring meals to my seat or room?

• My particular disabilities and needs are thus and so. What accommodation will be most comfortable and convenient?

Pictured here is Teri, who is making her first train trip, between Philadelphia and New York. She had called Amtrak several days in advance, told them she was in a wheelchair, and asked pertinent questions. Her call was referred within Amtrak to a special service desk, which coordinated her trip and called her back to discuss the accessibility of the stations. (Philadelphia's Thirtieth Street Station was for the most part barrier-free; New York's Pennsylvania Station is less so, but plans are underway to install an elevator from street level down to the tracks for use by persons with mobility problems.) Amtrak recommended that Teri take a train equipped with a specially designed seat and lavatory for wheelchair passengers. Services available include a red cap (porter) to await you at the station entrance and take you to the train.

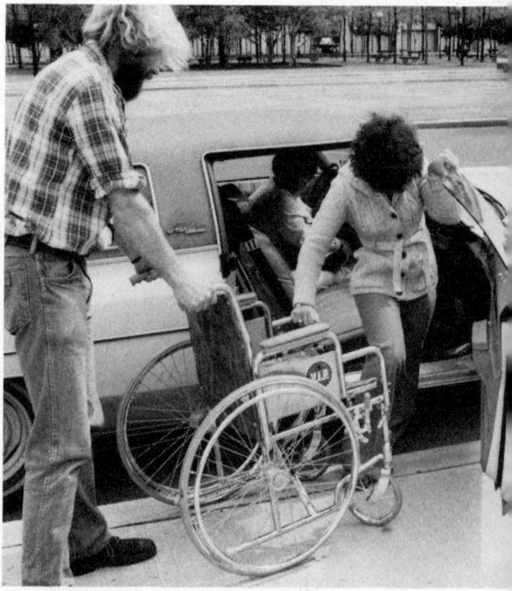

Teri does not need a red cap on arrival. Friends have driven her to the station.

She picks up her ticket at the ticket counter.

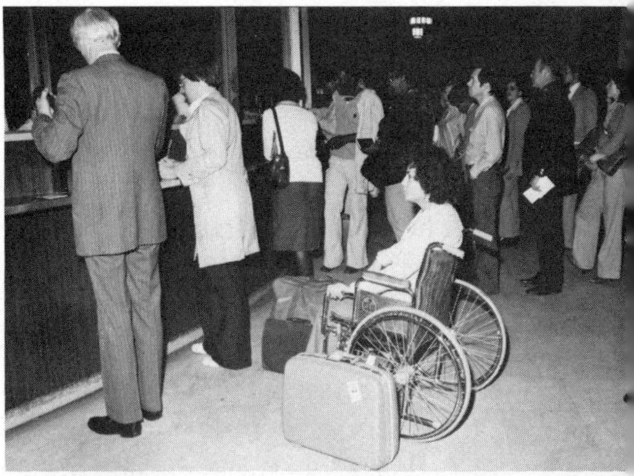

She then reports to the information desk. Amtrak is expecting her and a red cap arrives to escort her to the boarding platform by way of a freight elevator, often hard to locate and operate on your own.

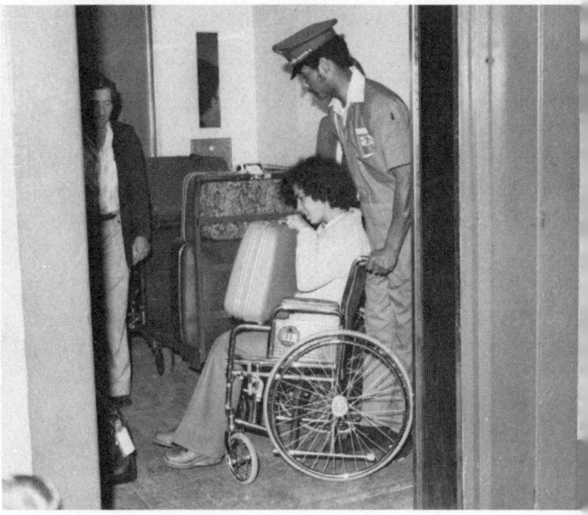

The seat designated for wheelchair riders on Amfleet trains is in coach class, generally not reserved accommodations on short-distance runs. When a disabled passenger travels, however, that seat becomes a reserved seat and the exact car and seat number are indicated on your ticket. The red cap then lines your chair up with the position on the platform where your car will stop. It is virtually impossible for an independent traveler to locate this position on his own, and crucially important that a wheelchair traveler be in the right place at the right time for boarding.

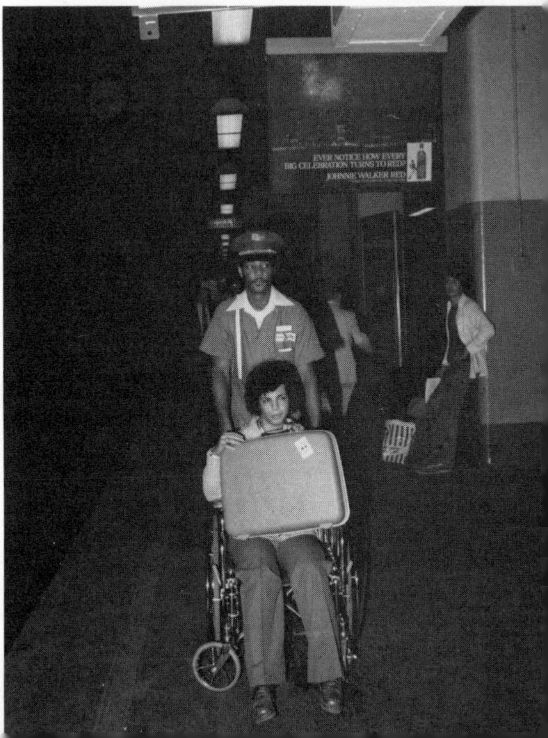

The train pulls in and out within minutes, so the red cap quickly maneuvers the chair onto and into the train and helps settle Teri into her seat. The Amtrak red cap service is free, but a tip of a dollar or two—depending on how much service has been rendered—is in order. (Have it ready and in your pocket. There is no time to fumble in your wallet before the train pulls out.)

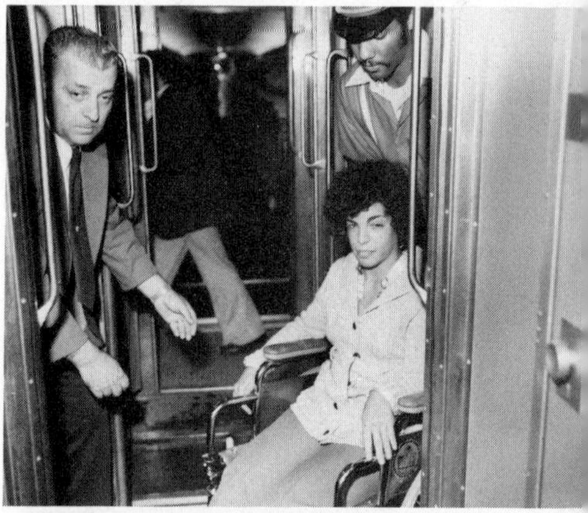

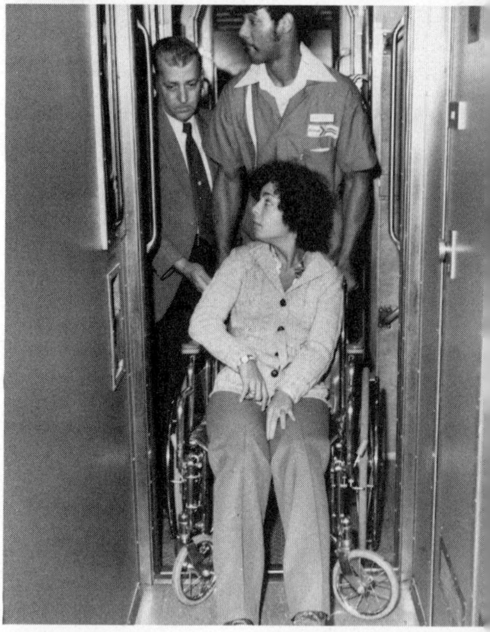

A space to store the wheelchair is just behind the passenger's swivel seat.

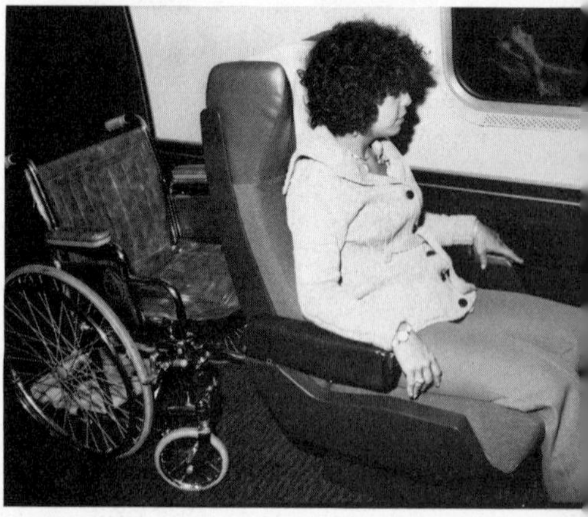

The aisle is twenty-six inches wide, but Teri is encouraged to stay in her train seat unless she wishes to use the lavatory across the aisle, designed for wheelchairs.

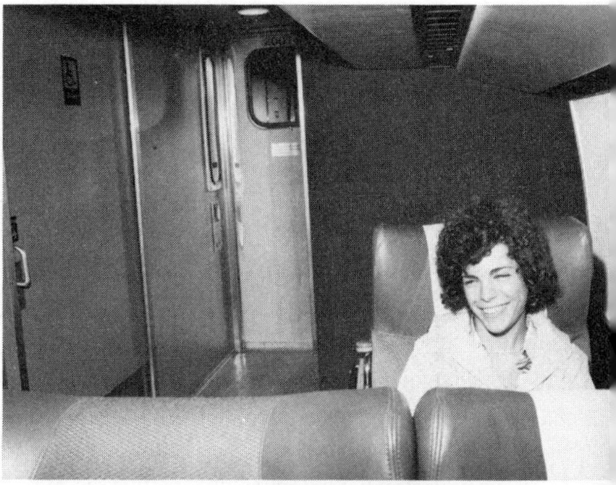

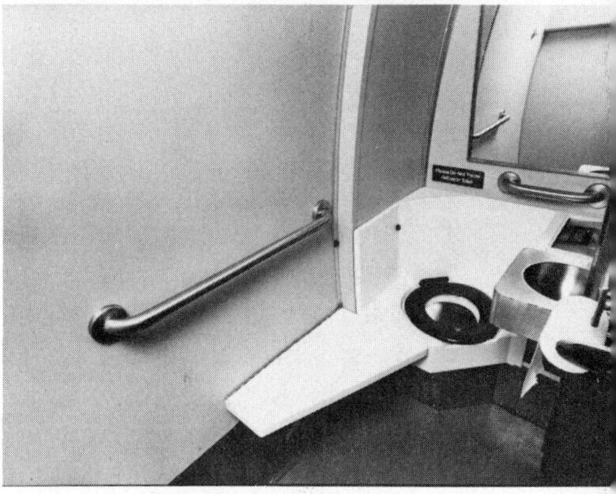

The conductor takes Teri's ticket and offers to bring her anything she might like to order from the snack bar. As a convenience, the special seat is in the food service coach.

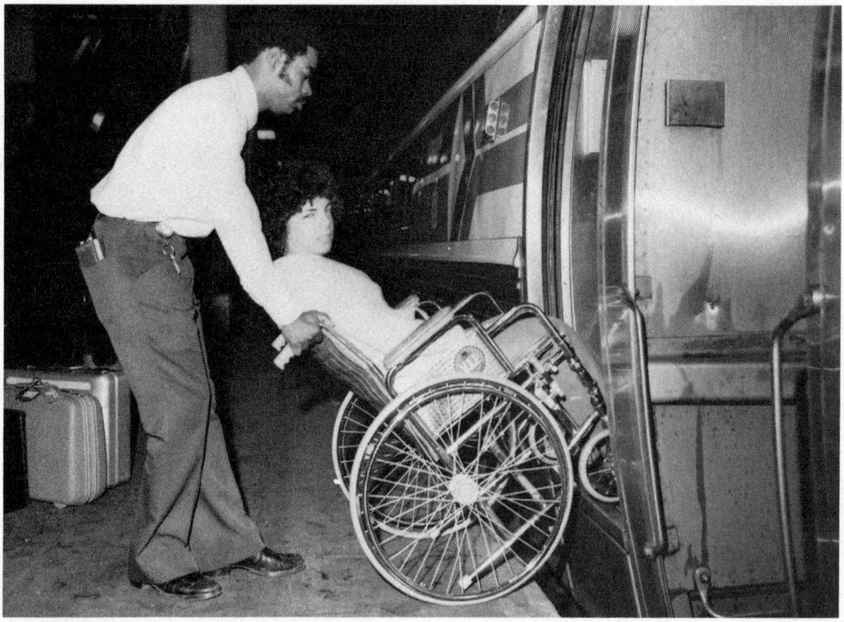

In New York a red cap had been assigned to meet Teri and assist her off the train. He does so in minutes. The train will continue to Boston. Amtrak personnel are trained in techniques of maneuvering wheelchairs and helping persons with mobility problems and blind persons, when assistance is requested.

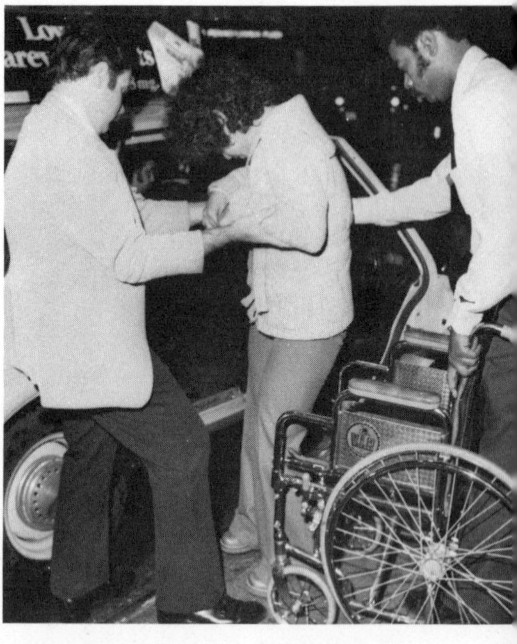

The red cap takes Teri up to the street by means of two elevators and finds her a cab. Again a tip is in order.

Not all Amtrak coaches are as modern as the one shown here, although 95 percent of passengers on short hauls are now riding in similar cars. Amtrak, which operates about 95 percent of the intercity trains in the United States, has a fivefold characterization of its equipment:

Amfleet—Coach class cars used nationwide on short-, medium-, and a few long-distance hauls. (Short haul is considered to be less than 500 miles; medium, 500 or more miles, but not overnight; and long, overnight.) The food service cars (called Amclub, Amcafé, or Amdinette) are fitted or being retrofitted with a special swivel seat whose armrest folds down, and with space behind for a wheelchair. A restroom that accommodates a wheelchair is across the aisle.

Rohr Turboliner—Seven runs between New York City and Buffalo, and New York/Albany and Montreal. The seat and restroom for the disabled are in the first class Turboclub car, although a handicapped person requiring this seat pays regular coach fare. The French Turboliners operating in the Chicago area, however, were not designed by Amtrak but were bought ready-made and do not have accessible restrooms.

Metroliner—The high-speed trains between Washington, D.C., and New York cut one hour off the timetable of Amfleet and conventional trains on that route. The coach fare at press time is $26.00 one-way, compared with $21.00 on Amfleet. The aisle width in Metroclub cars can take a wheelchair, but the lavatories cannot.

Conventional—An assortment of twenty-five- to thirty-year-old cars that Amtrak acquired along with management of the railroads. Used mostly on long-distance routes. Not ideal if you have mobility problems, but the windows in most sleeping cars are removable for boarding stretcher-borne passengers. A bedroom with convertible seats and a private bathroom (too small for wheelchairs) is the most comfortable arrangement for wheelchair passengers on conventional trains. Meals can be served in the compartments.

Superliner—Brand-new double-decker long-distance cars are expected to come on line in late 1978 or early 1979 with these features for disabled travelers: a swivel seat and special restroom in coach and one bedroom with accessible private bath in every sleeping car. These cars will appear first on the Chicago/Seattle *Empire Builder* and *North Coast Hiawatha*, and will subsequently replace old cars on the San Francisco *Zephyr* (Chicago/San Francisco), the Chicago/Los Angeles *Southwest Limited*, the New Orleans/L.A. *Sunset Limited*, and the L.A./Seattle *Coast Starlight.* When making reservations, check to see which trains have received the Superliner equipment.

The chart and route map reprinted on these pages, courtesy of Amtrak, may be useful in planning your trip. Note that "Height from platform to train vestibule" could bring the train entrance to platform level, which is the case at many major stations with elevated platforms.

SPECIAL SERVICES

In addition to trip coordination and red caps, Amtrak is also able to provide these services, with advance notice.

WHEELCHAIRS

Wheelchairs are available at almost 400 stations (out of a total of 524 Amtrak stations). If you are a senior citizen or are about to have a baby or just broke a leg or normally use crutches, a cane, or walker and don't feel up to covering the long distances at some stations, don't hesitate to ask for a wheelchair. Also remind Amtrak to have one waiting at your destination.

ASSISTANCE

Help getting on and off the train is available at many stations. Some stations are virtually unmanned, however, in which case you will be advised to have a companion who can provide the necessary assistance bring you to the station.

Amtrak is currently testing a loading chair device as well as a hydraulic chair lift, either or both of which may become standard equipment wherever the train entrance is higher than the platform.

Amtrak Equipment

	Amcafe, Amclub, Amdinette	Amcoach	Turboclub	Conventional coach*	Conventional sleeper*	Superliner coach	Superliner sleeper	Metrocoach	Metroclub
Height from platform to train vestibule**	51	51	51	51	51	18	18	level	
Doorway width to train vestibule	30	30	27	29	29	36	36	30	30
Doorway width into passenger area	30	30	32	26½	26½	30	30	29½	29½
Aisle width	26	23	30	20½-24	20½-24	na	na	25	33
Aisle width to special accommodation	33	na	30	na	na	30	30	na	na
Aisle width from special seat to food service area	26	na	na	na	na	na	na	na	na

All measurements are in inches.
na=not applicable
*The conventional equipment is a hodgepodge of different designs, and measurements vary; these are typical, but may not represent the extremes.
**Distance will vary from station to station. Specific information about particular stations and trains can be obtained by phoning the toll-free number listed later in this section.

Courtesy of Amtrak

RED CAPS

Bags can be handled whether or not you need any other assistance, at major stations.

FOR BLIND PASSENGERS

If you normally move about in public places unaided, you are not considered disabled by Amtrak and may travel with or without a guide dog (no fare) or a companion. A 25 percent discount is available to you and your companion provided you have certain coupons from the American Foundation for the Blind. (See General Information, Part IV, Section 1.) If you do need assistance, you should request it when making reservations, or mention it to the conductor when he collects your ticket. He can advise you of station stops and help you off the train.

FOR DEAF PASSENGERS

A Teletypewriter (TTY) at Amtrak central reservations office can communicate with customers who use such Teletypewriters. Call 800-523-6590 or 91; in Pennsylvania only, call 800-562-6960. Deaf passengers who need assistance may let the conductor know when he collects tickets. He can advise you personally when your stop is called. Amtrak personnel generally carry paper and pencils in order to communicate in writing if necessary.

MEDICAL AIDES

Amtrak can engage medical aides to accompany passengers who might need a nurse or other attendant en route, or who have no one to travel with them and cannot make the trip alone. There is no charge for the Amtrak service, but the traveler enters into a private agreement with the aide: the traveler pays for the services rendered and transportation costs.

STRETCHERS

When requested ten days in advance, it may be possible for stretcher-borne persons to travel in private bedrooms, being boarded through a removable window.

THE BASICS

MEALS

Fast foods at the snack bars in the food service cars are reasonable. Sample approximate prices: milk $.30, Cokes $.40, sandwiches $.80 to $1.75. In the dining cars the food is adequate, and complete dinners of meat or chicken range from $4.25 to $7.50. Beer, wine, and liquor are available.

On long-distance trains, Amtrak can provide special-diet meals if you notify them five days in advance.

DINERS

If you are hungry, go to the dining car as soon as meals are announced. Waits can be long. Also note that trains still observe the old custom of passengers writing out their own meal orders.

GRATUITIES

While the so-called Expedited Red Cap service that Amtrak offers is free, a tip to the red cap is in order. You may offer him a dollar or two if he has personally wheeled you down to the tracks and onto the train, or given other special considerations. The going rate for carrying your luggage is now $.35 to $.50 cents per bag, depending on the location (more generous in large Northeastern cities than in small Midwestern towns, for example). You do not tip conductors or anyone on a managerial level who gives you a hand. Dining car stewards are tipped 15 percent of the bill. If you are served in your seat or room because of your inability to get to the snack bar or diner, Amtrak waives a service charge, but you may wish to tip the person who serves you. Sleeping car attendants get a dollar a night.

BAGGAGE

On Amtrak you can take two standard suitcases per person if you are traveling coach in the passenger cars (more in private compartments); and three pieces weighing no more than 150 pounds total can be checked through (make sure that your train has a baggage car in this case). Identify all bags both outside and inside with name and address, as well as the address at your destination.

FARES

The ever-changing fares vary with the seasons and even the days of the week and the hours of the day. Whenever you are buying round-trip tickets be sure to *ask* if there are any special fares you qualify for. If you can be flexible about the days or hours you can travel, tell the agent. You stand to save 25 percent or more on certain runs on off days at off hours. Some experienced train riders always buy an excursion fare if they think they'll travel within its restrictions. You can always pay an additional fare to make the ticket valid, if necessary, but you won't be reimbursed on a regular round-trip ticket should your travel schedule ultimately qualify you for the lower excursion fare.

Here are representative New York to Chicago fares: $61 *rail passage* (coach), plus $49 for a single roomette (sleeper) or $92 for a double bedroom. Because the single is too compact, Amtrak offers disabled passengers a discount on its older long-distance equipment by waiving the 50 percent increase in rail passage that is normally charged for single occupancy of a double bedroom. Thus, on the New York–Chicago fare the unaccompanied disabled passenger would pay $153 for a double bedroom compared with $183.50, which a single ablebodied passenger would pay for the same accommodation. On the new Superliner sleepers, described above, disabled passengers will pay regular rates.

Children two to twelve pay half fare. Also ask about Family Fares. Note again that blind travelers (and one companion) holding coupons from the American Foundation for the Blind are entitled to a 25 percent discount.

RAILPASS

A U.S.A. Rail Pass valid for unlimited travel over the 26,000 route miles of Amtrak and Southern Railways, allows you to travel for fourteen contiguous days at $185, twenty-one days at $250, and thirty days at $295. These were 1977/78 winter rates. Summer rates tend to be higher. Ask about family railpass rates.

The railpass may or may not be a super duper saver. To determine whether the pass or straight tickets is your best buy do this: get railpass details and a timetable from Amtrak and plot your trip. How many days are involved? Now run through the trip and add up the cost of straight tickets for the same trip.

Example: You are planning a two-week trip with the routing: Springfield, Massachusetts, to Chicago to New Orleans to Orlando, Florida (via Birmingham), and back to Springfield (via New York). The fares total $279.75, so the railpass at $185 is your best buy. If you are making the Springfield-Chicago round trip, which adds up to $130, the pass is not the cheapest fare.

PACKAGES

Amtrak offers a wide range of tour packages. Applying your own travel know-how to them (get the folders at Amtrak ticket offices), figure out which ones suit you. Example: The Family Holiday Plans for Disney World, to be used in conjunction with Amtrak family fares, include two days at Disney World and two nights at your choice of four hotels listed on the tour folder. Either check the hotels offered against *Orlando's Guide for the Handicapped* (see Florida under the state listings), or check them against the hotel chain directories, or call their toll-free numbers (see the Hotels and Motels section in Part III). Which ones are accessible? The books show that, of the four hotels on the Family Holiday Plan, Dutch Inn, Howard Johnson's, and TraveLodge are accessible. (And when buying such a package, don't forget to tell Amtrak or your travel agent that you need an accessible room and to get confirmation on this. Make sure your train has the type of accommodation you wish.)

Another package example: This one is called the Rail, Road & City Adventure program. It offers holders of the railpass an opportunity to rent a Hertz sedan or intermediate-size car and stay overnight at a Holiday Inn in a number of cities at a fixed price. In Los Angeles it is a flat $35.95. Note that in Los Angeles the Holiday Inn room alone could run between $25 and $35 if bought separately. Applying the travel methodology set forth in this book, you can easily confirm that Hertz in L.A. has hand-control cars and that Holiday Inns have accessible rooms. Book them when you make your Amtrak arrangement and also follow up with a phone call or letter to Hertz and Holiday Inns stating your specific requirements.

TOLL FREE RESERVATIONS AND INFORMATION

Use the following numbers to call for Amtrak information and reservations. Unless a different area code is specified, first dial 1, where required, then 800.

Arkansas, Kentucky, 874-2775; Alabama, Georgia, Louisiana, Mississippi, North Carolina, South Carolina, Tennessee, 874-2800; Arizona, Colorado, Kansas, Idaho, Montana, Nebraska, Nevada, New Mexico, North Dakota, Oklahoma, Oregon, Utah, Wyoming, 421-8320; Delaware, Maryland, New Jersey, New York (except Buffalo, 716-523-5720, and New York City, 212-736-4545) 523-5700; Connecticut, District of Columbia, 523-5720; Indiana, Iowa, Wisconsin, Michigan (except Northern Michigan), 621-0353; Northern Michigan, Minnesota, Missouri, South Dakota, Washington, 421-8320; Massachusetts, New Hampshire, Rhode Island, Vermont, 523-5720; Virginia, West Virginia, 874-2775; California (except L.A., 213-624-0171), 648-3850; Florida (except Jacksonville, 904-731-1600), 342-2520; Maine, 523-5731; Ohio, 621-0317; Pennsylvania (except Philadelphia, 215-824-1600), 562-5380; Texas, 421-8320; Illinois (except Chicago, 312-786-1333), 972-9147.

Note again that deaf persons may communicate by means of Teletypewriters through these 800 numbers: 523-6590 or 91 nationwide except Pennsylvania, where the number is 562-6960.

BARRIER-FREE STATIONS

Many Amtrak stations can be used by nonambulatory passengers, but they may need assistance in getting into the terminal or down to the tracks. Some stations are semiaccessible: Union Station in Washington is an example of this. Passengers coming from or going north can use it, but the southbound tracks are inaccessible. About sixty stations are totally accessible, and there is an ongoing program to build or upgrade stations in that respect. Here is a partial list of the barrier-free stations:

- Arizona
  - Flagstaff
- California
  - Del Mar
  - Fullerton
  - Martinez
  - San Diego
- Connecticut
  - Berlin
  - Meriden
  - Old Saybrook
  - Thompsonville
  - Wallingford
  - Windsor
- Delaware
  - Wilmington
- Florida
  - Clearwater
  - Deland
  - Delray Beach
  - Ft. Lauderdale
  - Hollywood
  - Jacksonville
  - Miami
  - Orlando
  - St. Petersburg
  - Sanford
  - Waldo
  - Wildwood
  - Winterpark
- Georgia
  - Savannah
- Kentucky
  - Louisville
- Massachusetts
  - Boston
    - Back Bay
    - South Station
  - Springfield
- Montana
  - Belton
  - Libby
  - Miles City
  - Wolfe Point
- New Jersey
  - Trenton
- New York
  - New York
    - Grand Central
    - Penn Station
- North Carolina
  - Raleigh
- Ohio
  - Cleveland
- Oregon
  - Eugene
  - Klamath Falls
  - Portland
- Pennsylvania
  - Middletown

Pennsylvania (*cont'd.*)
  Philadelphia
    North Philadelphia
Rhode Island
  Westerly
Utah
  Brigham City
Virginia
  Richmond
  Roanoke
Washington
  Vancouver
West Virginia
  Bluefield
  Parkersburg

AMTRAK BOOKLET

Access Amtrak, a guide to services for the elderly and handicapped is available free from Amtrak at 400 North Capitol Street, N.W., Washington, D.C. 20001.

MISCELLANEOUS

Problems?—En route speak to the conductor. He is in charge of the train. At the station ask for the station service office, the station supervisor or—in smaller stations—the ticket clerk.

Wardrobe and Packing—Wear comfortable clothes. If you are taking an overnight trip and are traveling coach, women might take an at-home type of caftan or kimono to change into. Many cars on long-distance trains include a dressing room. Keep whatever you will need for the trip in one easy-to-handle suitcase or tote bag. This also applies to travelers in sleeping compartments. Keep a sweater at hand.

Altitude—If you have respiratory problems or a heart condition, check your Amtrak route against an atlas for altitude. (Trains often go through high mountains.) Amtrak can tell you the altitude for major cities en route.

THE RAILROADS

Amtrak, mandated by Congress in 1971 to run the nation's railroads, now operates most of the intercity trains in this country. For that reason, train travel in America is almost synonymous with Amtrak. In addition to Amtrak the principal railroads are the Southern and the Denver & Rio Grande Western. Their routes are identified on the map.

INTERCITY RAIL PASSENGER ROUTES
National Railroad Passenger Corporation

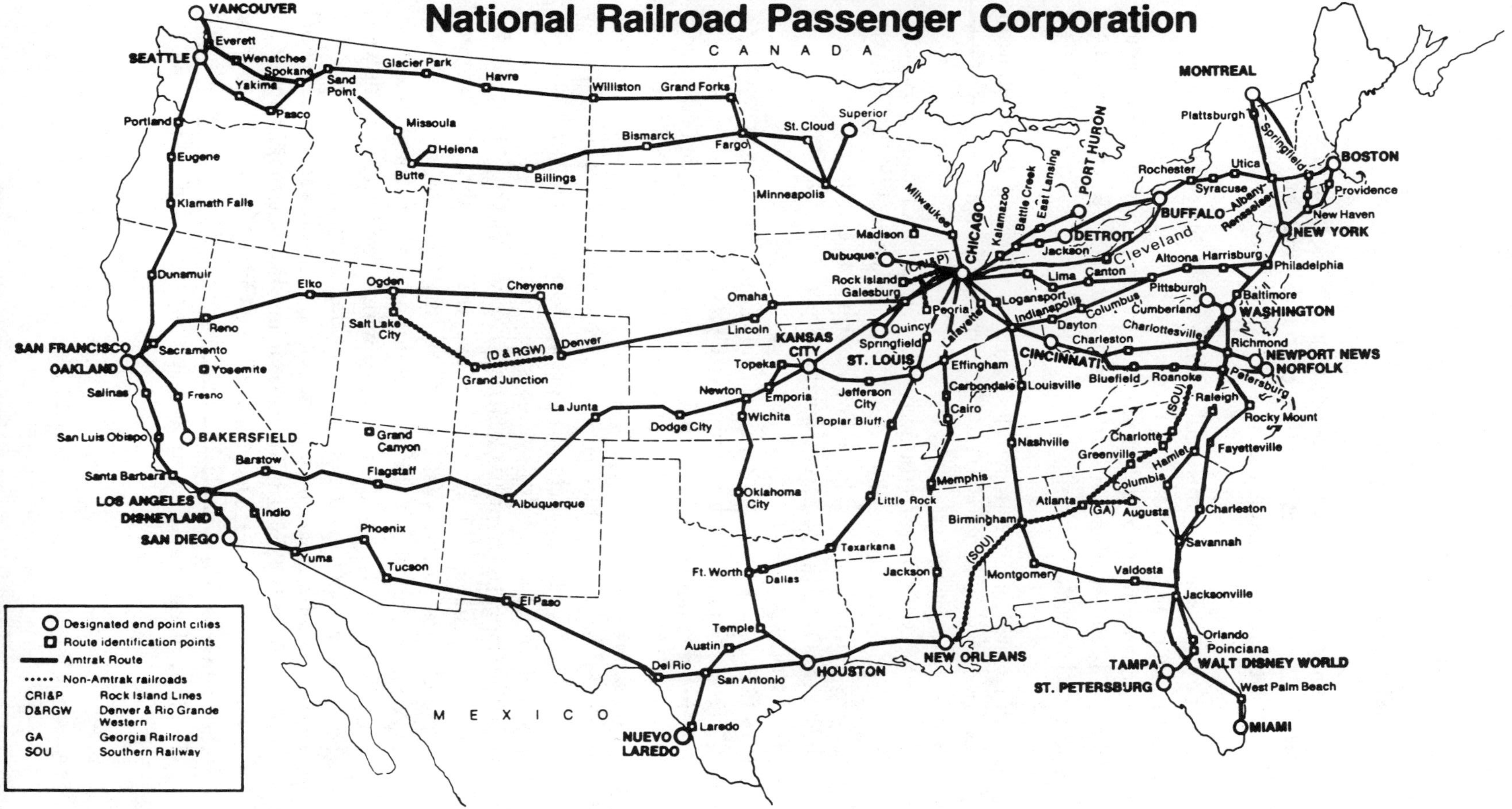

Rail travel offers the advantages of:

- Downtown-to-downtown convenience. A saving, too, if you use limos or ambulettes to a final central destination.
- Sleeping compartments.
- Scenery.
- Your choice of meals and mealtimes. By bus you eat when it stops and by plane you eat when served.
- A chance to relax and socialize. Most trains have large reclining seats, fold-down tables on seatbacks, foot rests or leg rests, and bars in the club cars.

What are the best train rides? Are you judging by equipment, scenery, service, or smoothness of the tracks? Listed below are ranking favorites, however:

- *Southwest Limited* (formerly *Super Chief*). Chicago/L.A. (and slated for the new Superline cars). Observation cars look out onto the desert, mountains, stars. Here you can sip coffee and orange juice in bed and watch the Kansas wheat fields catch the first rays of light. Fifty-two hours.
- *Coast Starlight.* L.A./Seattle. Along the Pacific coast and past Cascades National Park in Oregon. Thirty-one hours.
- *Silver Meteor.* N.Y./Miami. Running on very smooth tracks south of Washington. Twenty-five hours.
- *Empire Builder.* Chicago/Seattle. With a fine tradition and a credit to the new double-decker Superliner equipment. Through the evergreen Northwest including Glacier National Park, with fascinating rock formations. Fifty-six hours.
- *Southern Crescent.* Washington/New Orleans. Operated by Southern Railway. Makes three round trips weekly: Washington/New Orleans. Daily: Washington/Atlanta. Operates old equipment over rough roadbeds (and may run late) but has a devoted following, including railfans. The dining service with white linen, fresh flowers, heavy silver, and good Southern cooking is renowned, as are the friendly, professional conductors, porters, and stewards. No special facilities for the disabled. Fourteen hours Washington/Atlanta.
- *Western Zephyr.* Denver/Salt Lake City. The premier train of the Denver & Rio Grande Western that runs through snow-capped Rockies, along mountain streams and rocky canyons. Good dining

service. The thirty-year-old equipment may be difficult or impossible to negotiate if you are nonambulatory. Nine hours.

NON-AMTRAK LINES

The major non-Amtrak intercity lines are the Southern Railway (book through Amtrak), the Denver & Rio Grande Western (303-629-7300), and Auto-Train. The first two both operate conventional old equipment, which does not easily accommodate the disabled. Their personnel will give you a hand if you do opt for these trains.

Auto-Train offers the interesting prospect of saving 900 miles of driving between Lorton, Virginia (seventeen hours), or Louisville, Kentucky (twenty-two hours), and Sanford, Florida, near Orlando, while your car is being ferried and you ride the train. Rates are $99 per car and $79 per passenger in peak winter and holiday periods, with reduced fares for other than the first passenger at other times. Included in the fare are meals and entertainment or games. Deluxe double sleeping compartments are $85 per person in peak season.

Many wheelchair-bound travelers have ridden the Auto-Train, although chairs cannot move through the narrow aisles. The railroad recommends a bedroom with private bath for greatest comfort. Meals can be served at your coach seat or in your private bedroom if you are unable to go to the dining car. A straightback chair is used for boarding nonambulatory travelers.

Advise Auto-Train of special requirements when you reserve.

An Auto-Train/Eastern Airlines package allows your car to travel with Auto-Train while you fly. The package includes optional overnight hotel accommodations. Book through Eastern or a travel agent.

Auto-Train reservations and information: 800-424-1111; in Florida dial 1-800-424-1111; in the Washington, D.C., area, 785-4000. Auto-Train is at 1801 K Street, N.W., Washington, DC 20006.

Note: Any fares quoted above are samples and are subject to change.

4

AIRLINES

Here are twenty of the questions you are most likely to ask about air travel for handicapped passengers, at once the easiest and most complicated means of transportation.

1. *What do you mean by handicapped?*

The Federal Aviation Administration (FAA) identifies a handicapped passenger as one "who may need the assistance of another person to move expeditiously to an exit in the event of an emergency." There is no one Civil Aeronautics Board (CAB) definition; the various carriers have different definitions of "nonambulatory" and "physically handicapped." The most common definition of "nonambulatory" reads, in part, "Persons who are unable to walk or need support of another person to walk, but who are otherwise capable of caring for themselves." "Physically handicapped," as defined by several airlines, refers to "A person with any impairment or physical disability which would cause such a person to require special attention or assistance from carrier personnel." (See the charts below.)

2. *Is it possible for someone confined to a wheelchair or otherwise disabled to fly?*

Yes. One airline has stated it this way, "For anyone used to living alone and moving around his or her own neighborhood without assistance the experience of flying alone is one that can be undertaken with confidence." An airline may limit the number of unaccompanied amputees and paraplegics, however, to X number per flight, the number often being determined by the number of cabin or flight attendants (stewards and stewardesses) on the plane, as well as by the number of exits. (See Who May Fly elsewhere in this section.) In addition, any number may fly on most lines provided they are traveling with their own companions to assist them with meals or other personal needs, which the cabin attendants cannot do, or to help in the emergency evacuation of the aircraft. (The attendants may and often do lend a slight assist to any passenger, however.) On group tours made up of disabled individuals, large groups can travel (indeed entire wheelchair basketball teams do) provided there is an adequate number of ablebodied assistants in their group. Some airlines limit the length of a flight for nonambulatory passengers. Certain persons who may be asked to travel with an assistant include some quadriplegics, those unable to move to the lavatory (unless fitted with a catheter), deaf-and-blind, certain mentally retarded, mentally ill, or stretcher-borne passengers, as well as those requiring special oxygen. Also see the Medical Questions and Answers section in Part IV for medical conditions that may make flying inadvisable. Note that the captain (pilot) retains the authority to refuse the transport of *any* passengers whose condition would jeopardize their own well-being or that of the other passengers.

The number of disabled passengers accepted is related to how quickly the aircraft can be evacuated in an emergency and is usually based on the number of floor-level (nonwing) emergency exits. A wide-bodied plane, such as a Boeing 747, must be able to evacuate all passengers within ninety seconds, according to FAA regulations. This could include up to 14 nonambulatory/physically handicapped on the American Airlines 747, for example.

If you have never flown, make a short test flight to see how you like it before starting off on a long flight.

3. *How do I board the airplane?*

Airlines generally ask passengers who need special assistance to arrive at the airport forty-five minutes to an hour prior to flight time (up to ninety minutes early for international flights). This allows the airline time to preboard you, getting you settled and familiar with the aircraft before the other passengers board. Flight attendants will explain emergency evacuation procedures and answer any questions. A blind passenger, for example, will be guided through the plane with attention to its different features. A deaf person receives written instructions. Frontier Airlines gives out brochures outlining its emergency procedures, as well as a folder in Braille detailing the location of emergency exits. Ozark and Texas International Airlines also provide emergency information in Braille.

Boarding is done in one of several ways, depending on the airline, airport, and aircraft.

The preferred method is by jetway, a telescoping corridor that leads straight from the terminal to the plane door. (Here you may be transferred to a narrow chair that can be moved through the narrow plane aisle, or you may be boarded in your own chair, aisle space permitting.)

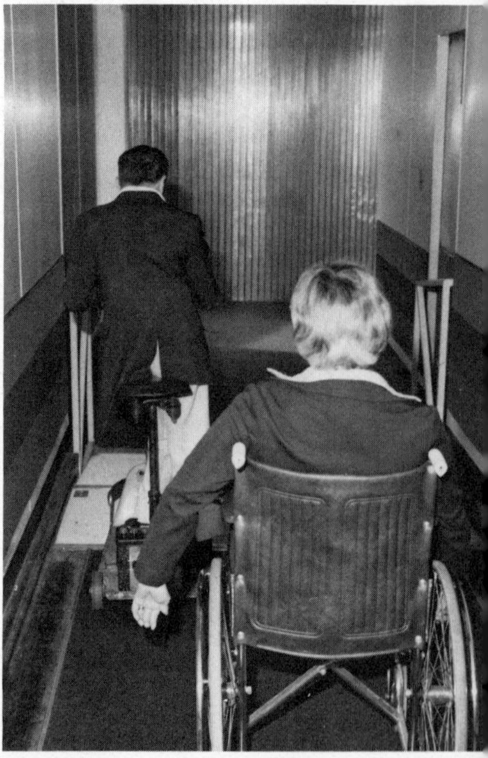

Photo by Lois Reamy

Forklift, cherry picker, catering truck—call it what you will.

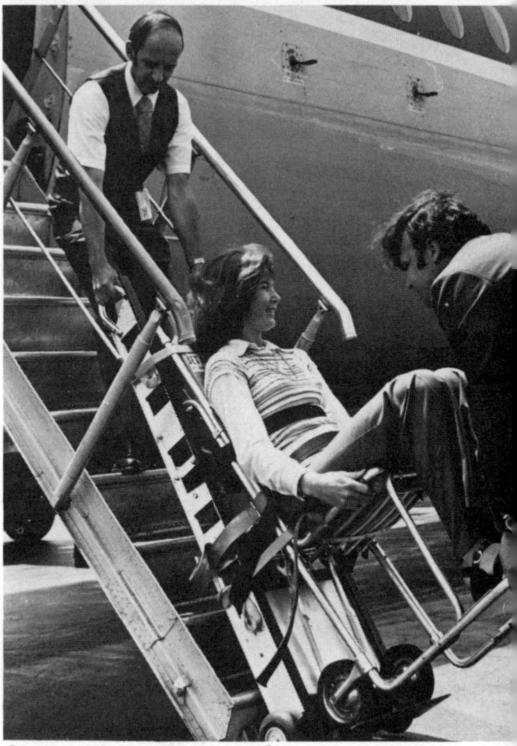

Courtesy Accent on Living ©

The "walking chair" or stairchair (also called airstair chair) shown here is Allegheny's version, called the "Manhandler."

TWA's "Handicapped Lift," an enclosed elevator-style vehicle that goes up and down like a cherry picker but which drives you straight from the boarding gate to the aircraft and keeps you dry in inclement weather. It is in operation at the following TWA terminals, which do not have jetways: Tucson, St. Louis, Albuquerque, Hartford, Cleveland, Columbus, Dayton, Las Vegas, Phoenix, Pittsburgh, and Louisville.

Trans World Airlines photo

Mobile lounge that elevates to the aircraft door and lowers to ground level to shuttle between plane and terminal. (This is one of the least-preferred methods with some disabled travelers, since they report that the lounges do not have tie-downs for chairs or convenient seats.)

Courtesy the Port of New York Authority, photo by D. Brewster

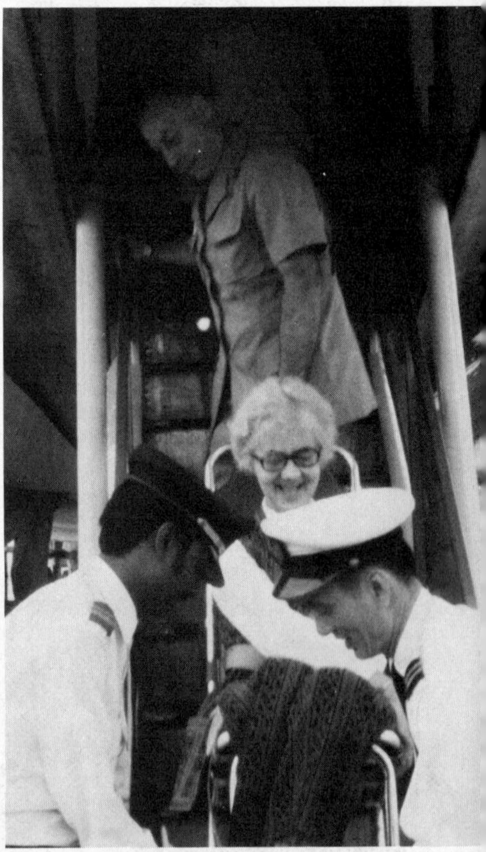

Courtesy Wings on Wheels

Last, and least favored, is two— or four—strong arms. At times you may be lifted bodily.

FAA-approved chair designed by a South Carolinian may soon appear on some airlines (TWA, Western, Frontier, Eastern, and Delta have expressed interest). You'd transfer from your chair to the Day Insert Travel Chair, be wheeled on board, and stay in the DIT-C, which fits into a conventional airline seat, for your flight. It can also enter the lavatory.

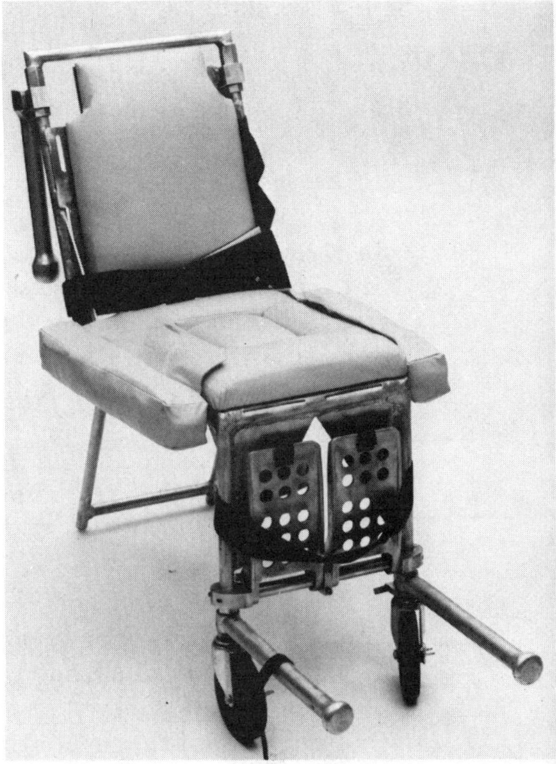

Courtesy YAD "Quality" Enterprises

The less sophisticated methods of enplaning and deplaning are likely to be found at the smaller airports or when you are flying on smaller aircraft. When flying in smaller aircraft, or into small airports, be sure to inquire about the boarding arrangements. Also bear in mind that even airports that do have jetways may not use them with every single flight. (June, featured in the Hawaii story elsewhere in this book, had checked airport accessibility in *Access Travel: Airports* [below] and was satisfied that Honolulu International Airport had jetways. It does, but her United Airlines charter flight did not park at one. Instead she and Bob deplaned by means of a cherry picker.)

4. *Can I remain in my wheelchair during the flight?*
No. According to the FAA, which sets most of the safety regulations for airlines, you must sit in the airplane seat, with your seat belt fastened for takeoff and landing. There are presently no U.S. airplanes with tie-downs and other support attachments to safeguard wheelchair passengers, although airlines and aircraft manufacturers are studying this possibility, especially for the next generation of aircraft that will probably appear in the mid-eighties.

5. *Will my wheelchair (crutches, walker, etc.) be located near my seat for use during a flight?*
The aisles are generally too narrow for a standard chair, and on crutches you may have to take the aisle sideways. Most likely your chair will be stowed in the pit and delivered to you when you deplane either at planeside (ideal and most common) or in the baggage claim area. In some cases, depending on the type of aircraft, an airline may fold your chair and stow it in the cabin. While this is not the custom, Western does it on occasion, as does United, which can place two folding chairs either in the first-class cloakroom of the Boeing-747 or in the video cabinet carryon baggage compartment of the DC-10. Canes, crutches, and walkers may be stored in an approved stowage compartment by the flight attendant and would not be used during an emergency evacuation. Some airlines might permit you to use them during the flight, however. If you have a cane that folds to a size convenient to keep with you, call it to the stewardess's attention.

6. *Can I sit wherever I wish?*

Yes and no. Be sure to state your preference. You might wish to request a seat assignment when you book your flight. If you work through a travel agent, discuss the airplane's configuration with him or her. He should have seating plans for the various aircraft of the various airlines. (The same aircraft may be slightly different depending on which airline flies it and even on the route.) If you are traveling with another person, you may like a row with only two seats. And you can choose between smoking and nonsmoking sections. The flight attendants know which rows are designated for the nonambulatory passengers, who, for example, may not sit in an emergency exit row, or in a section whose emergency exit is over a wing (a difficult way out in an emergency evacuation). On some lines, two nonambulatory passengers probably will not be assigned to seats in the same row. If you are blind, you may not sit by the emergency exit, where instructions for releasing the escape slide are printed. Otherwise, a blind passenger can probably sit just about anywhere. If you would like a seat near the lavatory or with as much legroom as possible for your bum knee, a letter from your physician might facilitate your request. (See questions dealing with seating under Medical Questions and Answers in Part IV.) If you can take only a limited number of steps, it is important to know the configuration of the airplane, because you may want to be near the lavatory. Also note that in some cases—because of the greater spaciousness—the lavatories may be farther from the seats in first class than in coach. Disabled persons are often assigned aisle seats.

7. *Must I be able to sit in an upright position?*

Passengers are generally required to have their seat backs in an upright position with seat belts fastened to protect them against the aircraft thrust at takeoff and landing, per Federal Regulation. The requirement does not apply to persons unable to sit erect for a medical reason, if these persons are carried in accordance with the operator's procedures and the seat back does not obstruct any passenger's access to the aisle or to an exit.

8. *Will the flight attendants help me to the lavatory?*

They sometimes lend support to someone who is not too steady, but are generally unable to assist the nonambulatory passenger. Until new aircraft come along with lavatories large enough to accommodate wheelchairs, getting to—and into—the lavatory will remain the single most difficult problem with the majority of nonambulatory passengers. There are various solutions, none of them great. Note that the organized tours designed for disabled travelers (see index for Flying Wheels, Rambling, and Wings on Wheels) all take along their own narrow chair for this purpose. Also note that a backless chair that collapses to eighteen by thirteen by nineteen inches, with a cushion at nineteen by four by fourteen inches, can even squeak through the lavatory door. Called the Norman Wheel Chair, it weighs twenty-five pounds total and is available from Falkenberg, 3612 S. W. Troy St., Portland, OR 97219, 503-246-5407. Being repriced at press time. Also see the Day Insert Travel Chair above and related question in the Medical Questions and Answers section in Part IV.

9. *Can I pull a curtain to conceal my seat?*

No. Seat backs are high, however, and a great number of travelers find privacy under an airline blanket.

10. *Will the airline provide a special diet?*

Yes. Certainly if it is a major scheduled carrier. For example, on four hours' notice United can oblige with these diets: bland, children, infant, diabetic, gluten free, high protein, hypoglycemic, low fat, low protein, low sodium, lactose restricted, low calorie, low cholesterol, and three vegetarian varieties. On twenty-four hours' notice they can readily dish up Hindu, kosher, Moslem, oriental, soul food, or Weight Watchers meals. Not all airlines are as versatile as United, but most can provide medically required diets, although they may require up to twenty-four hours' notice. If you have trouble managing food or if operations such as cutting meat present a problem, you might prefer to preorder a sandwich.

Although meals are served on flights of sufficient duration that coincide with mealtimes, and there are snacks on other flights of sufficient duration, at the time you book your flight ask if a meal will be served. You never pay for a meal on a U.S. airline.

11. *Must I travel first-class?*

No. When you call an airline and mention that you are disabled, the airline might suggest that you fly first-class. That's because the airlines believe you will be more comfortable in the wider seats and with more aisle space for getting in and out. There are also more flight attendants per passenger in first than in coach. You are not obliged to go first, and should not feel pressured to do so. On the other hand, if money is no object and you, too, think you'd be more comfortable, then do it. Comparative regular one-way fares: Atlanta to Miami, $100 first-class, $77 coach. Special low fares, carrying certain restrictions, are also available, such as a round-trip fare at $77.

12. *The airlines always advise disabled passengers* to notify them in advance—usually twenty-four hours—when they will be flying. So what if I just go out to the airport at the last minute and buy a ticket?*

A spot check of several airlines showed they would do their best to accommodate certain handicaps, even on the spur of the moment. By letting them know in advance, however, they can make it easier for you. For example, they like to reserve a convenient seat for you. Or you might be delayed until a narrow chair that is being used at another boarding gate becomes available. Or if there is a limit to the number of unaccompanied paraplegics or amputees that may fly, the number may have been filled. (At press time, while most airlines do have limits to the number of unaccompanied nonambulatory/physically handicapped passengers per flight—only Frontier Airlines has no restrictions—airline computers are not programmed to keep tabs. Thus, you could feasibly hold a confirmed reservation, go to the airport, and find that there was already a full complement of nonambulatory passengers who had arrived ahead of you. It is hoped this point will be cleared up over the next few months as the airlines continue to improve and standardize their procedures. Until then, arrive at the airport in good time. (See Airlines Are Up in the Air, below.)

* An Airport Transport Association sponsored meeting on carriage of handicapped persons (April 27, 1978) developed this list for recommendation to ATA members of types of passengers for whom advance notification might be required: nonambulatory; aero-stretcher; oxygen-assisted; respirator-assisted; infant (under seven days old); deaf or blind with or without dogs; deaf-and-blind, with or without dogs; pregnant, ninth month; mentally handicapped, with escort; unable-to-be-seated (nonstretcher); reclined-seat-required; nonstatic disease; requiring assistance; intravenous feeding required; jaw wired. Such requirements must be filed with the Civil Aeronautics Board when they become procedure and are published in the airline tariffs that travel professionals consult.

13. *Can I take my own oxygen for use on board?*

No. If packaged properly according to U.S. Department of Transportation (DOT) regulations (check with the airlines for packaging requirements), a personal oxygen supply can usually go as cargo. The airlines then can supply oxygen on twenty-four to seventy-two hours notice, depending on the carrier. The passenger may be required to travel with someone who can administer the oxygen. Standby emergency oxygen is available on air carriers. Also see related questions in Medical Questions and Answers in Part IV.

14. *Suppose a person requires two seats?*

He can book them and pay the full fare for one plus 50 percent fare for the second. For example, if the fare is $100 but he needs two seats, he will pay $150. On most equipment, the armrests dividing seats are removable. By flying at a nonpeak period (such as midday on a popular commuter route, or weekday as opposed to weekend), there's always a chance that nobody will occupy the adjacent seat and you can just spread out, free of charge. Sometimes the airline reservations agent will tell you how heavily a flight is booked.

15. *Who is responsible if my flight is delayed or we miss a connecting flight?*

The airline will make arrangements for you, which could range from booking you on the next convenient flight (even with a different line) to putting you up at a hotel for the night at its expense. In the event of a misconnection, the delivering carrier will be responsible for making your ongoing arrangements if it is at fault. That carrier is also responsible for delivering you to your connecting airline (i.e., actually placing you in the hands of the ground service personnel of that airline, even when it involves changing terminals). If a delay is due to a malfunction of the receiving airline, that airline will be responsible for you. As a disabled passenger you stand less chance of being "bumped" off an overbooked flight.

16. *If I have connecting flights, who tells the different carriers involved about my special needs?*

The originating airline is responsible for informing the connecting carriers that you need a wheelchair, a salt-free diet, or the like. To be on the safe side, however, you or your travel agent should advise the connecting carrier(s) yourselves.

17. *Who can assist me on the ground?*

Although some airports are beginning to offer disabled drivers long-term parking in short-term lots near the terminal, getting from your car to the terminal is often difficult if you drive to the airport. A shuttle bus usually swings through the long-term lot picking up drivers, but boarding that bus could be a hassle. You might find it more convenient to have a friend drive you to the airport, or to take a taxi.

At the terminal curb, you can usually find a skycap (an airport porter) to help with your baggage and chair. You may be able to actually check in with him. He may push you inside the terminal and take you to the boarding gates. When you arrive by plane, an airline ground service person will generally push you down to the baggage claim area, where skycaps are available if you wish help. At major airports the service staff is extremely adept with wheelchairs. A ground service person for United Airlines at the San Francisco airport reported that up to 250 wheelchair travelers come through a day. When you make reservations you may also tell the airline that you will need help with your luggage when you arrive. They will wire your destination.

18. *Should a nonambulatory person take a charter flight?*

If you want to. It is especially important in this instance to buy trip cancellation insurance, however. Read carefully the insurance section under General Information in Part IV. Keep in mind that charter aircraft are tightly configured to hold the greatest number of persons permitted. Popular charter aircraft, such as the DC-8-61, have no first-class section. If you require a special diet, you should advise the tour operator running the charter and get confirmation. Charter flights or complete charter tours are available on both the scheduled airlines (United, TWA, American, and the like, which all offer a schedule of flights), and the nonscheduled or supplemental lines (Overseas National, World, Trans International, for example) that supply aircraft to meet a one-time demand. There is always the possibility that a charter flight will be cancelled (usually because not enough persons signed up) or that there will be delays at the airport (this could happen on scheduled flights as well, although perhaps with less frequency). Because of the array of low fares now being offered by scheduled airlines—consider the Chickenfeed fare, the Super Saver, and the Peanut fare—charter flights may no longer be the great saving they once were. Many tour operators who were offering complete air/land arrangements have begun selling tour packages for the land portion only, to be built onto some of the new low fares.

Any person does well to avoid the so-called gray market—charter or even regular tickets being sold at unrealistically low prices, usually by a fly-by-night promoter or operator. These are the guys who often leave travelers stranded, creating sensational newspaper headlines. Your best indication that something is amiss is your own common sense. Gray-market operators tend to advertise in underground newspapers, have temporary office space, unlisted phone numbers, and other questionable business practices. The low-low fare may be your best tip-off. These operations sometimes are an outlet for stolen airline ticket stock. Sometimes they enter into unethical deals with airlines.

19. *Will I be asked to sign a waiver of my rights?*

Not with U.S. airlines, or with foreign carriers on flights that originate here. But there are reports that some foreign carriers flying outside the United States ask disabled passengers to sign a form absolving the airline from responsibility in the event of an accident. An attorney who specializes in aviation indicates that such a form "is not worth the paper it is written on," and he is of the opinion that the waiver would not be upheld in a court of law, if the airline in question had any affiliation in the United States (even as a domestic subsidiary of an international carrier that does fly here).

20. *What happens if my wheelchair is damaged in flight?*

This happens rarely, but it is a possibility. An airline has baggage insurance—usually up to $750 per passenger—that will cover damage to a chair. Make a practice of inspecting your chair (and baggage) immediately upon arrival. If the airline is to cover damage or loss, it must be reported before you leave the terminal.

If your chair or chair and baggage collectively are worth more than $750 (or the airline's maximum liability), at the check-in counter you should buy excess-value insurance, usually at a rate of ten cents per $100 coverage. (If your homeowner's insurance covers such damage, excess-value insurance will not be necessary, since you can collect only from one company.)

Airlines respond in different ways to the immediate needs of a wheelchair user whose chair has been damaged. One businessman who has charted more than 1.3 million air miles and whose chair has been damaged three times reported that in one case the airline's maintenance crew was able to repair the chair then and there; another time the airline lent him a chair to use in the city he was visiting until his own chair could be mended; the third time he was able to use his chair until he could have it repaired. In all cases the airlines covered the damage.

AIRLINES ARE UP IN THE AIR

As we go to press, the airlines are up in the air on a number of issues, as they work within the industry to standardize procedures for transporting disabled passengers. Differences include the length of a flight for which they will accept an unaccompanied nonambulatory person (some have a cutoff at four hours, others eight, still others none). Some airlines will not accept a nonambulatory passenger weighing more than 170 or 180 pounds; others have no weight restrictions. The airlines vary on how far in advance a handicapped person should book, how much notice he must give to have a special meal in flight, and how early he must check in for preboarding. Some airlines will accept a motorized wheelchair with a wet-cell battery (see discussion elsewhere in this section), others will not. Some airlines can provide oxygen by prearrangement, others cannot.

These are just some of the inconsistencies that have made air travel difficult for persons with limited mobility. This is especially true if connecting flights with different airlines are involved, although the originating carrier is responsible for ensuring that an individual can reach his destination before it accepts him for the first leg of the trip.

Last year the FAA issued a regulation to the effect that the U.S.

interstate airlines could not arbitrarily deny seats to disabled persons on the grounds that they were a safety hazard, but left it to each individual carrier to develop its own procedures for the air transportation of the handicapped, based upon their knowledge of their equipment, station facilities, and the like. The interstate carriers, in an attempt to standardize their procedures, were granted late last year a CAB rule waiver, which has allowed them to come together to work out common procedures, as well as an interline "language" to use when transmitting messages concerning disabled passengers from one airline to another. Furthermore, the Civil Aeronautics Board hopes to obtain a uniform number of handicapped passengers allowed per specified type of aircraft and has complained that the tariffs filed by the carriers concerning these passengers are in many ways unjustly discriminatory, especially in the area of numbers. At press time this has not been achieved. See Who May Fly, below.

Until the differences are resolved our best advice is as follows:

- Ask questions.
- Make reservations well in advance, giving as much information as possible about your disability and your needs and telling whether you will be accompanied by a person, or guide dog (that travels free) and whether you need the airline to supply a wheelchair, oxygen, or other equipment. If you use a motorized chair, discuss this.

If the inconsistencies are disturbing, bear in mind that in practice air travel usually goes relatively smoothly. The exceptions may be when flying on small airplanes into small airports, where the personnel could be inexperienced in helping disabled passengers.

WHO MAY FLY

The airline regulations for transportation of the handicapped/nonambulatory passengers that follow were effective April 20, 1978. For the latest procedures call the airlines or have your travel agent check one of the airline tariffs, such as *Squire's Tariff*.

Who May Travel Without a Companion*

Category	Air New England	Alaska	Allegheny	Aloha	American	Eastern	National	North Central	Northwest	Piedmont	Southern	Texas International	TWA	United	Hughes Airwest	Wein Air Alaska	Western	Ozark	Hawaiian
Nonambulatory: Persons who are not able to board and deplane from an aircraft unassisted or who are not able to move about the aircraft unassisted					●												●		
Nonambulatory: Persons who are unable to walk or need the support of another person to walk, but who are otherwise capable of caring for themselves without assistance throughout the flight. If a passenger can walk without the aidof another person, the passenger is not considered to be nonambulatory, regardless of degree of impairment. If a passenger uses a wheelchair for convenience, the passenger is not considered to be nonambulatory. A child is not considered a nonambulatory passenger unless the child has a restricting physical handicap, other than age. Via United, if the passenger can walk from his or her seat to the nearest emergency exit without the aid of another person, the passenger is not considered to be nonambulatory, regardless of degree of impairment.	●	●	●	●		●	●	●	●	●	●	●		●	●	●			
Nonambulatory: Persons who are unable to walk or need the support of another person to walk, but who are otherwise capable of caring for themselves without assistance throughout the flight. The passenger must be capable of evacuating from an aircraft without assistance in the case of an emergency. The passenger may evacuate through the use of his arms or any other method, as long as assistance is not required. The passenger must be capable of moving to and from the lavatory without assistance, unless fitted with a catheter or similar device.													●						
Physically handicapped: A person with any impairment or physical disability which would cause such person to require special attention or assistance from carrier personnel.		●		●						●		●			●	●		●	●
Deaf-*and*-blind passengers**	●		●		●	●	●	●	●		●			●			●	●	

*These passengers may travel without a companion provided they meet other requirements (see the table Requirements for Travelers Without a Companion), and provided that the maximum number of such passengers has not been exceeded (see the table Maximum Number of Nonambulatory/Physically Handicapped Passengers Who May Travel, per Flight to determine the maximum number for each airline).

**Alaska Airlines individually evaluates deaf-and-blind passengers.

Requirements for Travelers Without a Companion

Requirement	Air New England	Alaska Air	Allegheny	Aloha	American	Eastern	National	North Central	Northwest	Piedmont	Southern	Texas International	TWA	United	Hughes Airwest	Wein Air Alaska	Western	Ozark	Hawaiian
Twenty-four-hour advance booking	●	●	●	●	●	●	●	●	●		●						●	●	
Seventy-two-hour advance booking														●					
Must occupy seat in upright position		●	●	●			●			●	●	●			●		●	●	●
Must be able to move through aisle at floor level and be able to use fastened seat belt					●														
May be charged any additional expense for boarding and deplaning, although airline will arrange it.*		●		●										●					
May not travel if the maximum number of nonambulatory/physically handicapped passengers has been met**													●	●					
The maximum number of nonambulatory passengers** refers to accompanied and/or unaccompanied passengers. Carrier will make every effort to accommodate nonambulatory passengers in excess of the maximum numbers but will not be obligated to do so.					●		●												
The maximum number of nonambulatory passengers** refers to accompanied and/or unaccompanied passengers. Carrier will make every effort to accommodate nonambulatory passengers in excess of the maximum numbers but will not be obligated to do so. The total number of nonambulatory passengers on any given flight will not exceed the limitation of one such nonambulatory passenger per row per aisle.						●													
These carriers will make every reasonable effort to accommodate nonambulatory passengers in excess of the maximum numbers** but will not be obligated to do so.	●			●				●	●	●									

*Most likely to occur when small aircraft is in use, or when the airport is not equipped with modern boarding devices.

**See the following table, Maximum Number of Nonambulatory/Physically Handicapped Passengers Who May Travel, per Flight.

Maximum Number of Nonambulatory/Physically Handicapped Passengers Who May Travel, per Flight

Carrier	Aircraft Type	Maximum Number
Air New England	DHC-6	1
	FH-227	2
Alaska	B-727-100	2
	B-727-200	4
Allegheny	BAC1-11	2
	Beechcraft 99	1
	CV-580	1
	DeHavilland DH6	1
	DeHavilland TO	1
	DC-9-31	2
	DC-9-50	2
	Nord 262	1
	Nord M-298	1
Aloha	B-737	18
American	B-707	4
	B-727-023	3
	B-727-223	4
	DC-10	6
	B-747	14
Eastern	A-300	8
	B-727-100	2
	B-727-200	4
	DC-9	2
	L-1011	8
	L-188	2
Hughes Airwest	F27	1
	DC-9-10	2
	DC-9-30	2
	B-727-200	3
National	B-727	2
	DC-10	4
North Central	CV-580	1
	DC-9-32	3
	DC-9-50	3
Northwest	B-707-320-C	5
	B-727	4
	B-747	10
	DC-10	8

Maximum Number of Nonambulatory/Physically Handicapped Passengers Who May Travel, per Flight (continued)

Carrier	Aircraft Type	Maximum Number
Piedmont	B-727	4
	B-737	4
	YS-11	3
Southern	DC-9-15	3
	DC-9-31	3
	M-404	3
	Swearingen Metroliner	0
Texas International	CV-600	1
	DC-9-10	1
	DC-9-30	1
TWA	B-747	10
	L-1011	6
	B-707	4
	B-727-231 (long)	4
	B-727-31 (short)	3
	DC-9	2
United	B-727	4
	B-727-222	6
	B-737	4
	B-747	10
	DC-8	4
	DC-8-61	10
	DC-8-62	6
	DC-10	8
Wein Air Alaska	B-737-200C when seating configuration permits carriage of 26 passengers	1
	B-737-200C when configuration permits carriage of 74 passengers	2
	B-737-200C when configuration permits carriage of 112 passengers	3

Number of Attendants Required for Group Travel on TWA

Aircraft Type	Number of Passengers in Group	Minimum Number of Attendants Required	Additional Number of Passengers in Group	Additional Number of Attendants Required
B-747	2 through 10	1	1 through 10	1
L-1011	2 through 6	1	1 through 6	1
B-707	2 through 4	1	1 through 4	1
B-727 (Stretch)	2 through 4	1	1 through 4	1
B-727 (Non-stretch)	2 through 3	1	1 through 3	1
DC-9	2	1	1 or 2	1

TWA requires one attendant per passenger whose condition renders him incapable of caring for himself without assistance (and who will thus require no unreasonable attention or assistance from the airline employees), except for group travel, as listed above.

Among the airlines whose procedures are too disparate to include on the tables here are Frontier, Continental, Braniff, Reeve Aleutian, and Pan Am.

Frontier has no restrictions on the number of nonambulatory or handicapped passengers, or on their degree of disability, who can fly unaccompanied provided the passenger needs no special in flight personnel or equipment and is responsible for his own lavatory needs. The passenger must be able to use the normal seat and restraints (seat belt) during takeoff and landing.

Continental, Braniff, Reeve Aleutian, and Pan Am will refuse to transport anyone incapable of caring for himself without assistance unless he is accompanied by a companion responsible for caring for him en route and he will not require unreasonable attention or assistance from airline employees.

The maximum number of nonambulatory passengers accepted by Delta and Continental and the conditions under which they are accepted are given in the table on page 98.

Maximum Number of Nonambulatory Passengers Who May Travel, per Flight

Aircraft Type	Via Continental	Via Delta
B-727	4	—
B-727-95	—	3
B-727-232/295	—	4
DC-8-51	—	5
DC-8-61	—	5
DC-9-15	—	—
DC-9-31	—	—
DC-9-32	—	3
DC-10	8	—
L-1011	—	8
M-404	—	—
Swearingen Metroliner	—	—

Nonambulatory passengers are defined as passengers who are unable to walk or need the support of another person to walk, but who are otherwise capable of caring for themselves without assistance throughout the flight.

If a passenger can walk without the aid of another person, the passenger is not considered to be nonambulatory, regardless of the degree of impairment. If a passenger uses a wheelchair for convenience, the passenger is not considered to be nonambulatory. A child is not considered as a nonambulatory passenger unless the child has a restricting physical handicap, other than age.

TAKING A FLIGHT

Bob and June, who are inveterate travelers, have gotten air travel down to a science. If you have never flown—or not since you have become disabled—you can see how these experts do it.

Recorded here in pictures is their air trip via United to Hawaii, featured in this book.

Because of the logistics of leaving their car in the long-term parking lot and getting themselves to the terminal at Kennedy Airport, they take a taxi to the airport.

Curbside check-in facilitates matters. Wherever airlines offer it (often at the major airports), you can check your suitcases in with a skycap in front of the terminal. Be sure to watch that the bags are properly tagged for your destination, and do keep your baggage claim stub. The skycap, by the way, is identified by the skycap badge on his cap (tip him thirty-five to fifty cents per bag).

If there is no curbside check-in, you'll go to the counter, and a skycap may take your bags inside. In either case, you'll still have to go to the check-in counter, as Bob and June do, for your seat assignment. If you don't have your own chair and have requested use of the airline's chair, it is often produced at this point, unless you have arranged to have it available at the curb.

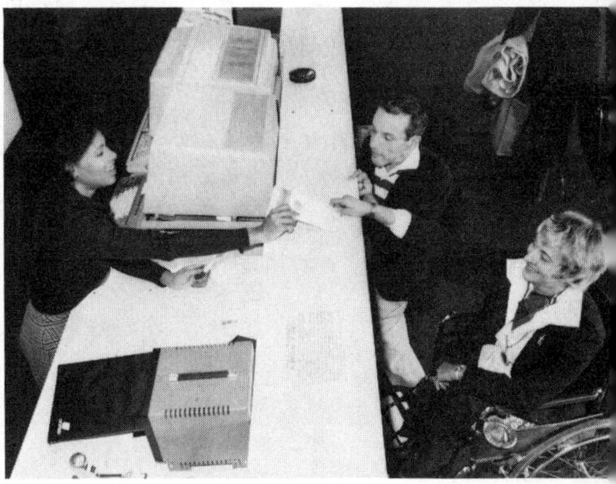

In many modern airports, the distance between the check-in counter and boarding areas—called *gates*—is vast, and you may prefer to have a skycap push you to the boarding gate. June takes advantage of this service provided by a skycap, whom she offers a tip. One or two dollars is appropriate, depending on the distance and the amount of time he spends with you. Never tip the airline personnel who push you, however.

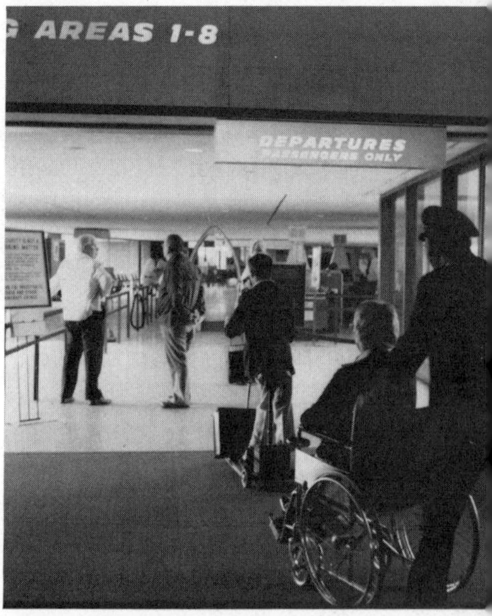

As a guard against skyjacking, all passengers must undergo a tight security check. June turns over all hand luggage, including her pocketbook, at a checkpoint, where it goes through a metal detector. (If you have film that you do not wish to have X-rayed, ask for a hand check.) Ambulatory passengers walk through a metal-detecting tunnel.

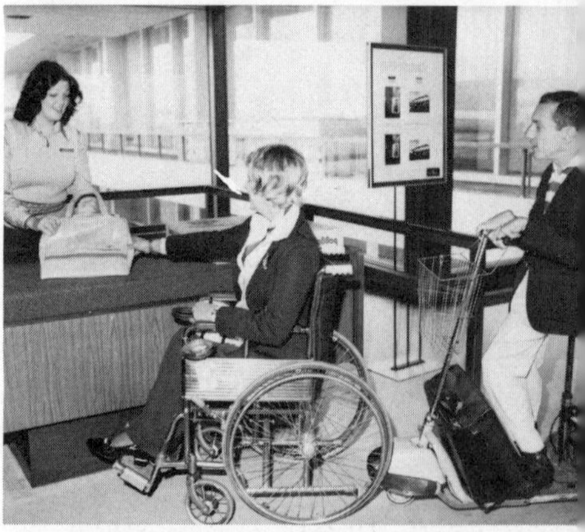

Bob and June are scanned with a hand-held device.

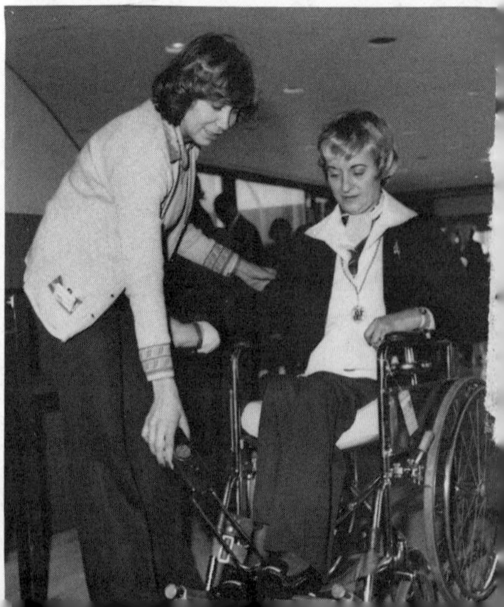

Cleared to board, they claim their hand luggage and follow the signs to their departure gate. Here a ground service person escorts them via a jetway to the airplane.

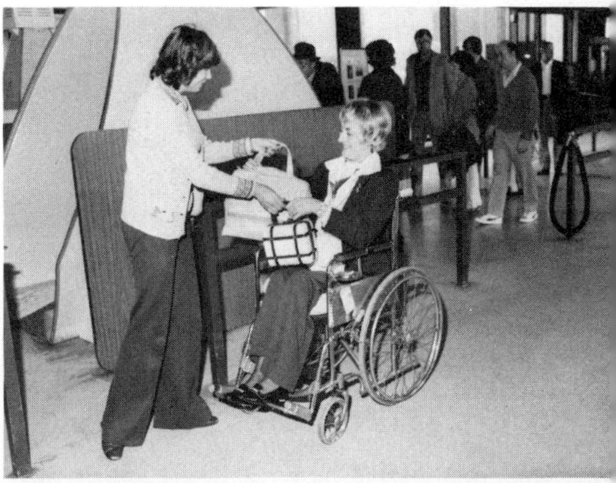

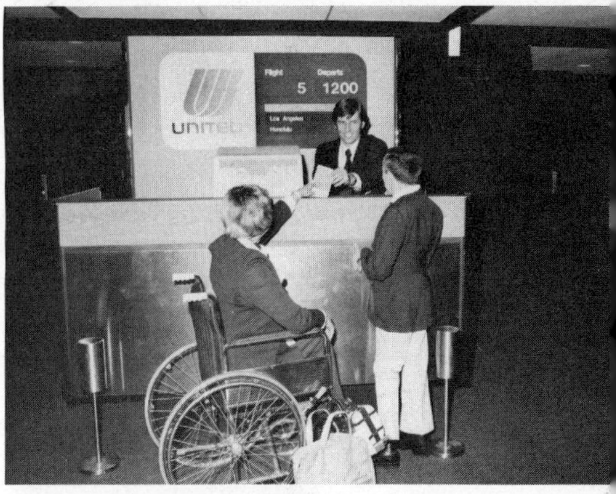

A narrow chair (also called a boarding chair, L-shaped chair, or aisle chair) is waiting. Always ask if it's possible to board in your own chair. If it can be maneuvered to your assigned seat, the airline usually complies.

Bob and June prepare the Amigo Chair to go into the pit, removing its special nonspillable gel battery and taping the terminals. (See Flying Wheelchairs, below.) The wheelchair will also go into the pit. June locks the arms and removes her cushion. Make sure that you tag the chairs with proper airline baggage tags, just as you do your suitcases. They should travel as Escort Luggage, meaning that

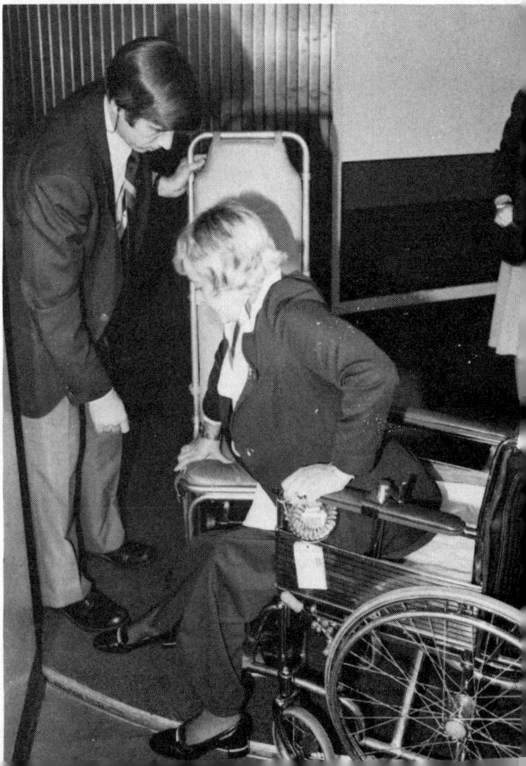

you will claim them at planeside, not in the baggage claim area. (Although it is rare in the United States, you will find if traveling abroad that you may be asked to give up your wheelchair at the time you check your suitcases—being assigned an airline wheelchair—and will retrieve your chair at the baggage claim area at your destination.) Be sure to check your chair through to any point where you will be leaving the plane and needing it or making a connecting flight, not to your final destination. (If you will be leaving the plane only to use the terminal restroom, as June does in Los Angeles, it is better to leave your chair in the pit and use an airline chair.)

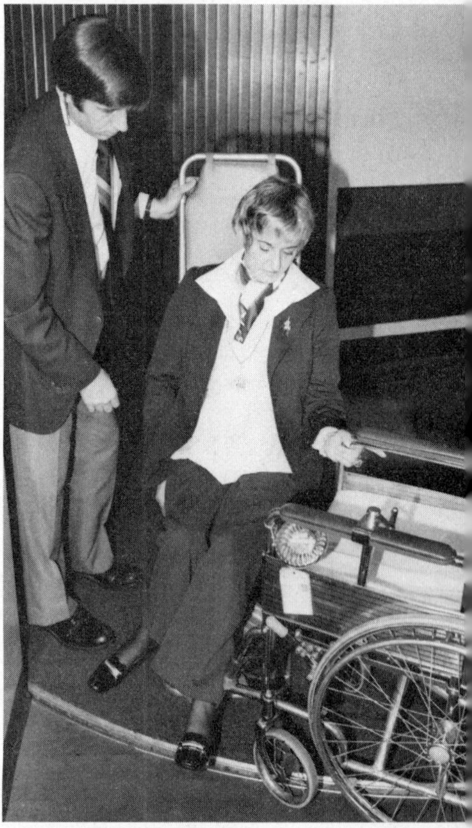

Onto the plane and into the seat. On this DC-8-61 stretch, passengers in standard chairs who are assigned front-row seats next to the entrance can often board in their own chairs. From her seat, June can touch the lavatory door, but being postpolio and unable to take a single step, she cannot use it. Bob and June cannot see the in flight movie from these front-row seats, which have every other advantage.

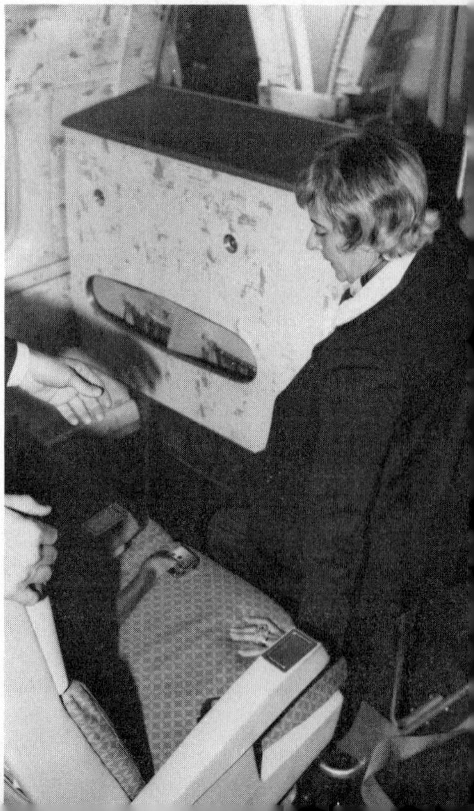

The stewardess asks, "How can I best serve you?" She is required to do so by the FAA, but she also happens to be a considerate young woman. June thanks her politely. Bob needs help fastening his seat belt. The stewardess gives him and June a personal safety briefing on the aircraft.

Airborne.

Photo by Lois Reamy

About a half hour out of Los Angeles, June reminds the flight attendant to ask the pilot to ask the tower to ask United to have a wheelchair waiting in Los Angeles so that she can use the terminal restroom

The chair is waiting, per arrangement.

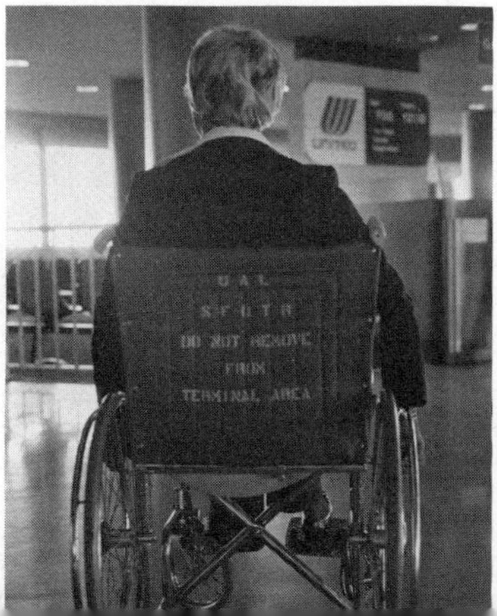

Photo by Lois Reamy

RETURN TO NEW YORK

Arriving passengers who are disabled are usually last to leave the plane. This allows the other passengers, always in a rush, to deplane. It also allows time for your wheelchair to be unloaded and set up planeside, waiting for you. If you need a "pusher" tell the airline.

Look for signs and arrows that lead to the baggage claim area. It may be wise to ask if there are any steps or escalators on the conventional route. Sometimes (as happened on Bob and June's return to the United Airlines terminal at JFK) it is necessary to be directed or escorted to the claim area via a service elevator.

Remember your flight number. Bags usually arrive within minutes at a carousel that is identified by that number. At the carousel (circular conveyor belt), skycaps are waiting to take passengers' bags or otherwise assist you.

The skycap finds a taxi and helps Bob and June get settled. The skycap is tipped. If he helps fold a chair or lift an Amigo scooter into the trunk or provides other services, you may wish to tip him extra.

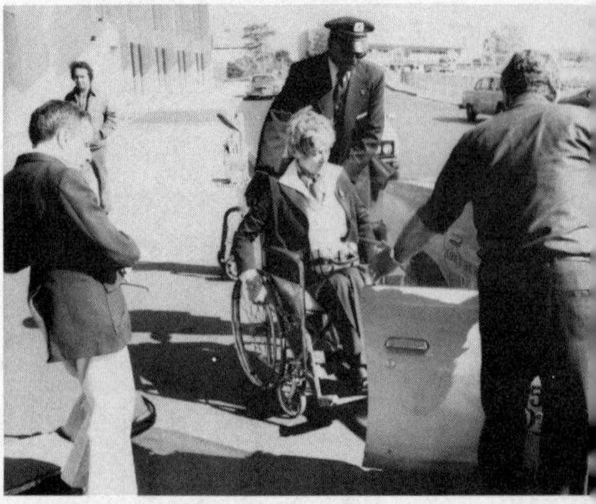

FLYING WHEELCHAIRS

To restate the points made in the picture story on the care and handling of a wheelchair:

ATTENTION
This is very important to a
physically handicapped person
Please handle with extreme care.
NOTE: PLEASE DO NOT DROP. TO LIFT,
GRAB FRONT BUMPER + UNDER BACK
END.
THANK YOU

Photo by Lois Reamy

• Be sure that it is properly tagged with the airline's ticket coded for your destination, and that your name is clearly printed on it as well as on a tape that is secured to the chair.

• You may ask if the chair can travel in a storage compartment in the cabin. The rare airline allows this; most do not.

• Before it goes into the pit, remove any loose parts, such as cushions or saddlebags, and take them with you. Lock the arms.

Motorized chairs present special problems. Because of the corrosive nature of wet-cell electric storage batteries, most airlines will not accept them. You might consider converting to a nonspillable battery. If you have a wheelchair with a nonspillable battery, be sure to call this fact to the airline's attention, as such batteries are not prohibited when removed from the wheelchair, and do not come under FAA regulations.

At press time, we know that United, TWA, and Western will, with certain stipulations, accept some wet-cell batteries. TWA will accept only nonspillable batteries, which must be removed from the chair and securely packaged by the passenger. Wet-cell batteries must be completely and securely boxed for protection against short circuits and corrosive spillage. This means that they must be nonspillable to prevent leakage regardless of their position. Meeting these requirements, the battery may be accepted as checked baggage or carried on board for under-seat storage or placed in a carry-on rack.

Western requires nonspillable batteries to be removed and packed in a leak-proof box which protects battery terminals. In the rare instance when a motorized chair travels in the cabin, the battery can remain in its mount.

United will accept a chair with a spillable wet-cell battery when the battery is disconnected and the terminals are taped, provided the battery remains *in* the wheelchair. (Removal of batteries voids this provision with United.) The chair cannot exceed thirty-seven inches in overall height.

When traveling with a motorized chair, take along a roll of electrical tape for taping the terminals.

PRACTICAL INFORMATION

SAVOIR FARES

Because of the great diversity of ever-changing air fares, the best advice comes from the CAB, which suggests that before you book a flight, you ask your travel agent or the airline a number of questions, headed off by:

1. What is the lowest individual discount fare available between points A and B?
2. How can I qualify for this fare?
3. What are the conditions and restrictions governing this fare?

Other questions and definitions of the types of fares are presented concisely in a folder entitled *Consumer Facts on Air Fares.*

A booklet, *Air Travelers' Fly-Rights*, is also recommended reading for prospective air passengers. This goes into some detail on what happens if you get "bumped" when a flight is overbooked (not as likely to happen to a disabled as to an ablebodied passenger, however) and what to do with an unused ticket.

Another useful publication is *consumer guide to international air travel.* All three are available from the Civil Aeronautics Board, Washington, DC 20428.

How to Fly is a folder that includes a great deal of practical information. Subheadings include "Health and Age No Barrier to Airline Travel." Among the hints offered is this: "Tuck your napkin under your chin when eating on a plane. Sudden downdrafts, updrafts or turbulence could make you spill food or drink on your clothing." Available from Air Transport Association of America (ATA) at 1709 New York Ave., NW, Washington, DC 20006.

Domestic airlines (those flying within the United States) publish current summaries of air fares for their top destinations from the major cities on their routes. They are available at ticket offices. The "Consumer Fact Sheet on Air Fares" is also available from the CAB, above.

While *TravelAbility* deals primarily with travel in America, it should be noted that publications explaining national and international charter possibilities include TWA's Charter Program Guide, available from travel agents, and *JAX FAX*, which your travel agent probably uses. TWA also has an updated booklet on air travel for handicapped individuals, available from its ticket offices.

DISCOUNT FARES?

In 1977, Congress granted the airlines permission to offer discount standby fares to certain groups, including the elderly and handicapped. At press time, Allegheny, TWA, United on certain flights except intra-California, Delta, Aloha Airlines, and Hawaiian Air are offering senior citizen discounts. No one yet has a discount fare for handicapped passengers. One problem here is the definition of handicapped. Certain definitions are very broad. Watch for developments in this department. If standby fares are offered, use logic to determine which flights will be less heavily booked. For example, routes traveled by businessmen might be a good midday or weekend bet, and you might have better luck with tourist routes—such as New York to Miami—midweek.

HOW TO READ AN AIRLINE TICKET

Make a practice of looking over your ticket as soon as you receive it. Be sure that everything is in order and that you understand it. If you have questions, ask your travel agent or the airline ticket agent.

The best way to read a ticket is like a book. Each page in the ticket is called a coupon and represents a change of aircraft (to a connecting flight) or a different leg of your journey. Each page shows a carbon copy of your entire routing with one particular segment that stands out.

Never tamper with a ticket. If any part of it needs to be rewritten, take it to the agent who issued it or to the airline ticket counter.

Also make a practice of knowing the terms of your contract with the carrier, which are printed on the ticket, and read the ticket envelope, which gives baggage information, telephone numbers, and the like.

The major points for you to check on your ticket are shown on the sample ticket.

BAGGAGE

For domestic and overseas flights, each passenger has the free baggage allowance of two suitcases, one of which does not exceed sixty-two inches total measurements (arrived at by adding together

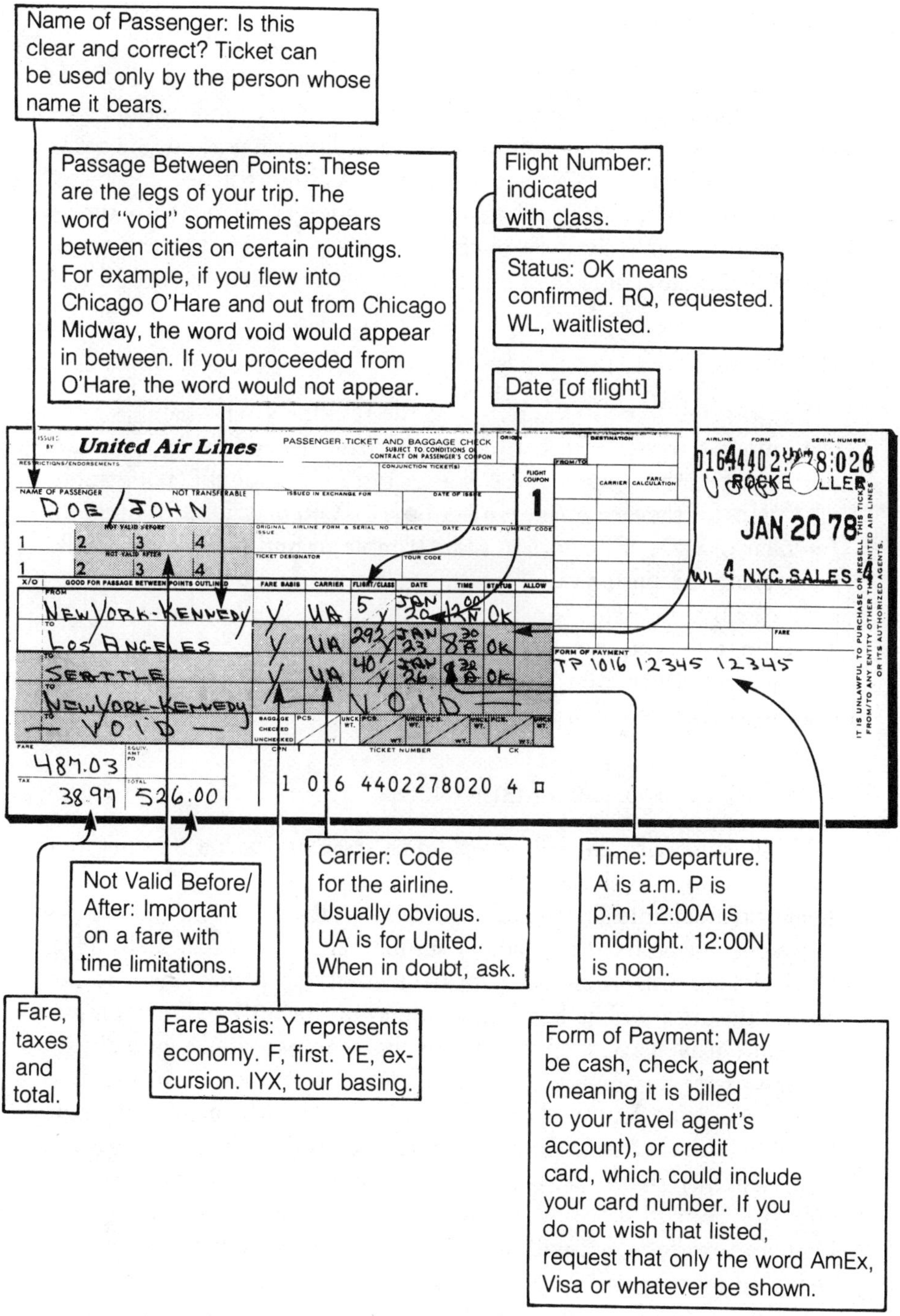
Name of Passenger: Is this clear and correct? Ticket can be used only by the person whose name it bears.
Passage Between Points: These are the legs of your trip. The word "void" sometimes appears between cities on certain routings. For example, if you flew into Chicago O'Hare and out from Chicago Midway, the word void would appear in between. If you proceeded from O'Hare, the word would not appear.
Flight Number: indicated with class.
Status: OK means confirmed. RQ, requested. WL, waitlisted.
Date [of flight]
United Air Lines
PASSENGER TICKET AND BAGGAGE CHECK
NAME OF PASSENGER
NOT TRANSFERABLE
DOE/JOHN
NOT VALID BEFORE
NOT VALID AFTER
GOOD FOR PASSAGE BETWEEN POINTS OUTLINED
FARE BASIS
CARRIER
FLIGHT/CLASS
DATE
TIME
STATUS
ALLOW
NEW YORK-KENNEDY
LOS ANGELES
SEATTLE
NEW YORK-KENNEDY
VOID
FARE
487.03
TAX
38.97
TOTAL
526.00
TICKET NUMBER
1 016 4402278020 4
JAN 20 78
NYC SALES
FORM OF PAYMENT
TP 1016 12345 12345
Not Valid Before/After: Important on a fare with time limitations.
Carrier: Code for the airline. Usually obvious. UA is for United. When in doubt, ask.
Time: Departure. A is a.m. P is p.m. 12:00A is midnight. 12:00N is noon.
Fare, taxes and total.
Fare Basis: Y represents economy. F, first. YE, excursion. IYX, tour basing.
Form of Payment: May be cash, check, agent (meaning it is billed to your travel agent's account), or credit card, which could include your card number. If you do not wish that listed, request that only the word AmEx, Visa or whatever be shown.

the length, width and depth) and the other not exceeding fifty-two inches. Hand luggage which can be stored in the under-seat space should not exceed forty-five inches overall dimensions, and one over-the-arm type garment bag is also allowed. Within Europe and many foreign countries, the free baggage allowance is by weight—forty-four pounds coach, sixty-six pounds first class—so for overseas travel it is probably advisable to consider the weight of your bags.

TIPPING

You tip the skycap (the porter at the terminal) who handles your bags about thirty-five to fifty cents per bag, depending on the location, and whether or not there is a set rate. (If in doubt, you simply ask, "What is the customary tip per bag?") You may wish to tip more (a dollar or two) if he goes to some trouble to find you a taxi, handle your chair, or push you through the terminal. You can recognize a skycap by the badge on his cap (also make a mental note of his name, in case you get separated). Otherwise, there is no tipping: you never tip airline ground personnel or the stewards or stewardesses who serve your meals.

STRETCHERS AND AIR AMBULANCES

While some airlines will accept some stretcher-borne patients, not all airlines do, and those that do may not be able to handle them on all aircraft. Suitable aircraft must be fitted with equipment that allows a stretcher to be fixed in place. The number of seats that a stretcher replaces varies, as does the compartment of the plane where it can go and the airfare. The last is determined by the airline. For example, an airline may place the stretcher in the coach section, while charging the passenger for four first-class adult fares. Another airline may charge the equivalent of six full fares. And while it is mandatory that a qualified attendant accompany a stretcher patient, the airlines vary as to whether one or two attendants are allowed for the inclusive fare the patient is paying. Airlines may have other regulations: United, for example, will not transport a stretcher-borne person weighing more than 190 pounds, nor one for a trip of less than 700 miles, nor one on a trip that involves connecting flights within its own system. United requires seventy-two hours prior notice. Other airlines have their own provisions.

The following U.S. airlines are known to transport persons on stretchers with certain provisions: Alaska, Aloha, Braniff, Delta, Hawaiian, Hughes Airwest, Northwest, Reeve Aleutian, TWA, United, Western, and Pan American, if international transport is required.

An alternative is the air ambulance services that are usually equipped with emergency standby equipment; Airborne Intensive Care's Learjets, for example, have equipment similar to a hospital's intensive care unit, and Airborne is in air-to-ground telecommunication with a hospital emergency room. Air ambulances offer the advantages of no long waits on the ground, whereas on a commercial airliner the stretcher is the first to be boarded and the last to leave. But air ambulances are expensive. A recent Golden Jet airways flight from San Diego to Birmingham, complete with necessary medical attendants, cost in the vicinity of $6,000, compared with the $664 L.A.-to-Birmingham rate it might have cost on a commercial airliner had that been possible. (There is no direct service from San Diego to Birmingham, however, and no connecting flights could be arranged.)

Among the air ambulance services are Airborne Intensive Care, 1911 Harrison Ave., Rockford, IL 61101, 800-435-8090; Golden Jet Airways, Los Angeles Airport, P.O. Box 90253, Los Angeles, CA 90009, 213-670-1976; and Air Medic. The latter is licensed as an "indirect air carrier" by the CAB (it actually owns no aircraft) but can supply stretchers, aero-nurses, life-sustaining equipment, and other medical services for patients traveling by commercial airline, or can arrange a charter through 138 operators nationwide. Air Medic, 12517 Chandler Blvd., North Hollywood, CA 91607, 800-423-2667; in California 213-985-2020; in Alaska and Hawaii 800-423-2700.

Also check your local telephone Yellow Pages for air ambulances.

A military airlift may also be requested when no commercial airlift is available or adequate. In extreme emergencies, the Aerospace Rescue and Recovery Service may be called upon (at no charge). Local police or hospitals know how to contact the nearest unit. The Military Airlift Command Aeromedical Evacuation can be scheduled, at a cost to the individual. The request must be approved by the

Directorate of Transportation, Headquarters, United States Air Force, Washington, D.C. 202-697-9560 or 697-0375; night, 697-7220.

Also see Medical Questions and Answers and the discussion of insurance under General Information, both in Part IV.

HINTS

Useful hints for air travelers are scattered throughout this chapter and throughout the book, especially in the sections Why Plan a Trip? Medical Questions and Answers, Hotels and Motels, and General Information.

Here are other hints to use in arranging your own flight, or to pass along to your travel agent:

• Try to avoid travel rush days and hours (e.g., holiday weekends, early Friday evenings in summer, and the like).

• Take a day flight whenever possible.

• Airlines reservations systems can also book hotels and rental cars for you, and the airline tour desks can book entire tour packages. TWA's tour catalog lists tours packaged by Wings on Wheels for handicapped travelers.

• Because nonambulatory passengers are usually the last to deplane, be sure to allow additional time to make a connecting flight.

• Also ask the travel agent or reservations agent to check the *Official Airline Guide* (*OAG*) for a change of equipment, even though the flight number does not change. For example, American Airlines flight 625, New York to St. Thomas, actually changes from a Boeing 727 or 707 to a forty-eight seat Convair 440 at St. Croix and then flies to St. Thomas, although the flight number never changes.

• Try to book a nonstop flight whenever possible. Next best is a direct flight (although it stops you don't change planes).

• Information prepared primarily for airline personnel might be of interest to you and includes: *Seeing Eye Dogs As Air Travelers,* available from The Seeing Eye, Morristown, NJ 07960; and the FAA advisory circular AC No. 120-32, *Air Transportation of Handicapped Persons*, available from the Department of Transportation, Federal Aviation Administration, Washington, DC 20591.

• Keep abreast of airline innovations that can make travel easier.

• An airline may be able to store the special requirements of its credit card holders, especially those in the frequent-traveler category. This could eliminate spelling out all of your needs every time you make a reservation.

AIRCRAFT

The ideal commercial airliner for the disabled passenger has not been built yet. Meanwhile, the wide-bodies—the Boeing 747, DC-10, and L-1011—are your best bets for all-around comfort. Second best are the Boeing 707, DC-8, and DC-9, although less spacious. For the most part, airplane aisles will be no wider than twenty-two inches, except for some in first class. The special-design narrow chair is most often used in boarding nonambulatory passengers, although on some planes, depending on your seat assignment, you can board in your own chair. Aisles are difficult to negotiate on crutches, since a user must generally walk sideways.

The same aircraft may have quite different interior configurations, depending on the airline and the route. For that reason, it is useless to run blueprints here or recommend specific seat numbers.

Airplane lavatories—sometimes called Blue Rooms, although there is nothing poetic about them—have been discussed repeatedly elsewhere. They are generally inaccessible to nonambulatory travelers.

MAJOR U.S. CARRIERS

About twenty interstate airlines fly within the United States. Some of them, such as United, American, and TWA, fly nationwide. Others, as their names suggest, are regional: Western, Frontier, Southern, Allegheny. If you are not working through a travel agent, your Yellow Pages will show the airlines that serve your local airport.

If an airline's reservations or special services desk cannot provide the information or answers you need, ask for the number of its consumer affairs department.

Addresses and phone numbers for the major airlines are listed in *Travel tips for the handicapped*, available from the United States Travel Service, Department of Commerce, Washington, DC 20230.

AIRLINE JARGON

The language of the airlines is reprinted from *Inside United Airlines*, courtesy of that airline.

ATA — Air Transport Association—founded in 1936 as an official spokesman for the industry.

board — Get on the airplane.

bulkhead — Part of the aircraft dividing sections of the plane. Bulkheads have fasteners for baby bassinets.

CAB — Civil Aeronautics Board—a federal agency that regulates airline rules and rates and awards air routes.

ceiling — A reference to visibility—such as a low cloud cover.

charter — Temporary hiring of an aircraft for the movement of passengers or cargo.

circling — Flying in a set pattern until cleared to land.

container — A special device in which baggage is stored, protected, and handled as a unit in transit on a flight.

D.B. — Denied Boarding—when a passenger cannot be accommodated because there are more confirmed customers than seats available on a flight.

deplane — Get off the airplane.

direct — A flight that goes to your planned destination, but makes stops on the way.

diversion — Landing at a city other than your planned destination.

downline — The next airplane stop—or your destination.

en route — Flying—on the way to your destination.

ETA — Estimated time of arrival.

ETD — Estimated time of departure.

FAA — Federal Aviation Administration—the government regulatory agency concerned with aviation safety.

flight segment	A portion of the passenger's itinerary from Point A to Point B.
interline	Travel via two or more carriers.
involuntary	A change in travel plans which may be occasioned by irregular flight operations.
irregular operation	A multitude of delayed flights usually caused by adverse weather conditions.
itinerary	A record of your journey—a list of your flights.
joint fare	A single through-rate involving travel via two or more carriers.
mechanical	Delay caused by a mechanical breakdown.
misconnect	Late arrival at a specific point and planned connecting flight has left without you.
no-op	Flight cancelled—will not operate.
no-show	Passenger with confirmed reservation who does not arrive for flight.
non-stop	A flight that goes to your planned destination without making stops.
offline	Travel on carriers other than the originating airline.
online	Travel solely on one airline.
pit	The belly of the aircraft where baggage and cargo is stored. [Also called the hold.]
reroute	Rewrite passenger tickets to permit passenger to travel to destination by a route other than originally planned.
skycap	At major terminals, skycaps are available to assist passengers with check-in, luggage, and, if needed, assistance to the airplane.
stacked-up	A delay in landing caused by heavy air traffic (a multitude of flights waiting their turn for landing clearance).
standby	Passenger not confirmed on flight—standing by for a seat if it becomes available.

stopover — Passenger destination or any city on itinerary where a passenger willingly stops for four hours or more.

tariff — Publication containing airline regulatory rules and rates.

through — Passenger who continues to destination on flight which makes stops enroute.

tower — Controls the flow of air traffic in and out of airport—air traffic controllers are employed by FAA.

upline — Station you just came from—or originating point.

waitlist — Is used by reservations to list passengers for sold-out flights. [The airline's computer may hold the passenger's name for waitlist, and if there is a cancellation, the individual is put on the flight.]

AIRPORTS

Airports in the United States range from a glorified shed beside a tarmac to vast satellite terminals, where the shortest distance between two points is often by way of stairs, escalators, or moving corridors that are hard to get onto unless you can step lively. (Inquire about elevators.) Other airport obstacles could include inaccessible restrooms and restaurants, as well as out-of-reach telephones and water fountains. Announcements over the loud speakers are often hard for anyone to understand, and posted flight information may be hard to locate and read. Even so, the airports are making progress in the way of accessibility. This is documented by the *Access Travel* survey, which showed 118 terminals worldwide that were accessible in varying degrees in its first edition in late 1976. The updated version which came out less than a year later included more than one hundred additional terminals. Much of the increase was within the United States.

As you travel, keep your own notes on which airports you prefer, and choose them when you have the choice. One wheelchair traveler who often visits Washington, D.C., avoids Dulles Airport because he does not like the motor lounge for transfers between plane and terminal. He prefers National Airport's jetways. On the other hand, a person who walks, but with difficulty, might welcome the motor lounge, which eliminates what would be lengthy corridors.

Get to know your own city's airport(s). If it is at all sizeable, and you are not familiar with it, you might have lunch there, watch the planes take off, and explore the facilities as an outing some day *before* you plan to travel.

Airport accessibility maps and/or text indicating parking arrangements, curb ramps, public washrooms, and the like are available for Chicago's O'Hare and the three New York area airports, JFK, La Guardia, and Newark. Write to Department of Aviation, Room 1111, City Hall, Chicago, IL 60602, for O'Hare's *airport guide for the handicapped;* and to the Port Authority of New York and New Jersey, Aviation Public Service Division, Rm. 65 North, 1 World Trade Center, New York, NY 10048, or call 212-466-7503, for a booklet on all three New York airports. Also see airports chart.

The Portland (Oregon) International Airport, after a terminal expansion, last year received the Oregon Easter Seal Society's National Handicapped Awareness Award as well as a certificate from the state Architectural Barriers Council for its features that include reserved parking for disabled drivers.

The Atlanta Airport by comparison has been described by one wheelchair traveler as "a nightmare for the unwary, inexperienced handicapped traveler." It is, however, undergoing major renovation and expansion designed to be barrier-free. An accessibility map of the Dallas/Ft. Worth Airport is included in *Access Dallas* (see Texas under state listings).

The barrier-free Metro public transportation system in Washington, D.C., connects National Airport with the city itself.

The Traveler's Aid counter of Denver Stapleton Airport provides a TVphone for use by persons with impaired hearing.

The FAA, in cooperation with the United States Architectural and Transportation Barriers Compliance Board, the Airport Operators Council International, and the Reuben H. Donnelley Corporation, has published an updated directory of features, facilities, and services for handicapped air travelers at 220 terminals in twenty-seven countries. Called *Access Travel: Airports*, copies are available from Consumer Information Center, Dept. 619-F, Pueblo, CO 81009. Reprinted here by permission of the Federal Aviation Administration is the accessibility information for the large hub airports in the United States.

Accessibility Information

How to Use This Chart
Facilities for each airport terminal are listed on six consecutive pages: be sure to check columns listed under your terminal on all pages. A ruler, colored pencil, or crayon can help align or highlight data in columns under each terminal.

	ATLANTA, GA.	BOSTON, MA.	CHICAGO, IL. (MIDWAY)
PARKING			
Parking spaces reserved for handicapped	●	S	
Directional signing to reserved spaces	●	●	
Spaces level and at least 12 feet wide	●	●	
Spaces within 200 feet of terminal entrance		●	
Spaces protected from weather		S	
Parking meters and tickets accessible to driver	●	●	●
Level or ramped path from parking to entrance	●	●	
EXTERIOR CIRCULATION			
Vehicular and passenger traffic separated	●	●	
All walkways at least 5 feet wide	●	●	●
Stairs and ramps at all changes of level	S	S	NA
Handrails on all ramps and stairs	●	●	
Curb cuts at all pedestrian crossings	●	S	
All ramps at least 5 feet wide	●	●	●
All ramp slopes 8.3% or less		●	●
All ramps indicated by accessibility symbol		S	
All ramps protected from snow and ice	●	S	
All ramp surfaces nonslip		●	●
Ramps over 30 feet long have level rest landings		NA	NA
Ramps have level landings at turns	NA	NA	NA
Ramps have handrails on both sides	●	NA	
ARRIVAL AND DEPARTURE			
Level vehicle loading/unloading areas close to building entrances	●	●	●
Loading/unloading areas protected from weather	●	S	●
INTERIOR CIRCULATION			
Building entrances and exits level with automatic door	●	●	●
Public areas in building accessible by level/ramped route	●	●	●
Public corridors at least 5 feet wide and obstruction-free	●	●	●
ELEVATORS			
Public elevators accessible on level path	●	●	NA
Public elevators to all floors, including garage	●	●	NA
Elevators at least 5 by 5 feet inside measurement	S	S	NA
Elevator door opening at least 3 feet	●	●	NA

															NEW YORK, N.Y. (JFK)															
CHICAGO, IL. (O'HARE)	CLEVELAND, OH.	DALLAS/FT. WORTH, TX.	DENVER, CO.	DETROIT, MI.	HONOLULU, HI.	HOUSTON, TX. (HOBBY)	HOUSTON, TX. (INTERCONTINENTAL)	KANSAS CITY, MO.	LAS VEGAS, NV.	LOS ANGELES, CA.	MIAMI, FL.	MINNEAPOLIS/ST. PAUL, MN.	NEWARK, N.J.	NEW ORLEANS, LA.	AMERICAN AIRLINES	BRITISH AIRWAYS	EASTERN AIRLINES	INTERNATIONAL TERMINAL	NATIONAL AIRLINES	NORTHWEST AIRLINES	TRANS WORLD AIRLINES	UNITED AIR LINES	NEW YORK, N.Y. (LAGUARDIA)	PHILADELPHIA, PA.	PITTSBURGH, PA.	ST. LOUIS, MO.	SAN FRANCISCO, CA.	SEATTLE/TACOMA, WA.	TAMPA, FL.	WASHINGTON, D.C. (NATIONAL)
●		S	●	●	●					●	●	●	●	●	NA		●			●		●	●	●		●	●	●	●	●
●					●						●	●	●	●	NA								●	●		●	●			●
●	●	●	●	●	●					●	●	●	●	●	NA							●		●		●	●	●	●	●
●	●	●	●	●	●		●		●	●	●	●	●	●	NA		●			●		●	●	●		●	●	●	●	●
●	S	S			●		●		●	S	●	●	●		NA					●			●	●		●	S	●	●	
●	●	●	●		●			●	●	●	●	●	●	●	NA		NA					NA	●			●	●	●	●	NA
●	●	●	●	●	●				●	●	●	●	●	●	NA		●						●	●	●	●	●		●	●
●	●	●		●	●			●	●	●	S		●	●	●		●	●	●				●	●	●	●	●	●		S
●	●	●	●	●	●			●	●	●	●	●	●	●	●	●	●	●	●	●	●	●	●	●	●	●	●	●	●	S
●		●		●	●				●	●	●	NA	EI	●	●		●		NA	●	NA	●			●	●	●		●	●
●	●	●		●	●		●	●	●	●	S	NA	●		●	NA	●	●	NA	●		●	●		●	●	●		●	●
●	S	●		●	●				●	●	●	●	●	●	NA		●	●			●	●	●	●		●	●	●	S	●
●	NA	NA		●	●				●	●	●	●	NA	●	NA	NA	●	NA	NA	●	NA	●	NA	●		●	●		●	●
●	NA	NA		●					●	●	●	●	NA	●	NA	NA	●	NA	NA	●	NA	●	NA	●	●	●	●	●	●	●
●	NA	NA								●			NA		NA	NA		NA	NA		NA		NA	●						
●	●	NA					●		NA	NA	●		NA	NA	NA	NA	●	NA	NA		NA	●	NA	●		●	●	●	NA	●
●	●	NA			●				●	●	●	●	NA	●	NA	NA	●	NA	NA		NA	●	NA	●		●	●	●	●	●
NA	●	NA	●				NA		●	●	NA	NA	NA	NA	NA	NA	●	NA	NA	●	NA	NA	NA	NA	NA		NA	●	NA	NA
NA	●	NA	●	●	●		NA		●	●	NA	●	NA	NA	NA	NA	●	NA	NA	●	NA	NA	NA		NA	●	NA	●	NA	NA
NA	●	NA			●		NA		●	S	NA	S	NA		NA	NA	●	NA	NA	●	NA	NA	NA		NA	●	●		●	●
●	●	●	●	●	●	●	●	●	●	●	●	●	●	●	●	●	●	●	●	●	●	●	●	●	●	●	●	●	●	●
●	●	●		●	●		●	●	●	●	●		●	●	●	●	●	●	●	●	●	●	●	●	●	●	●	●	●	S
●	●	●	●	●	●	●	●	●	●	●	●	●	●	●	●	●	●	●	●	●	●	●	●	●	●	●	●	●	●	●
●	●	●		●	●		●	●	●	●	●	●	●	●	●	●	●	●	●	●	●	●	●	●	●	●	●	●	●	S
●	●	●	●	●	●	●	●	●	●	●	●	●	●	●	●	●	●	●	●	●	●	●	●	●	●	●	●	●	●	●
●	●	●		●	●	NA	●	●	●	●	●	NA	●	●	●	●	●	●	●	●	●	●	●	●	●	●	●	●	●	●
●	●	●		●	●	NA	●	●	●	●	●	●	●	●	NA	●	●	●	●		●	●	●	●	●	●	●	●	●	●
	●	●		●	●	NA	●	●	●	●	●	●	●	●	●	●	●	●	●	●	●	●	●	●	●	●	●	●	●	●
●	●	●	●	●	●	NA	●	●	●	●	●	●	●	●	●	●	●	●	●	●	●	●	●	●	●	●	●	●	●	●

Accessibility Information (continued)

	ATLANTA, GA.	BOSTON, MA.	CHICAGO, IL. (MIDWAY)
Elevators (continued)			
Elevator doors have automatic safety reopening device	●	●	NA
Elevator controls no more than 4 feet above floor		S	NA
Elevator controls have raised lettering		S	NA
STAIRS			
Ramp or elevator available as alternate to stairs or escalators	●	●	
Stairways free of projecting noses	●	●	
Stairway riser height 7 inches or less	●	●	
Handrails on both sides	●	●	
INTERIOR RAMPS			
At least 5 feet wide	●	●	●
Slopes 8.3% or less	●	●	●
Ramp approaches indicated by accessibility symbol		S	
Level area at least 5 feet by 5 feet at top and bottom of ramps	●	●	●
Ramps over 30 feet long have level rest landings	NA	NA	NA
Landings at turning points	NA	NA	NA
Handrails on both sides		NA	
DOORS			
Level passages at least 5 feet between adjacent doorways	●	●	●
Doors have clear opening at least 3 feet	●	●	●
Thresholds level with floor	●	●	●
Lever handles instead of knobs		●	
Wall mounted paging phones not over 3 feet above floor	NA	NA	
BOARDING			
Ramp or level loading bridges [jetways] to aircraft	S	●	
ACCOMMODATIONS			
Special transportation to other airport buildings	NA	●	NA
Car rental agencies which can provide hand-controlled cars	H7 A7	H7	H7
Accessible hotel accommodations in airport complex		●	
Vending machine controls identified with raised lettering			
Dining tables have at least 29-inch clearance above floor	●	S	●
Drinking fountains accessible to/usable by handicapped	S	S	●
REST ROOMS AND TOILETS			
Accessible rest rooms and toilets available	●	●	●
With 5 by 5 feet turning space	●	●	●

															NEW YORK, N.Y. (JFK)															
CHICAGO, IL. (O'HARE)	CLEVELAND, OH.	DALLAS/FT. WORTH, TX.	DENVER, CO.	DETROIT, MI.	HONOLULU, HI.	HOUSTON, TX. (HOBBY)	HOUSTON, TX. (INTERCONTINENTAL)	KANSAS CITY, MO.	LAS VEGAS, NV.	LOS ANGELES, CA.	MIAMI, FL.	MINNEAPOLIS/ST. PAUL, MN.	NEWARK, N.J.	NEW ORLEANS, LA.	AMERICAN AIRLINES	BRITISH AIRWAYS	EASTERN AIRLINES	INTERNATIONAL TERMINAL	NATIONAL AIRLINES	NORTHWEST AIRLINES	TRANS WORLD AIRLINES	UNITED AIR LINES	NEW YORK, N.Y. (LAGUARDIA)	PHILADELPHIA, PA.	PITTSBURGH, PA.	ST. LOUIS, MO.	SAN FRANCISCO, CA.	SEATTLE/TACOMA, WA.	TAMPA, FL.	WASHINGTON, D.C. (NATIONAL)
●	●	●	●	●	●	NA	●	●	●	●	●	●	●	●	●	●			●	●	●	●		●	●	●	●	●	●	●
	S	●				NA			●	●	S				NA		●		●	●		●		●	●		●		●	●
	S	●		●		NA		NA						●								●					●			
●	●	●		●	●		●	●	●	●	●	●	●	●		●	●	●	●	●	●	●	●	●	●	●	●	●	●	●
●	●	●				●	●	●		●	●	●		●	●	●	●	●	●	●	●	●	●	●	●	●	●		●	●
●	●	●	●	●	●		●	●	●	●	●	●	●	●	●	●	●		●	●	●	●		●	●		●	●	●	●
●	●	●		●	●	●	●	●	●	●	●	●	●	●	●	●	●		●		●	●	●	●	●	●	●	●	●	●
●	●	NA	●	●	●	●	NA	NA	●	NA	●	NA	NA	●	●	●	●	NA	●	●	●	NA		NA	●	●	●	●	NA	S
●	●	NA	●	●		●	NA	NA	●	NA	●	NA	NA	●	●	●	●	NA	●	●	●	NA	●	NA	●	●	●	●	NA	●
●		NA					NA	NA		NA		NA	NA					NA				NA		NA	NA				NA	
●	●	NA	●	●	●	●	NA	NA	●	NA	●	NA	NA	NA	●	●	●	NA	●	●	●	NA	●	NA	NA	●	●	●	NA	●
NA	●	NA		●		●	NA	NA	●	NA	NA	NA	NA		NA		●	NA		●	●	NA		NA	NA		NA	●	NA	NA
NA	●	NA	●	●	●	●	NA	NA	●	NA	S	NA	NA	NA	NA	●	●	NA	NA	●	NA	NA	●	NA	●	●	NA	●	NA	NA
NA	S	NA			●	●	NA	NA	●	NA	S	NA	NA		NA		●	NA				NA	●	NA	●	●	●		NA	S
●	●	●		●	●	●	●	●	●	●	●	●	●		●	●	●	●	●	●	●	●	●	●	●	●	●	●	●	●
●	S	●	●	●	●		●	●	●	●	●	●	●	●	●	●	●	●	●	●	●	●	●	●	●	●	●	●	●	●
●	●	●	●	●	●	●	●	●	●	●	●	●	●	●	●	●	●	●	●	●	●	●	●	●	●	●	●	●	●	●
		S		●			●		●		●	●	S	S	●	●	●	S			●				●		●		S	NA
●				●	●				●			●																		S
●	S	●	●	●	●	S	●	●	●	●	●	●	●	S	●	●	●	●	●	●	●	●	5	●	●		●	●	●	S
●	●	●		●	●		●	●		●		●		NA	NA	6	6	●	●	●	●	●		●	NA	NA	●	●	●	●
●	A7	H7 A7		A7 H7		A7	A7 H7	H A7	H7	H7 A7 N7		A7	A7	A	NA	A7	H7 A7	A7		A7	A7 H7		A7	A7 H7		A7	H7 A7 N7	H7 A7	H7 A7	H7 A7 N7
●	●	●		●			●	●			●				●	●	●	●	●	●	●	●		●	●		●		●	
NA																														
●		●	●		●		●	●	●	●	●	●		●	NA	●	●	●		●	●	●	●		●	●	●	●	●	S
	S	●	●	●	●			●	●	●	●	●	●		●				●		●		●	●	●	●	●	●	●	●
●	●	●	●	S	●	●	●	●	●	●	●	●	●	S	●	●	●	●	●	●	●		●	●	●		●	●	●	●
●	●	●	●	●	●	●	●	●	●	●	●	●	●	S	●	●	S	●	●	●	●		●	●	●	●	●	●	●	●

Accessibility Information (continued)

	ATLANTA, GA.	BOSTON, MA.	CHICAGO, IL. (MIDWAY)
Rest Rooms and Toilets (continued)			
With at least one stall 3 feet wide	●	●	●
With at least one stall 4 feet 8 inches deep	●	S	●
With at least one stall with out-swinging 32-inch door	●	S	●
With grab bars	●	●	●
With 29-inch clearance under lavatories	●	S	
With mirrors, towels, etc. not over 40 inches above floor	●	S	
PHONES			
Phone with coin slot not over 48 inches high in each phone bank		S	
Phone with amplifier available in each bank of telephones			
Raised lettering on telephone operating instructions		S	
SERVICES			
Brochures available on facilities for handicapped persons			
Medical services available	●	●	9
Escort service available from airport or airlines	●	●	

Reprinted by permission of the Federal Aviation Administration

Explanatory Notes:
A—Avis. H—Hertz. N—National Car Rental. CW—Covered walkway. El—Elevator available. NA—Not applicable. S—In some locations, but not all. 5—All gates except Boston and Washington shuttle. 6—Special van with ramps. 7—Advance notice required, preferably two weeks. 8—On call. 9—First Aid only. 10—Remodeling in progress, 1977.

															NEW YORK, N.Y. (JFK)															
CHICAGO, IL. (O'HARE)	CLEVELAND, OH.	DALLAS/FT. WORTH, TX.	DENVER, CO.	DETROIT, MI.	HONOLULU, HI.	HOUSTON, TX. (HOBBY)	HOUSTON, TX. (INTERCONTINENTAL)	KANSAS CITY, MO.	LAS VEGAS, NV.	LOS ANGELES, CA.	MIAMI, FL.	MINNEAPOLIS/ST. PAUL, MN.	NEWARK, N.J.	NEW ORLEANS, LA.	AMERICAN AIRLINES	BRITISH AIRWAYS	EASTERN AIRLINES	INTERNATIONAL TERMINAL	NATIONAL AIRLINES	NORTHWEST AIRLINES	TRANS WORLD AIRLINES	UNITED AIR LINES	NEW YORK, N.Y. (LAGUARDIA)	PHILADELPHIA, PA.	PITTSBURGH, PA.	ST. LOUIS, MO.	SAN FRANCISCO, CA.	SEATTLE/TACOMA, WA.	TAMPA, FL.	WASHINGTON, D.C. (NATIONAL)
●	S	●	●		●		●	●	●	●	●	●	●	S	●			●	●	●	●	●	●	●	●		●	●	●	●
●		●	●		●		●	●	●	●	●	●	●	S	●	●	●	●	●				●	●	●		●	●	●	●
●	S	●	●		●		●		●	●	●	●	●	S	●	●		●	●				●	●	●		●	●	●	●
●		●	●		●			●	●	●	●	●	●	S	●			●	●				●	●	●		●	●	●	●
		●							●			●			●		S		●	●		●			●		●		●	
		S		S					●		●		●					S			●		●	●	●	S	●	●		
S		S			●	S	●		●	●	●	●	S					S	●	●		●	S	●	S	●	●	●		S
S	S	S		●			●		●	●		●	S					S					S				●		S	S
																												●		
●		●								●		●												●			●			
9	8/9	●	●	●	●		●		●	●	●	●	●	●	●	●	●	●		8	8	8	●	●	9	8	●	●	9	●
●	●	●	●	●	●	●			●	●	●	●	●	●	●	●	●	●		●		NA	●	●	●	●	●	●	●	●

5

CRUISES

Three principals star in the photo reportage on these pages:

Dot, who uses a wheelchair a good part of the time, her niece Janis, and the *Cunard QE2*. The ship plays an important role in this chapter because this is not just any ship. Aside from being the largest passenger ship in the world, with accommodation for 1,700 passengers and 1,000 crew, this ship from the drawing board stage on was designed with attention to wheelchair passengers. This was possible because of the huge scale—*QE2* is 963 feet long—permitting flexibility in stateroom design and more fluid space in the public areas. (The *Cunard Countess* and *Cunard Princess*, sister ships, are 536 feet long and are not barrier-free, although they are newer than *QE2*, which made her maiden voyage in 1969.) But except for the sports deck and the signal deck, every part of *QE2*'s public areas is accessible.

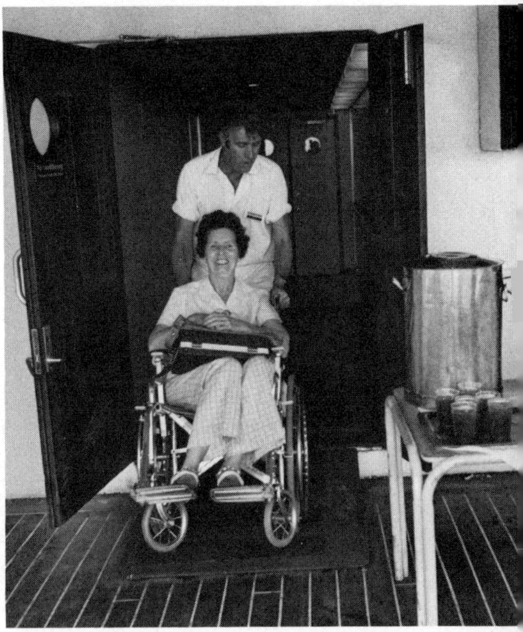

Ramps replace or complement steps in all public areas. Sometimes there is even an accommodating push.

Four staterooms are designed specifically for persons confined to chairs. These rooms include a spacious bathroom with no riser in the doorway, a door that opens outward so as not to block the plumbing, and grab bars at the toilet and tub. Five more rooms can be modified. And at least sixteen additional rooms can possibly take a wheelchair.

The hospital is staffed by specially trained nurses, two doctors, one of whom is a surgeon, and a dentist.

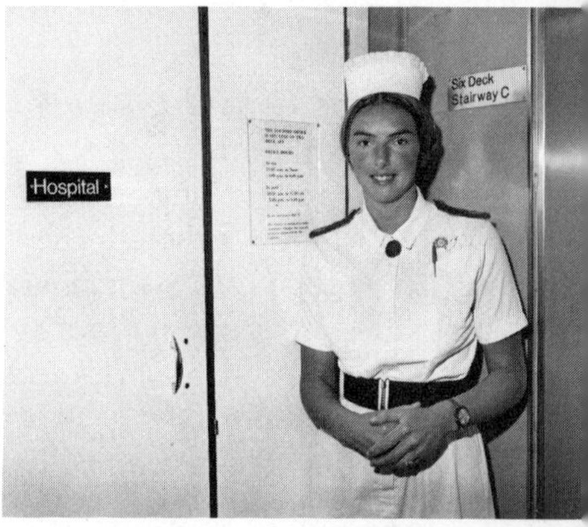

It is fully equipped, and it's said by Cunard to be the most complete hospital on any passenger ship. A pharmacy is also on board.

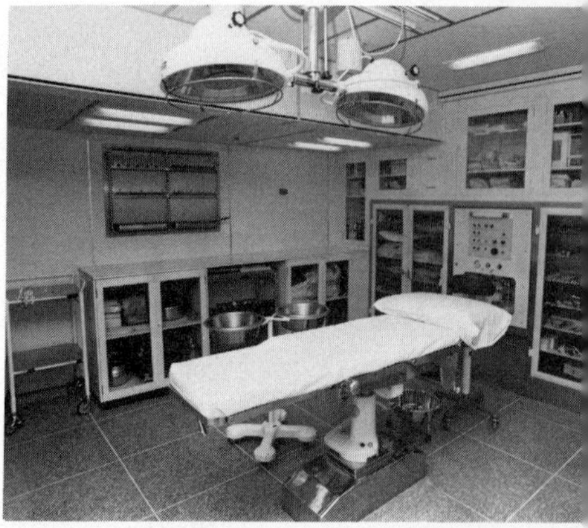

In addition, a physiotherapy room is staffed by a physiotherapist (for cruises only, not in use on transatlantic voyages). Here one can continue a regimen of heat treatments or other therapy.

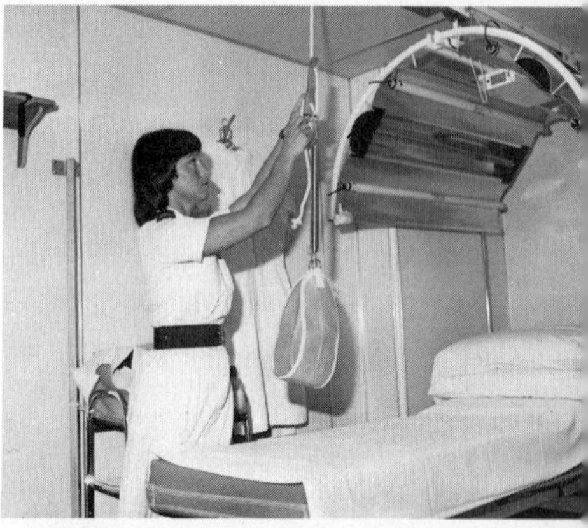

Dot generally begins her day with breakfast in bed, served by her cabin steward. (On some ships, breakfast is also served on deck.)

The joy of cruising to many people lies in the personal attention by the staff and the diversity of entertainment—including dancing and nightclub acts—and activities that you can choose from. Dot skips the bridge, bingo, and Chinese cooking lessons offered on her particular sailing in favor of basking in the sun. Hamburgers are served poolside and a buffet is also set up for lunching *al fresco*.

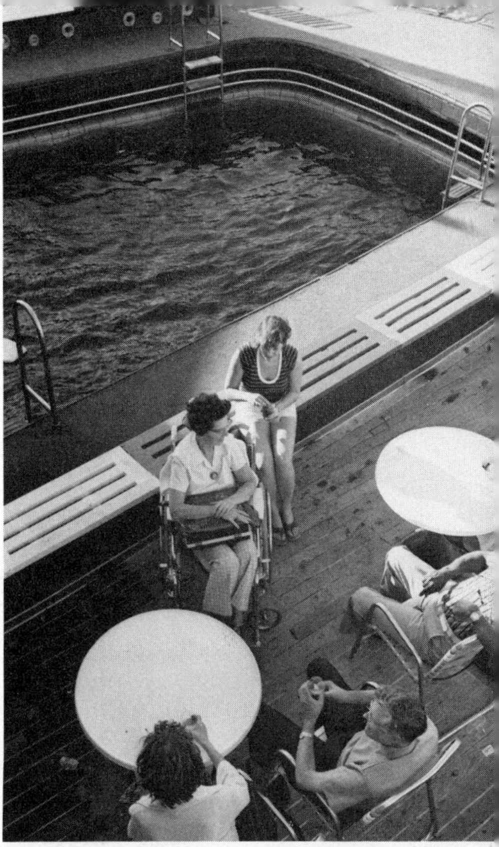

Dinner is lavish. At a table carefully selected by her travel agency (Flying Wheels Tours) as convenient to the dining room's accessible entrance, and yet not out of the way, the dining room steward confers with Dot over a menu that runs through eight courses.

The wine steward can recommend the perfect complement—a crisp Chablis with the oysters, a robust Burgundy with the prime ribs of beef—or serve a single glass of table wine.

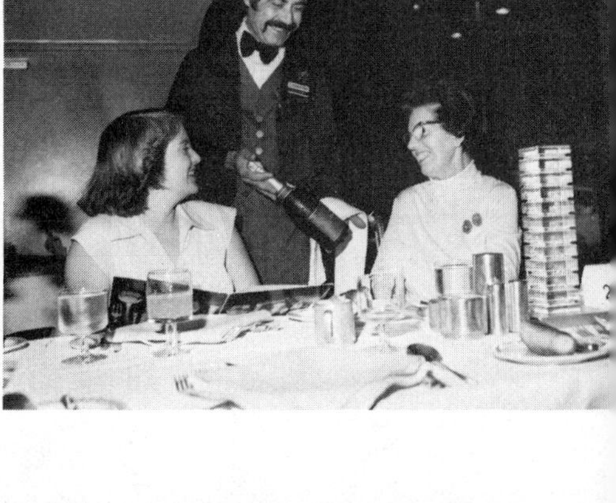

The highlight of any cruise: the Captain's Party. Here Captain Robert Arnott welcomes Dot and Janis to the *QE2*.

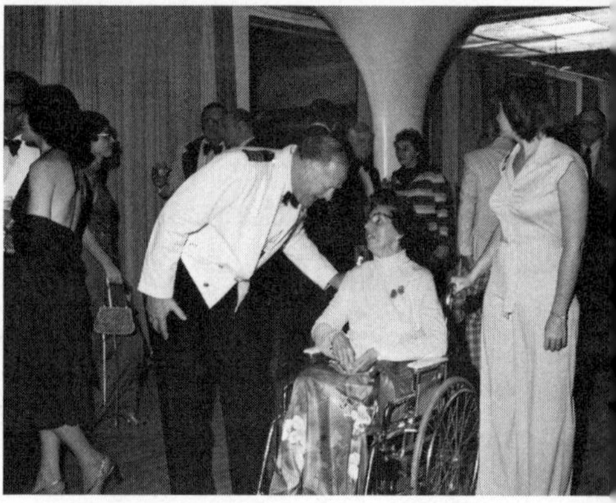

PART 2
GOING ASHORE

Majestic ocean queens, galas, sumptuous spreads . . . while some are drawn to the ships themselves, it is the colorful ports-of-call that ultimately draw others to cruising. Getting from the ship to those ports is achieved in one of two ways, by launch or by gangplank.

The ship drops anchor, as *QE2* does at St. Thomas, and the passengers are ferried ashore by launch (also called a *tender*). While precarious at times, there is never a risk. The ablebodied seamen who handle you and your chair inspire confidence. Steps are suspended over the side and the men lift Dot, chair and all. From the ladder into the

launch they lift her bodily. (If the sea were rough and there were any risk, a disabled person might be asked to remain on board ship.)

By far the more common and popular means of going ashore is via the gangplank when the ship docks, as *QE2* does at San Juan, Puerto Rico.

Because the regular passenger ramp is from a door higher on the hull, Dot asks to disembark via the lower ramp from the crew's quarters. Again, she is in able hands.

Initial embarkation and final debarkation are usually at modern ports, such as New York's new Passenger Ship Terminal, where the ship docks and you simply go ashore on one level. Here, undergoing a Customs check at the New York pier upon return, Janis has asked the Customs inspector to come to them, rather than their having to queue up.

Photo by Lois Reamy

A LINE ON CRUISES

Dot, a retired schoolteacher, taught as far afield as Hawaii, Saipan, and Europe before she suffered a disabling disease twelve years ago. Even so, she has not stopped traveling. She had had three vacations in the Caribbean before the cruise. Her special message here is that even persons with average incomes can probably afford a cruise.

She has a point. Cruises have enjoyed an enormous popularity in recent years and one reason for this is their excellent value: the same high standard of service and good food would be hard to find except at a luxury resort where you would pay top dollar. Furthermore, cruises take you to one island paradise after another, but you are free to sit out anything you wish. Rates vary, of course, according to the ship itself, the class of accommodation, the season, and the duration. A seven-day cruise with a standard outside twin cabin may average $570 per person on the Carnival Lines to $800 to $900 on *QE2*.

When researching the right cruise for you consider the ship's accessibility. Bear in mind that while *QE2* and the *Vistafjord* (see below) are among the most barrier-free ships afloat, many other ships are well able to accommodate persons with disabilities, and may be willing to remove bathroom doors, put in temporary ramps, and the like, when requested. Do check out any ship you are considering. And do consider any ship that appeals to you.

One veteran cruise-goer who has enjoyed three cruises always sends this letter to the line she is considering. This she does over and above her travel agent's thorough arrangements. You could use her letter as a model.

Amend the letter to include any special questions you have regarding special diets, whether you can use a motorized wheelchair on board, whether there is a laundromat or laundry service, and other particulars.

Pay special attention to Question 8 in the letter. Some ships require nobody to sign a waiver. Some ships require all passengers to sign a waiver. And certain ships require only disabled passengers to sign a form absolving the company from responsibility in the event of certain accidents.

1 Fortieth Avenue
Euclid, NJ 00000
January 24, 1978

Reservations Manager
Holland America Cruises
2 Pennsylvania Plaza
New York, NY 10001

Gentlemen:

My aunt and I are planning a cruise on the_________________[name of ship] for_______________[dates], and I would like to obtain some specific information before we make definite reservations.

Because I am confined to a wheelchair and my aunt is a senior citizen, we must check on various matters. Therefore, could you please advise us on the following:

1. Width of elevator doors and whether the elevators offer access to all parts of the ship.
2. Width of stateroom and lavatory doors. Do the doors open outward, or otherwise not block the plumbing? Are there risers at these doorways? If so, could they be ramped in our room?
3. Do any staterooms have an extra basin in the room, to eliminate some trips into the bathroom? Do the bathrooms have a tub rather than shower? What is the location and cost of such rooms? Are they near the elevator? Are there sharp turns from passageway into stateroom?
4. Are any sections of the ship "off-limits" to a wheelchair user because of stairs, narrow doorways, or other obstacles?
5. Could a ramp be placed at one of the outside decks if they have steps or risers?
6. Is it necessary to use a launch to go to the islands on the______________[dates] cruise? Is it difficult for a wheelchair occupant to use the stairs down to the launch? Will help be available to take me on and off the ship? If the gangplank used by passengers is too steep for a wheelchair user, is the one used by the crew any lower and could I use it?
7. Will I have to sign a waiver of my rights discharging the ship line from responsibility in the event of an accident?
8. Will I be asked to preboard on sailing day and will you provide particulars on departure and arrival, as well as information on the accessibility of the pier?

Inasmuch as I hope to have a smooth sailing, your cooperation in providing this information that could prevent any possible difficulties would be most helpful and greatly appreciated.

I look forward to your kind reply.

Sincerely yours,

Marie R.

Further points to consider in choosing the right cruise are:

• Point of origin. Major cruise ports in the United States are New York, Miami, Port Everglades, Los Angeles, San Francisco, San Juan, and New Orleans. Occasional ships sail from Norfolk and Philadelphia. Do you prefer sailing from a city close to home? Or will you fly to meet the ship? Most cruise lines offer a fly/cruise rate that includes a low airfare to the city of embarkation. Do you prefer to spend your entire time in calm Caribbean waters, for example, or do you wish to spend a total of three to four days in getting to and from the sunny islands for the convenience of sailing from home?

• Ports of call. Ships out of American ports commonly sail to Alaska, Mexico, Central and South America, Hawaii, Bermuda and the Bahamas in the Atlantic, and to the Caribbean. The latter is the world's number one cruising ground, vaunted for a fine year-round climate and island gems, each with its own accent ranging from syncopated English to Creole French. If going ashore by launch does not appeal to you, once you have selected a cruise itinerary with islands you'd like to visit, check with the cruise line to see if the ship in question will dock or anchor on that particular sailing. The dates may make a difference. While *QE2* never docks at St. Thomas, for example, because she is too big for the port, other ships do. But due to the limited number of berths, a small ship that docks on one sailing may have to anchor on the next because other ships reserved earlier. Some ships are on a fixed year-in, year-out schedule and always dock.

The cruiselines do not always know until arrival whether a ship will dock or anchor. Also see Ports-of-Call at the end of this section.

• Special interests. The range of interests now featured on cruises is astonishing. Dot's cruise offered yoga lessons, Chinese cooking classes, dance lessons, and a golf clinic, to name a few. A medical group was also convening aboard ship. Some lines offer theme cruises such as football, classical or jazz music festivals, oceanography films and lectures, bridge, and photography. Some cruises are also designed for senior citizens, with health and beauty lectures that appeal to mature persons. So what's your line?

• Health inspections. At press time, many ships (including some of those mentioned in this chapter) have been failing some or most of the sanitation inspections made by the quarantine division of the U.S. Center for Disease Control. Ships are frequently inspected and rated on their water, refrigeration, food preparation, potential contamination of food, personal cleanliness of food handlers, and general cleanliness and repair. No penalty is imposed for ships that do not measure up. Outbreaks of gastrointestinal illness on ships are often traced to contaminated ice, improperly refrigerated meat, or the like. Before you settle on a cruise—especially if you are highly prone to infection—you may wish to check with the Center for Disease Control to find out how your chosen ship measures up. John Yashuk at the Center will send you the six-month rating for all ships inspected (showing whether or not they were accorded the eighty-five points necessary to pass inspection), or a full inspection report on two or three ships once you have narrowed down your choices. Mr. Yashuk is at the U.S. Center for Disease Control, 1015 North America Way, Rm. 107, Miami, FL 33132, 305-350-4307.

The following ships have passed every inspection included in the Center's last report issued prior to press time: *Vistafjord*, *Skyward*, *Southward*, *Starward*, and *Nordic Prince*.

It is believed by some persons in the travel industry that recent media attention to the sanitary conditions on ships will cause them to shape up.

WIDE WORLD OF SHIPS

Up to seventy or eighty ships under a multitude of flags sail from U.S. ports during any cruise season, mid-December to mid-April. A number of these ships also enjoy a year-round season. Most major newspapers and travel magazines run a couple of cruise sections or supplements a year that include both editorial coverage and advertisements on what's available. Up-to-date information is imperative, since most itineraries and rates vary from season to season. Travel agents can be most helpful in this department. Aside from having a supply of tantalizing cruise folders, they usually know what's what with the ships.

The degree of accessibility varies, so determine your requirements and inquire about any ship. For example, one woman who has a commode chair made out okay on the *Doric*, which had a sink in the room, even though her chair could not get into the bathroom. She was, of course, traveling with a companion. If you can walk or can take even a few steps, you have a wide world of ships to choose from, since you can forget about the restrictive risers (three- or four-inch sills at stateroom, bathroom, and other doors) as well as the narrow bathroom doors that often open inward and block the plumbing. Some wheelies, ascertaining that a ship's public areas are generally accessible or that a cruiseline is willing to ramp a few areas, have managed to cruise on their chosen ships through their own resourcefulness. One woman cruising with her sister took along her own plastic commode as well as a plastic washbasin. Not ideal? No, but these individuals were able to take a cruise that suited them in terms of price, special interest, or itinerary.

The ships below are among those that have transported persons in wheelchairs and with varying degrees of mobility. The extent of accessibility varies. Bathrooms on the Carnival and Home Lines, for example, are probably inaccessible to wheelchairs. And ramps to public areas may be requested. Inquire with respect to your needs.

Carnival Cruise Lines, 820 Biscayne Blvd., Miami, FL 33132, 305-377-4751. *Carnivale*, which has all public rooms on one deck, and *Mardi Gras* (primarily out of Miami to San Juan, St. Thomas, and St. Maarten, and to Nassau, San Juan, and St. Thomas, respectively). Coming in October 1978 is the *Festivale*, expected to be semiaccessible.

Cunard Line, 555 Fifth Ave., New York, NY 10017, 212-983-2500. *QE2* fully accessible (out of New York to the Caribbean during cruise season, also extensive world cruises; transatlantic in summer). The *Cunard Countess* (year-round Caribbean cruises out of San Juan) and the *Cunard Princess* (generally New York to Bermuda) would suit ambulatory persons *only*.

Holland America Cruises, 2 Pennsylvania Plaza, New York, NY 10001, 212-760-3800. *Rotterdam* and *Statendam* (from New York to Bermuda and/or the Caribbean). Also *Prinsendam* out of Vancouver to Alaska. Address accessibility information requests to the Marine Hotel Department.

Home Lines, 1 World Trade Center, New York, New York, 10048, 212-432-1414. *Doric* and *Oceanic* (out of New York to Bermuda and Nassau).

Courtesy the Norwegian America Line

The Norwegian America Line's *Vistafjord* is accessible

Norwegian America Line, 29 Broadway, New York, NY 10006, 212-422-3900, *Vistafjord* (from Port Everglades to Caribbean, including a Barbados connection plan that has an overnight in a Barbados hotel and a return flight to Florida; also transatlantic and European cruise season). Ship caters to an older crowd. Public rooms and decks are level. Totally accessible except for one outside deck, which has a riser at entrance. No risers on bathroom doors. Staterooms whose baths have tubs are spacious enough for wheelchairs with a narrowing device. Free oxygen in staterooms on request.

Norwegian Caribbean Lines, 1 Biscayne Tower, Miami, FL 33131, 305-358-6670, *Skyward, Southward, Starward* (from Miami for cruises to the Bahamas or to Caribbean ports). Requires you to put your wheelchair in the hold and use theirs by prearrangement. Bathrooms not accessible to wheelchairs. Requests that disabled persons travel with a companion able to provide any personal care necessary. *Skyward* recommended by the company because she always docks rather than anchors.

Royal Caribbean Cruise Line, 903 South America Way, Miami, FL 33132, 305-379-2601. *Nordic Prince* (from Miami to Caribbean ports year-round).

PRACTICAL INFORMATION

TRIP COSTS

The cruise price includes the voyage, stateroom, all meals—up to six a day, counting breakfast, mid-morning bouillon, lunch, tea, dinner, and midnight supper—and entertainment. Complimentary wine with dinner is served on some lines, especially those flying under the flag of wine-drinking countries. On others, you may buy wine. All movies and instructions (dance lessons, yoga, and the like) are included.

For extras you pay extra. Drinks at the bar, for example, are usually less than you'd pay ashore. At special galas such as the Captain's Party, drinks are free. Typical rates for sauna or steambath are $5; for massage $12; for wash-and-set $10 and up (make appointments early); and for a man's haircut, $4 to $5. (Tip as you would at home.) If you like bingo (often a dollar a card) or the ship's casino, budget accordingly. Also allow for shopping on shipboard and ashore.

Organized shore excursions range from sightseeing by car, or a combination boatride/picnic, to a night club tour, which usually takes in three clubs, throwing in several drinks for the price. Excursion rates vary from one line to another. Ask in advance for the excursion options and their cost.

Organized shore excursions are not necessary. You can shop or browse in the little ports, or take off on your own to the nearest beach. Persons with limited mobility often do better to make their own sightseeing arrangements locally. If you have not decided in advance what you wish to do on each island, study the booklet of organized shore excursions likely to be in your stateroom for adaptable ideas. Also see Ports-of-Call, below.

Tipping is a big item on most cruises. Your line may offer tipping guidelines. If not, you might ask the ship line or your travel agent what the customary tips are. Otherwise, you may tip at the minimum rate of $1.50 a day per passenger to the dining room waiter and the cabin steward and accordingly to others who serve you, including the deck steward if you take an assigned deck chair and let him pamper you with refreshments (on some decks you are strictly on your own). Tip the wine steward 15 percent of your total wine bill on the last night. You may leave the barman a tip whenever you order, as you would in a regular bar. Or if you keep a running tab charged to your room, you may give him 15 percent when you pay the bill. Whenever stewards work in pairs (i.e., in some dining rooms and staterooms), you may tip each one a dollar a day, or $1.50 per day for both of them, giving the entire amount to the one in charge and mentioning that it is for them both. If there is a busboy who clears the table. $.75 a day is sufficient.

Tipping the *maitre d'* is optional. If he makes any special arrangements for you a gratuity is in order. Tips are customarily placed in neat envelopes (take them or pick them up at the ship's office) and handed to the recipients with thanks the last night out. On a cruise of more than a week or ten days, you might tip weekly. Some of the more informal ships have a system whereby each passenger puts the equivalent of five dollars a day in the kitty.

If someone provides extra attention—helping with your chair or indulging you with room service or running little errands—you may wish to offer an additional gratuity. Never tip the ship's officers.

It saves time on board if you estimate in advance how much you will need and take a supply of crisp bills in one- , five- , and ten-dollar denominations from home for tipping purposes.

The porters who handle your bags when you arrive at the pier, both outward and inward bound, should be tipped $.50 to $.75 per bag at the pier. Your ship line will send advance information regarding this and other boarding procedures. If you are traveling on a fly/sail package whereby the ship line meets your plane and takes you to the pier, it is highly unlikely that you will need porters. The ship line usually takes care of your bags.

Note: On the rare line, such as Holland America, with a no-tipping-required policy, a small tip (appreciably less than on other lines) may be offered.

WHEELCHAIRS AND CRUTCHES

Wheelchairs for use on shipboard "should be no more than twenty-four inches wide and should be collapsible," according to the Cunard Line. Going ashore by launch could pose problems for motorized chairs on cruises. Cunard will store your motorized chair in the hold on transatlantic crossings, however, and lend you a manual chair to use at sea. Norwegian Caribbean always requires you to use its chair and stow yours in the hold. Other lines may have similar requirements, so check first. Also note that while it seems highly unusual, some islands may not allow motorized chairs to operate without a permit. Bermuda, for one, allows motorized chairs only under the authority of a permit granted in advance of arrival by the Minister of Transport, P.O. Box 718, Hamilton 5, Bermuda.

Users of motorized chairs should check both with their ship line and with the islands they plan to visit to make sure they will be accepted.

If you need a wheelchair only for covering the long distances at the ship terminal, ask the line to have one waiting at the pier. If you will need a chair for the duration of the cruise or crossing, the ship line may advise you to bring your own.

Persons who use crutches should bear in mind that maneuvering with them can be treacherous on rough seas, or on steps during calm seas. You might take along a backup chair or plan to use one from the ship's hospital for emergencies.

WARDROBE/PACKING

On tropical cruises women wear their loveliest summer clothes (floating caftans, long skirts with silk blouses or halters, and pretty dinner dresses) for special evenings. Men wear black-tie or a dark business suit with a conservative tie for dress-up evenings, and otherwise wear a jacket and tie to dinner. On some of the more informal lines that are breaking with tradition, however, sports jackets and slacks and leisure suits are acceptable. If in doubt, men especially should ask their cruise line or travel agent. For less formal evenings, women tend to dress in their nicest patio pants and long skirts or Sunday dresses. On Dot's seven-day cruise, three evenings were formal. As a rule, you do not dress on the first or last night or on the evenings in port. The ship's agenda distributed daily indicates expected dinner attire.

You may wear casual clothes into the dining room for breakfast or lunch (shorts and swimsuits being the exception). Most ships also serve a poolside lunch. For daytime on the ship, dress casually. Women should plan to wear a pantsuit or an attractive dress, and men, slacks and a sports shirt when you go ashore. Take a sunhat or buy one at an island straw market.

Pack a few winter clothes and have a warm coat and cap to wear on deck if you are sailing in winter from a northern port. Take along sweaters and/or shawls for air-conditioned days and breezy nights.

The number of suitcases is unlimited (except for fly/sails) but too many suitcases can clutter up a small stateroom. Passengers who can personally handle all their luggage are permitted to disembark ahead of those who must wait for their gear to be delivered to the pier. Baggage is generally collected the evening before you return to port, so take an overnight case that you can manage yourself.

HINTS

- Never call a ship a "boat." Anyway not in front of the vessel's officers and crew.
- Never leave any valuables in your stateroom. Place them in the ship's vault.
- Request a stateroom near an elevator that goes right to the center of the activities.
- Check beforehand on voltage and whether you may use electrical devices in your stateroom. (There is usually a special outlet for shavers.)

• Ships may have two seatings for dinner (this is especially true on transatlantic crossings; not likely on a cruise). The early seating may be at 7 or 7:30; the later one around 9. If you like to eat early or want time to work up an appetite for the Lucullan midnight buffet, choose the early seating. If you like to relax with a drink before dinner, choose the later one. Some ships—especially on cruises—may have only one seating. In either case, reserve a table when you make your reservation, requesting that it be conveniently located near the entrance but not out of the way. The number of your table should be in the stateroom when you arrive. This saves waiting in line for a table assignment before your first meal.

• If you have a medical condition, such as diabetes, be sure to advise the ship line when you make your reservation so that the hospital can be prepared for any emergency that might arise.

• If you have never sailed, consider booking a short cruise—a week or a weekend—before taking off on a voyage of several weeks or months. Some lines offer the popular "Cruise to Nowhere," often just a weekend excursion from New York City out into the Atlantic and back.

• Persons who live near a major port may have an opportunity to case their prospective ship while in port. Ask the ship line.

• Bon voyage parties are great to throw for friends to see you off. Possibly the only ship that does not permit them is the *QE2* (for security reasons). Do check before you invite anyone.

• Do not be surprised if a line asks you to fill out a medical questionnaire. Some of them do. Among other things, this helps them to select the most suitable stateroom for you. A line may ask persons who are nonambulatory or have other disabilities to travel with a companion.

• Once you know the specifications of your stateroom, determine if a chair such as the Norman Chair (see the Airlines section in Part II) or a secretary's posture chair (see General Information in Part IV) would be useful.

• The physical fitness director of the *QE2* suggests that particularly with the nonstop meals served on shipboard, passengers should exercise some good sense and control. He suggests eating a light lunch, skipping tea, and being prudent about the midnight buffet (usually the chef's masterpiece). He also suggests that passengers exercise some every day: a lap or two around the deck before breakfast and again *slowly* before retiring. If you cannot run or walk, you can always roll. The sea air is part of it.

PORTS-OF-CALL

Because most cruises out of U.S. ports are bound for the Caribbean islands, this section deals mainly with those ever-green idylls in that ever-blue sea.

When you go ashore you might do well to make your own arrangements with a local taxi driver, rather than take a prearranged shore excursion. Taxis often look just like private cars, and you'll find them lined up along the quay whenever a ship is in. Look for one that suits you.

Taxis have a history of "taking" independent travelers. Have a fair idea of the rates (the cruise director can help you) and make a firm deal in advance. The driver will take you to accessible points of interest at your own pace and return you to the quay when you've seen enough. When a ship rides at anchor, the launches run back and forth all day.

Dot choosing a taxi

Dot's ship called at St. Thomas and San Juan. On St. Thomas she and Janis paid the driver about fifteen dollars (for two) for a morning's drive to view the scenery. They stopped at Mountain Top, an apartment complex with a popular bar, where they had wide vistas down to the sea and banana daiquiris. Shops are also here and there is a special ground-level entrance for persons with limited mobility. After lunch at Sparky's, Dot went Christmas shopping in the duty-free stores and boutiques that line the streets of Charlotte Amalie. Drawbacks for a disabled person are the rugged sidewalks and curbs, a step up into many shops, and the difficulty in finding accessible restrooms. (Dot and Janis went into a travel agency and asked if its facilities were accessible and if they might use them. Affirmative.) Even the Visitors Bureau across from the pier is one flight up. The new Coral World—an aquarium and much more—is ramped throughout. The exception may be its underwater observatory. Five dollars admission.

St. Thomas would be difficult for a lone wheelie from a cruise ship. With a "pusher" he might also take a ferry to neighboring St. John Island, a nature preserve, for the day at Virgin Islands National Park. The restaurant at the Cinnamon Bay campsite is inaccessible but one may ask at the luxury Caneel Bay Plantation hotel if it is possible to lunch in the accessible dining room. Also see the *Access/National Parks* guide (check index) for accessible National Park Service sites in the Caribbean.

In San Juan all ships dock at the modern piers unless more than four ships are in port at once. Old San Juan, a picturesque Spanish Colonial town to drive through, is quite hilly and slopes down to the harbor. Sidewalks are narrow, curbs are vertical, and many streets are cobblestone-paved. Taking all this into account, Dot and Janis again hired a taxi (about ten dollars) for a drive through town and beyond to see some of the beautiful beaches, where tall palms edge the long stretches of silky sand that in turn edge the sea. El Morro, the cliché fortress that dates from the sixteenth century, is generally barrier-free. Dot and Janis toured it and returned to *QE2* for lunch and a sunny afternoon on deck.

Anyone needing group land arrangements in Puerto Rico should contact the tourist office, which notes that major tour operators have successfully served handicapped travelers in the past. For both St.

Dot and Janis on the streets of Charlotte Amalie

Thomas and Puerto Rico contacts, see the state listings. Also check the index for island references. Hotels that are accessible to the wheelchair-bound could afford a respite while you are visiting the islands. Barrier-free hotels on Puerto Rico are also likely to have barrier-free casinos.

OTHER POPULAR PORTS

The following information has been supplied by the respective tourist boards:

Antigua—A Holiday Inn on the southern side of the island, the Jolly Beach Hotel, and the White Sands, described as a "very English hotel" near St. John's, are said to be barrier-free. Docking for two ships. Others anchor. Antigua Department of Tourism, P.O. Box 363, High St. and Corn Alley, St. John's, Antigua, West Indies. (By the way, drop the "u." It's pronounced An-ti′-gah.)

Bahamas—Streets and sidewalks around Prince George Dock (where ships dock) in downtown Nassau are accessible. The Skyline South Ocean Beach Hotel & Golf Club has ground floor rooms, said to be accessible. Holiday Inn also has special rooms. Ministry of Tourism, Nassau Court, P.O. Box N 3701, Nassau, N.P. Bahamas.

Bermuda—An information sheet is entitled *Handicapped Visitors—Facilities in Bermuda.* Bermuda News Bureau, 630 Fifth Ave., New York, NY 10020, 212-246-6053.

Grenada—The port of St. George's, one of the most scenic in the Caribbean, does have a pier where ships dock. Among those that anchor are the *Vistafjord, Statendam,* and *Rotterdam.* The Grenada Tourist Board, P.O. Box No. 293, St. George's, Grenada, West Indies.

St. Vincent—*QE2* is among the ships which cannot berth but must anchor. *Vistafjord* can dock when a berth is available. Streets around the harbor are generally accessible to persons with chairs, canes, or crutches. Among the most suitable hotels for nonambulatory persons are Coconut Beach, Indian Bay, and Sunset Shores. Accessible to persons using canes and crutches are also the Grand View, Treasure Island, and Tropic Breeze. St. Vincent Tourist Board, P.O. Box 834, St. Vincent, West Indies.

St. Kitts—All ships currently anchor but plans are underway to build a deepwater harbor. Wheelchairs can be pushed or persons could get along on crutches in some streets around the harbor. Hoteliers make arrangements for their disabled guests to go sightseeing and shopping. The Royal St. Kitts Hotel has facilities that are almost ground level and *perhaps* could facilitate disabled guests. St. Kitts (Nevis and Anguilla) Tourist Board, P. O. Box 132, Basseterre, St. Kitts, West Indies.

Caribbean Tourist Association—General information on Antigua, Aruba, Barbados, Belize, Bonaire, Cayman Islands, Curaçao, Dominica, the French West Indies (notably Martinique, Guadeloupe,

St. Martin, and St. Barts), Haiti, Jamaica, Puerto Rico, Montserrat, St. Kitts/Nevis/Anguilla, St. Vincent and the Grenadines, Turks and Caicos, U.S. Virgins, Venezuela, and Surinam is available from the Caribbean Tourist Association, 20 East 46th St., New York, NY 10017, 212-MU2-0435. Specify island or islands.

St. Lucia Tourist Board—At 220 East 42nd St., New York, NY 10017, 212-867-2950.

St. Maarten—Information available from Sontheimer and Company, 445 Park Ave., New York, NY 10022, 212-688-8350.

Mexico—Among the Mexican National Tourist Council offices in the United States are those at 405 Park Ave., New York, NY 10020, 212-755-7689; Cain Tower, Peachtree St., N.E., Atlanta, GA 30303, 404-659-2409; John Hancock Center, Chicago, IL 60611, 312-224-3743; 3106 Wilshire Blvd., Los Angeles, CA 90010, 213-385-6438; 100 N. Biscayne Blvd., Miami, FL 33132, 305-371-8037; and 1156 Fifteenth St., N.W., Washington, DC 20006, 202-296-2594.

Panama—Panama Government Tourist Bureau, 630 Fifth Ave., New York, NY 10020, 212-246-5841.

Also see trip cancellation insurance under General Information, and Medical Questions and Answers, both in Part IV.

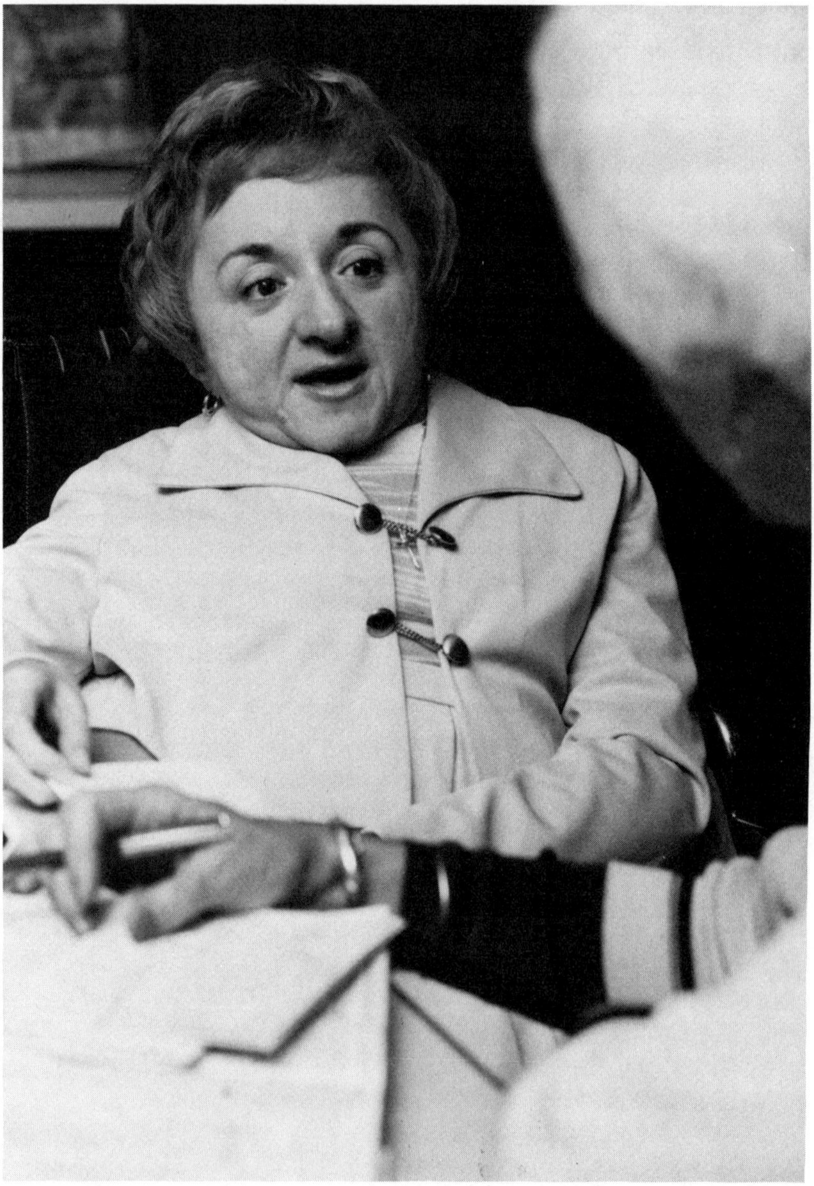

"We'd like a motel with an adjacent restaurant. This helps in bad weather and it's great for breakfast," a prospective traveler tells her travel agent (page 16).

Part III

WHERE TO GO
AND
WHERE TO STAY

1

HAWAII: A PERFECT PLACE TO GO

Hawaii is the one destination we have chosen to treat in depth. Aside from being almost everybody's dream trip, it also gets an A for Accessibility in our book, for with a reasonable amount of advance planning you can take in all the scenic beauty and major attractions of this tropical setting.

Furthermore, Hawaii—sunning itself year-round in the Pacific 2,400 miles off the California coast—offers the appeal of an exotic destination with the security of being in the United States: you already know the language and the money, you can buy familiar brands of almost anything, you know what you are eating unless you deliberately order the Hawaiian or Polynesian specialties with unpronounceable names, you can call home for about three dollars or less for as many minutes, and most U.S. medical insurance plans are honored here.

Another big plus for the popular island of Oahu is a little company called Handi-Cabs of the Pacific, whose ambulettes allow you to tour without leaving your chair. Equipped with ramps or lifts and tie-downs, the vans provide taxi and sightseeing services at rates competitive with the conventional taxi and tour-bus companies. Self-drive cars with hand controls and limousines are also available.

Low-priced vacation packages which range from about $400 to $500 for one week at a Waikiki hotel, including round-trip flights from New York (lower from the West Coast), also bring Hawaii within financial reach of many vacationers. If you need any extras—transportation via ambulette or a rental car with hand controls, for example—you personally add them on. Higher-priced group tours complete with medical attendants are also available from several tour operators, who likewise offer tours for the blind and persons requiring hospital visits for dialysis.

Flying time to Honolulu International Airport is about eleven hours from New York (allowing a one-hour stop in California when passengers who wish can use the airport's restrooms that accommodate wheelchairs), nine hours from Chicago (also with a stop), and five hours from the West Coast.

When you deplane at Honolulu International either by jetway or forklift (sometimes used by charter flights), you are at one of the most beautiful and accessible airports anywhere in the world. Here ramps like rainbow bridges blend into the architecture and oriental gardens. If you are traveling on a group plan, you will be welcomed with the traditional flower *lei* placed around your neck and a friendly "*Aloha*" from an island beauty, and your vacation officially begins.

Hawaii is actually a chain of 132 islands, six of which are known to tourists. But usually when we refer to Hawaii we are talking about Oahu, which aptly means "the gathering place." For this is where Honolulu, Pearl Harbor, Waikiki, and the action are to be found, along with 82 percent of the islands' 800,000 population, and most of the three million annual tourists.

And when we talk about Hawaii's accessibility, we are actually thinking of the tourist attractions of Oahu.

Waikiki is "the strip" here, and for a mile or so, white high-rise hotels flank, face, or butt each other for a combined total of 25,000 rooms. A number of them are well suited for wheelchair guests either by design or accident. In this year-round resort thicket just around the shore from the landmark Diamond Head, you will find accommodations ranging from the glamourous new Hyatt Regency with a cooling waterfall and sidewalk café in the open-air lobby, to standard hotels. You will also find fine restaurants or fast food chains such as

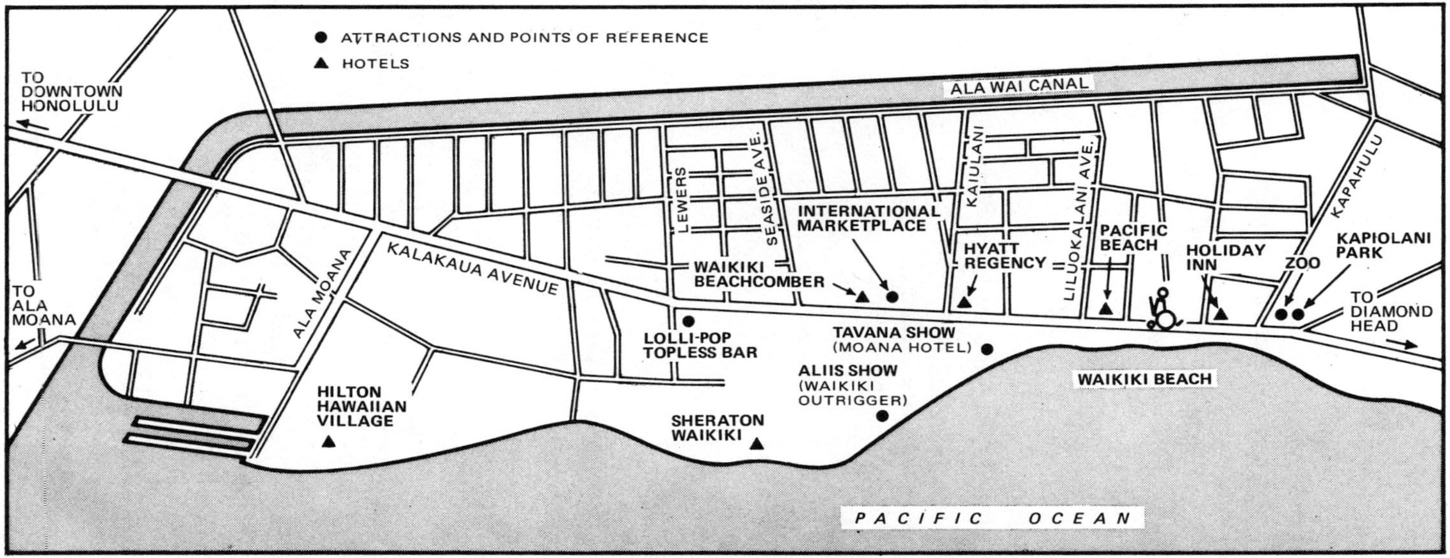
ATTRACTIONS AND POINTS OF REFERENCE
HOTELS
TO DOWNTOWN HONOLULU
TO ALA MOANA
ALA WAI CANAL
ALA MOANA
KALAKAUA AVENUE
LEWERS
SEASIDE AVE.
KAIULANI
LILIUOKALANI AVE.
KAPAHULU
INTERNATIONAL MARKETPLACE
WAIKIKI BEACHCOMBER
HYATT REGENCY
PACIFIC BEACH
HOLIDAY INN
ZOO
KAPIOLANI PARK
TO DIAMOND HEAD
LOLLI-POP TOPLESS BAR
TAVANA SHOW (MOANA HOTEL)
ALIIS SHOW (WAIKIKI OUTRIGGER)
HILTON HAWAIIAN VILLAGE
SHERATON WAIKIKI
WAIKIKI BEACH
PACIFIC OCEAN

BARRIER-FREE WAIKIKI

Pizza Hut and McDonald's, with eighty Oahu locations where a Big Mac goes for eighty-eight cents.

Most of the top-notch evening entertainment is staged in the Waikiki hotels, where you might catch a nightclub act from the mainland, or one of the local fixtures. These fixtures might be the Tavana show of Polynesian dancers at the Sheraton Moana Hotel; The Aliis, six Hawaiian guys who collectively play thirty instruments, sing a little, and clown a lot for a good show at the Waikiki Outrigger; and Al Harrington at the Hilton Hawaiian Village, where he hosts a variation of the *luau* feast (or cocktails) and entertains. You saw him first as Ben Kokua on *Hawaii Five-O*.

Sunset or nighttime cabaret cruises aboard big sailboats (usually catamarans) off the glittering tiara coast put you in an island mood. Cocktails and/or dinner are served to the silky sound of Hawaiian music and the tonic of a sea breeze. A windjammer luncheon sail drops anchor offshore for a swim in the salty Pacific or sunning on deck in full view of Waikiki. Narrated cruises of Pearl Harbor are offered as part of daytime excursions—a study in blue—aboard the *Hawaii State* or as a U.S. Navy launch ride out to the Arizona Memorial. In this peaceful harbor bordered by royal palms and backed by lavender mountains, the Japanese wiped out the American fleet anchored here on December 7, 1941—"a day that will live in infamy"—and drew the United States into the war in the Pacific.

Ala Moana (meaning By the Sea) is the ultimate shopping center. One of the largest in the world, Ala Moana's 155 stores cover fifty acres landscaped with gardens, fountains, sculpture, and tropical fish ponds. Stores include Hawaiian specialty shops and mainland and Japanese chain department stores. At the adjacent Ala Moana Building is La Ronde, the first revolving restaurant in America.

Waikiki center nearby also supports a huge number of shops all selling the same things: coral jewelry, carved bowls and trays of monkeypod wood (often marked "Made in the Philippines"), puka shell necklaces, *muumuus*, aloha shirts, chocolate-covered macadamia nuts, *muumuus*, puka, carved bowls, puka, macadamia nuts, *muumuus*, coral, monkeypod, puka, puka, coral, aloha shirts, carved coral, and puka in quantities that finally blur the vision. But it is fun to browse, bargain, and buy, especially at the International Marketplace, an open air emporium of eighty-seven shops shaded by huge banyan trees that drop roots from their branches, creating a small forest from a single tree.

Within minutes you can leave the high-rise hubbub behind, for opposite the Hyatt Regency begins an unobstructed stretch of sidewalk by the sea where you can stroll, ramble, or perform wheelies for that matter, and watch the surf and surfers and crisp white sailboats by day or a many-splendored sunset by evening.

In Waikiki about 90 percent of the sidewalk curbs have been *properly* ramped for smooth sailing. The curb-cuts run all the way from the zoo to within a couple of blocks of the Hilton Hawaiian Village. And while some of the public restrooms are accessible, some still are not. But the hotels are all in close proximity, and at press time there is an effort afoot to make accessible, and identify as such, more facilities.

In downtown Honolulu many of the sidewalks have also been ramped. No parking privileges are accorded disabled drivers except at certain parking lots.

Sightseeing in Honolulu takes you past modern office buildings, through a little Chinatown, and into the tawdry red-light district, called Hotel Street, with establishments named Caesar's Bath Palace, Topless Girls Girls, and Ida's Massage Studio. The Iolani Palace (where *Hawaii Five-O* offices are set) is the only royal palace in America and a remnant from the last century when the Alii royal family ruled the islands. A statue of King Kamehameha draped in gold is another reminder. The impressive state capitol designed by John Carl Warnecke represents the creation of the islands, with pillars like palm trees and a volcano-cone-shaped crown.

Oahu's number two attraction is the National Memorial Cemetery of the Pacific in Punchbowl Crater overlooking Honolulu, in solemn contrast to attraction number one, Waikiki. At Punchbowl are 112 acres of graves of the 25,000 American military dead from the Spanish-American War to the Vietnam War. The Court of the Missing here is engraved with the names of 26,280 more who are lost, missing, or buried at sea. A memorial building is faced with tableaux depicting the Pacific war theaters from Pearl Harbor through Korea. From time to time a carillon peals familiar hymns.

As you strike out across the twenty-six-by-forty-mile island its volcanic origins become apparent in the cone-shaped mountains and strange, ribbed mountainsides that create great depth of landscape. North from Honolulu the central highway rolls through miles of sugar and pineapple plantations. At roadside pineapple joints you can stop for chunks of sweet, juicy fruit. The fields finally slope off to the ocean for picture-perfect vistas of the sea and villages where life is slow and horseback riding is a mode of transportation.

The daredevil surfing beaches of Waimea and Sunset are along this north shore where an unpacific ocean pounds at the coast with waves up to twenty to forty feet in winter. This is where the surf "pipelines," or hollow tubelike waves, are so enormous a Mack truck could clear them and not get wet.

The north shore is sometimes likened to the less-hurried, verdant Outer Islands: the Hawaii of the travel posters where the foliage is waxlike and hibiscus comes in true Kodachrome colors of red, pink, and yellow.

Lunch on a day trip might be at the Kuilima Hyatt on the ocean or the Kahuku Sugar World, a former sugar mill now in business as a mini theme park. Shops and restaurants are easily accessible, but the hour-long tour is impassable in places if you have mobility problems.

The renowned Polynesian Cultural Center at Laie, an enterprise of the Mormon Church, is on the windward coast about thirty-five miles from Honolulu. Here are recreated villages of Samoa, Tonga, Tahiti, Fiji, and Hawaii, and of the Marquesans and Maoris, where the life and crafts are demonstrated. The gravel paths might be hard to push or walk on, but touring by electric cart or outrigger canoe are possible solutions.

The Outer Islands are Hawaii (also called the Big Island), with active volcanoes; Maui (the Valley Island); Kauai (the Garden Island); and Molokai (the Friendly Island) and its sidekick, Lanai, which is owned entirely by the Dole Corporation and has a single hotel.

These islands are superb if you are seeking peace and quiet, deserted palm-fringed beaches, gin-clear waters for snorkeling and skindiving, golf courses carved around ancient lava flows, and tropical scenery with few commercial interruptions.

One disabled veteran who makes his home in Honolulu reported on a happy vacation spent at the Maui Surf Hotel where he "sat in the sun and drank a lot."

Naturalists usually enjoy the Outer Islands, especially the Big Island and Maui, which have national parks that are accessible in varying degrees to persons with limited mobility. On the Big Island are City of Refuge National Historical Park, once a sacred precinct of the royal family, and Volcanoes National Park, featuring two of the world's most active volcanoes, sometimes shooting off their fireworks (average elevation below 4,000 feet). Haleakala National Park on Maui (average elevation above 8,000 feet), has the dormant Haleakala volcano, a particularly large and scenic crater. Overnight hikes (June through August) and horseback trips into the crater are offered. Persons with respiratory or heart problems are cautioned about the high altitudes and volcanic fumes.

Except for Lanai with its one hotel, the Outer Islands all have rooms that will accommodate wheelchair guests. By prearrangement you can rent an Avis car with hand controls on any of the islands except Lanai, or you can take your own hand controls and attach them to a rental car (the agency permitting). There is no Handi-Cab type of service, but limos and taxis, as well as tour buses, serve the islands. Hilo airport on the Big Island has jetways, the other airports board and deplane nonambulatory passengers by forklift.

If you do plan to visit one or more of the Outer Islands, keep in mind that every day you check out of a hotel, go to the airport, take a plane (even for a forty-five-minute flight), deplane, and check in at another hotel must be counted as a travel day.

Hawaiians can be full-blooded islanders with golden skin and straight black hair, Chinese, Japanese, Filipinos, whites or blacks from the mainland, or any combination thereof, sometimes resulting in rare beauty. While English is spoken here, the language is spiked with fascinating Hawaiian words from an alphabet having only twelve sounds. Thus, there are a lot of repetitions. That all-purpose word *aloha*, for example, means welcome, love, and goodbye.

TRIP PLANNING

These travel notes are based on a weeklong vacation spent in Hawaii with Bob and June, a well-traveled New York and Ft. Lauderdale couple. She is in a chair and he walks or ambulates via an Amigo

Bob and June in Hawaii *Photo by Lois Reamy*

Chair. They have toured most of Western Europe, Israel, and Morocco on six trips abroad and traveled extensively in the United States and on eight Caribbean islands. They rated Hawaii as their number one vacation choice in terms of barrier-free architecture, variety of accessible attractions, range of amenities offering good value at every style and price, helpfulness of local people, shopping, scenic beauty, and climate. They had always wanted to visit Hawaii, June being a romantic and Bob a military history buff. Both also enjoy sidewalk cafés, boat rides, photography, top-rate nightclub acts, shopping, and sightseeing.

Two or three months before their trip, Bob wrote for background information to the Hawaii Visitors Bureau and the Veterans Administration in Hawaii stating their mobility limitations. He perused the information, listed appealing attractions, and wrote in turn to them, asking if they were accessible. He contacted Handi-Cabs of the Pacific and made selections from its tour offerings. He studied hotel options his vacation package plan offered and selected from them on the basis of accessibility and situation. Then he set up an itinerary with some movable pieces and some fixtures. Fixtures included any events that were offered only on particular days and any tours he wanted to prebook with Handi-Cabs. He scheduled orientation tours early and saved one highlight—the windjammer cruise—till the end. He also planned a relaxing program and early evening for the first day. When you travel from east to west, expect to get sleepy early: your body clocks are still operating on hometown time. Anyone with similar taste could adapt this model itinerary to his/her specifications.

BOB AND JUNE'S ITINERARY

Asterisk represents use of Handi-Cab van.

First Day	Arrive Honolulu afternoon. Transfer to Sheraton-Waikiki by prearrangement with Handi-Cab.* Hotel check-in. Orientation to Waikiki. Sunset cocktails and dinner at hotel's towering Hanohano Room. Early bedtime.
Second Day	Lunch at Fisherman's Wharf Restaurant. Narrated cruise of Pearl Harbor aboard *Hawaii State.** Al Harrington *luau* dinner show at Hilton Hawaiian Village.*
Third Day	Full-day tour of island customized to include Honolulu and north shore with lunch at Kuilima Hyatt and return via windward coast.* Dinner at hotel coffee shop.

Fourth Day	Sunning by hotel pool. Lunch at hotel. Exploring Ala Moana shopping center.* Sunset dinner at La Ronde revolving restaurant in Ala Moana Building. The Aliis show at Waikiki Outrigger Hotel.
Fifth Day	Lunch and fashion show at Hyatt Regency Terrace Grille. Window-shopping at hotel shops. Dinner and show (Inkspots on tour) at Sheraton-Waikiki.
Sixth Day	Waikiki at leisure. Shopping at International Marketplace. Lunch with friend at hotel coffee shop. Sunning by pool. Dinner at hotel. Lolli-Pop topless bar four blocks from hotel.
Seventh Day	Begin packing. Windjammer lunch cruise (conventional taxi to/from pier; Amigo Chair not used). Sidewalk café-sitting (four hours) with new friends at Harry's Bar by waterfall in Hyatt Regency. Dinner with friends at Waikiki-Sheraton. Midnight promenade with two friends along the oceanfront.
Eighth Day	Shop for souvenirs. Order pineapples delivered to airport. Pack. Transfer to airport.* Afternoon departure.

THE BASICS: ATTRACTIONS

Here are details on some feasible attractions. Listed are some that Bob and June opted for, some they did not.

All rates quoted below, effective at press time, are subject to change.

CRUISES

On these boat trips ablebodied deckhands will assist at boardings where there is a step up to boarding ramp or boat. The head (rest room) is down below.

Catamaran Dinner Cruises—Aboard the *Ale Ale Kai* (ample flat deck for wheelchair parties). Two hours. Watch sun go down or moon come up over Diamond Head. Entertainment. Buffet dinner (crew will serve passengers in chairs). Open bar on *mai tais* and other drinks. Departs Fisherman's Wharf at 5:30 and 8:30 P.M. $17.50 per person. Reservations 538-3680 or 537-6355. Contact: Aikane Catamarans, 404 Piikoi St., Honolulu, HI 96814. *Sea Spree*, with meals served at tables, may be preferred if you lack muscle coordination. Special menu available if entire boat is chartered. Same departure times as *Ale Ale Kai*. $19 adults, $13 children under twelve. Reservations 923-1888. Contact: Kalama Cruises, P.O. Box 8453, Honolulu, HI 96815.

Hawaii State—Two-and-a-half-hour narrated cruise from Fisherman's Wharf covers Pearl Harbor. Large ferry-type boat. Ample flat decks for wheelchairs. Daily departures 9:30 A.M. and 1:30 P.M. Adults $7, children under twelve $3.50; special military rates. Reservations 536-3641. Paradise Cruise, Ltd., P.O. Box 8491, Honolulu, HI 96815.

U.S. Navy Pearl Harbor Cruise—Via launch to the Arizona Memorial. Disabled must be lifted in and out of small boat by ablebodied seamen. Stops at Arizona Memorial. Departs from Pearl City beyond the airport (allow at least a half hour by private transportation from Waikiki hotel to pier). Half-hour tour runs every thirty minutes Tues.–Sun. 9 A.M. to 3 P.M. Telephone 471-3901. Free.

Windjammer Picnic Sail—Traditional sailing vessels drop anchor in full view of Waikiki for picnic on deck or swimming off side. Two and a half hours. Entertainment and nonstop *mai tais* or soft drinks.

Smaller windjammer can accommodate two chairs; larger one, more. Daily sailings at 11 A.M. from Fisherman's Wharf. Adults $14.50, children under twelve $11.50. Reservations 521-0036. Windjammer Cruises, 1085 Ala Moana Blvd., Honolulu, HI 96814.

SIGHTSEEING

Kahuka Sugar Mill—Old sugar plant converted to a souvenir marketplace of thirty shops and restaurants with a Tinkertoy look in primary colors, antique train and cars. Admission free. Restrooms are accessible. Possible lunch stop on island tour to north shore. $3.50 adults, $2.25 ages five to twelve charged for tour of Sugar World mini theme park. Not all of tour is barrier-free. Tours daily 10 A.M. to 4:30 P.M. Telephone 293-8541. Kahuku Sugar Mill, Operations Office, P.O. Box 297, Kahuku, HI 96731.

Kodak Hula Show—Hawaiian and Tahitian pageant. Photographer's delight. Near the zoo in Kapiolani Park. Restrooms accessible. Tues.–Fri. 10 A.M. Admission free.

Paradise Park—A huge birdcage descends via steep ramp (help recommended on uphill climb) past birds of brilliant plumage to an enchanting aviary. Birds ride bicycles, perform other stunts. Must return to vehicle and drive to upper level for restaurant and gift shop. Daily 9:30 A.M. to 5:30 P.M. Adults $3.50, children four to twelve $2. Top of Manoa Rd. Telephone 988-2141. Paradise Park, 3737 Manoa Rd., Honolulu, HI 96822.

Polynesian Cultural Center—About thirty-five miles from Honolulu at Laie on windward coast. Covers forty-two acres. Seven villages recreated represent the culture and crafts at as many Pacific islands. Demonstrations, pageants, fashion shows, and nighttime *luaus* featured. Samoan fire dance a hit. Paths not smooth. Tour by electric cart or outrigger canoe, $1 extra. Daily except Sun. For adults and children under twelve, respectively, admission is $4.50 and $2.25, dinner $5.50 and $2.75, evening show $7.50 and $3.75. Reservations 923-1861. Polynesian Cultural Center, Reservations Office, Laie, Hawaii 96762.

Waioli Tea Room—Near Paradise Park. This Salvation Army enterprise features the relocated Little Grass Shack where Robert Louis Stevenson lived in 1893. Located in a green, green valley with frequent rain. A chorus of Waioli girls may sing the Doxology grace in Hawaiian (not always available). Meals served in three dining rooms 11 A.M. to 2 P.M. daily except Sun. Coffee hut serves macadamia-nut brownies and mango bread in season and other goodies baked on the premises and is open 8 A.M. to 4 P.M. except during lunch hours. Typical $3.50 lunch in tea room is salad, half a fried chicken, homemade bread, pie, and beverage. Restrooms accessible. Waioli Tea Room, 3016 Oahu Ave., Honolulu.

Sea Life Park—One of best shows put on by sea animals anywhere. Porpoise dances the hula. Beautiful tropical setting, natural Pacific tanks, evocative Polynesian gardens. At Makapuu Point. Daily 9:30 A.M. to 5 P.M. Adults $3.95, children seven to twelve $2.25, younger free. Telephone 923-1531. Sea Life Park, 2222 Kalakaua Ave., Honolulu, HI 96815.

Zoo—At edge of Waikiki (opposite Holiday Inn). Fifteen hundred assorted animals including only snake on the island. Superb collection of tropical birds. Accessible restrooms with grab bars. Daily 9 A.M. to 5 P.M. At 151 Kapahulu Ave., telephone 923-7723. Free.

RESTAURANTS/NIGHTLIFE

Al Harrington Luau—Island variety show hosted by Al Harrington (formerly Ben Kokua of *Hawaii Five-O*). Nightly except Sat. Dinner *luau* at 6 P.M. ($16.50) and cocktail show 10:30 P.M. ($9.50). Dome at Hilton Hawaiian Village. Reservations 947-2607.

Aliis—Six island guys play thirty instruments, sing, and ad lib. Nightly except Thurs. at 9 and 11 (Sun. 9 P.M. only; Sat. an additional 1 A.M. show without cover). Cover charge $3; two-drink minimum. Fantasy drinks $4–$4.50. Restrooms inaccessible. Waikiki Outrigger Hotel. Reservations 923-0711.

Fisherman's Wharf Restaurant—Lunch: entrees $2.95 up. Dinner: complete meal $4.95 up. Right at Fisherman's Wharf. Restrooms accessible to standard wheelchair using narrowing device. Reservation 538-3808.

La Ronde—Atop Ala Moana Building. Revolving restaurant twenty-three stories high turns 360 degrees every hour for circlorama view of ocean, city, mountains. Daily for lunch 11 A.M. to 2 P.M.; Happy Hour Mon.–Fri., 4 to 6 P.M. when bar brands start at $.95; dinner 5 to 10 P.M. and open for drinks until 11:30 P.M. Best view is an hour before sunset. Dinner entrees from $6.50 to $13.95. Lower-priced luncheon menu features salads and sandwiches. Twentieth floor restrooms accessible. Reservations 941-9138.

Lolli-Pop Topless Bar—No cover. No minimum. Drinks $2.50. Kalakaua Ave. near Lewers St.

Oceania—Floating but stationary dragon-encrusted pagoda (made in Hong Kong) serving Chinese (reservations 531-1666), international (Empire Room reservations 524-4880), and American (521-8796) cuisines in respective restaurants. Daily 11 A.M. through dinner and show. At Pier 6, Honolulu Harbor, HI 96813. One step to entrance ramp.

Tavana—Polyesian show and buffet dinner, 7 and 8:30 P.M. daily. Dinner $18.75 adults, $13.50 children. Or cocktails only at $11.50 adults and $7.50 (soft drinks) children. Enter through Surfrider Hotel next door. On beach level at Sheraton Moana Hotel. Reservations 922-3111.

CHILDREN

Mokulani Tours—Offers six tours for children with itineraries ranging from two to four and a half hours. Program includes visits to Sea Life Park, Kahuku Sugar Mill, or Paradise Park, a glass-bottom-boat ride, buffet dinner and magic show, and a day at the zoo. Pick up and return children to hotel. Prices from $5.75 to $22 usually include one meal. Babysitting at $2.50 an hour also offered. Mokulani Tours, P.O. Box 849, Kailua, HI 96734, 806-261-8116.

Note that many hotels offer supervised children's activities that range from sand castle competition and treasure hunts to stringing flowers into *leis*. Such programs may be seasonal. Check. They may be gratis or charge a nominal fee or as much as ten dollars, the rate at the Kuilima Hyatt's Kamp Kuilima. This is a program for seven- to twelve-year-olds and includes nature hikes, arts and crafts, swimming, surfboard paddling, and snorkeling. Available to guests at the Kuilima or Hyatt Regency (which has a daily shuttle service to the Kuilima). Offered year-round: daily in summer and on weekends the rest of the year.

LOCAL TOURS AND TRANSPORTATION

Handi-Cabs of the Pacific (HC-P)—Offers door-through-door service between hotels and attractions for base rate of $3 per pickup including one mile; $.80 each additional mile. An airport-to-hotel (prebooked) transfer is $12 minimum (two wheelchairs maximum). Group rates offered on a charter basis. Ambulatory companions free. Drivers and guides are trained to handle chairs and give other assistance. Six vans equipped with electric lift or ramp. Offers a ground tour program that includes: three-hour Honolulu city tour with Punchbowl National Cemetery, $5.25 per person based on a party of eight, or $42 minimum; eight-hour island circle at $14 per person based on a party of eight (four chairs, four ambulatory), or a $112 minimum, lunch not included. Other offerings are Polynesian Cultural Center, *Hawaii State* Pearl Harbor cruise, Sea Life Park, nightclub tour, Al Harrington luau, Oceania Floating Restaurant dinner show. Handi-Cab plan often works out to less than buying components. *Ale Ale Kai* moonlight sail regularly listed at $17.50 is offered at $19.50 by HC-P, *including* transportation to/from boat. (A conventional taxi to/from pier for anyone unable to use the boat's motorcoach pickup service runs well above $2.) HC-P points out that it makes *everything* on the island accessible by means of its trained drivers. If you have a special interest that appears to be inaccessible, check with HC-P.

Complete rate and tour schedule available from Handi-Cabs of the Pacific, P.O. Box 22428, Honolulu, HI 96822; telephone 808-524-3866.

The Handi-Van—Honolulu Mass Transit operates transportation at $.50 one way to holders of a special TheBusPass, which may not be practical for short-term tourists, since disabled persons must apply for the pass and there could be a wait. Mass Transit Div., Dept. of Transportation Services, City and County of Honolulu, 650 S. King St., Honolulu, HI 96813.

Conventional Sightseeing—Tour desks in hotel lobbies book conventional or customized tours by motorcoach or minibus.

Limousines—$16 and up per hour per car seating up to eight to twelve passengers. Driver is guide. Contact: Charley's limos, 955-3381; Ted Grandstedt, 949-6885.

Taxis—Rates are $.80 for first ⅛ mile, $.10 each additional ⅛ mile. Honolulu International Airport to Waikiki hotels runs about $8 on the meter. Charley's taxi tours of Hawaii are $17.70 per hour with two hour minimum. Reservations 955-3381.

Public Bus—Called TheBus. Twenty-five-cent fare. You can circle island for that.

Hand Controls and Wheelchair Rental and Repair—Lowell Grant at 919 Halekauwila St. (Honolulu, HI 96814), near Fisherman's Wharf, telephone 533-2794 or 524-2279, carries the MPS line of hand controls and will rent them. Also rents and repairs chairs.

Car Rental—Hertz, Avis, and Budget are among possibilities. Only Avis has hand controls, one left-, one right-hand set available. Specify two or four doors. Advance booking required. Avis rates effective at press time, $175 a week for intermediate-size car, $189 sedan, unlimited mileage. (Also see Car Rental in index.) Daily rates from $26.95 and $28.95 respectively. Will also supply hand-control cars on major Outer Islands. Hand controls can be brought along or rented locally (see item *above*) and attached to Budget (intermediate cars from $109.50 a week), and to Hertz, when arranged beforehand through manager of your Hertz office at home (not Hertz reservation system). Regular gas is running $.68 to $.78 a gallon.

AIRLINES, AIRFARES, AND PACKAGES

Hawaii is served from the mainland by American, Braniff, Continental, Northwest Orient, Pan American, United, and Western. All fly to Honolulu. Continental, United, Northwest Orient, and Western also serve Hilo on the Big Island. Inter-island flights are usually via Aloha Airlines or Hawaiian Air. Both airlines offer an average 35 percent discount to persons 65 and over (on daytime flights on a standby basis). Short-distance flightseeing is offered locally aboard small aircraft. Honolulu International and Hilo airports each have jetways for boarding, as well as conventional boarding platforms, where disabled passengers may be required to use forklifts. The array of airfares now available is mystifying, but you can often find an air/hotel package with a suitable flight at a saving of hundreds of dollars on the airfare alone. Shop around. Bob would have paid $568 for the lowest regular coach fare (effective at the time he flew), while his entire Hawaiian Holidays air/hotel package cost $499 per person (double-occupancy basis) with seven nights' accommodations at the Sheraton-Waikiki (his double room there was listed at $50 a day for two). By buying the separate components, each would have paid $743 plus tax for the same arrangements. Airlines also provide package tours of Hawaii; information on this is available from an airline's tour desk. Also look into the airlines' Tour Basing Fares. If you are buying a regular round-trip airline ticket, you can island-hop at an additional Common Fare of $13 per island (not applicable to charter fares).

TOUR OPERATORS

Collect the various tour folders. The following are among the largest operators: Aloha Hawaii, 516 Fifth Ave., New York, NY 10036, telephone 800-621-1012, or in New York City 212-764-3030; American Express, 150 East 42nd St., New York, NY 10017; Hawaiian Holidays, 800-221-2510 (CT, DE, MA, NH, NJ, Eastern PA, RI, VT), 800-221-2216 (AL, FL, GA, ME, MD, NC, SC, VA, DC, Western PA, WV), and 212-867-3900 for New York City, or write 711 Third Ave., New York, NY 10017; MacKenzie, 800-367-5190.

How to Choose a Package—Compare several. Described below are the author's choices of hotels in Hawaii where the traveler with limited mobility might be happiest. Most tours offer several hotel options. See if one of the hotels below, or another meeting your requirements, is available on the package you favor. You may also ask if a hotel substitution is possible.

GUIDED TOURS

These companies are among those with organized guided tours of Hawaii for disabled clients: Flying Wheels Tours, 143 W. Bridge St., Box 382, Owatonna, MN 55060, telephone 507-451-5005; Rambling Tours, Box 1304, Hallandale, FL 33009, telephone 305-456-2161 (includes Hawaii on its Orient package); Wings on Wheels, 19429 Forty-fourth St. W., Lynnwood, WA 98036, telephone 206-776-1184. Also note that trips for groups or individuals requiring dialysis have been offered by Wings on Wheels and by Varan Travel, a retail travel agency at 94 North Ave., Garwood, NJ 07027, telephone 201-789-0063. From Canada, tours are offered by Calladine & Baldry, Dufferin St. & Hwy. 401, Toronto, M6A 2T9, Ontario.

HOTELS

The *Hotel Guide* available from the Hawaii Visitors Bureau (see Information *below*) has coded 162 hotels with a *W* for wheelchair, implying varying degrees of accessibility. *W* hotels are located on all the tourist islands except Lanai.

Hotels listed below are the author's choice in terms of accessibility and attractiveness of guestrooms and public areas, proximity to sight-seeing and entertainment attractions, and range of services. Hotels are also selected for appeal to representative life-styles and budgets. This or any hotel list can best be used in conjunction with packaged tours as described above in Airlines, Airfares, and Packages. In any case, you may be well advised to check with the hotel management on specific requirements.

Rates below, effective at press time and subject to change, are European Plan (without meals). A 4 percent state tax is additional. *Lanai rooms*, described in some hotel literature, refers to rooms with balcony or terrace. Hotels have a doctor in-house or on call. Most offer a full range of services, including beauty salon and barber.

WAIKIKI

(Waikiki) Beachcomber—In heart of Waikiki near International Marketplace and across street from ocean. Four wheelchair rooms on twenty-first floor, some with balconies and sea views; connecting rooms, spacious baths with thirty-two-inch doors, grab bars at tubs. Refrigerators, air conditioning, color TV. Laundromat and grocery store on premises. Parking for disabled. Some public areas, including pool, inaccessible. Double: $30–$38; $6 each additional person; under two free. Crib charge $5. Reservations and information: Island Holidays Resorts, Central Reservations Office, P.O. Box 8519, 2222 Kalakaua Ave., Honolulu, HI 96815, 808-922-6121; cable ISLEPALMS.

Hyatt Regency Waikiki—1,260 rooms in forty-story twin towers. Across street from ocean. Most glamorous Waikiki hotel, built at cost of $100 million and opened 1976. Waterfall and gardens in open-air lobby. Seventy shops, eight restaurants and bars. Twenty-four rooms designed for disabled guests, twelve with bathroom grab bars and ocean views; all twenty-four with thirty-two-inch door clearance. Connecting rooms available. Disabled guests use executive elevator to second floor (in lieu of stairways), general elevators connecting all other

Courtesy Hyatt Regency Waikiki

The hotel strip at Waikiki is highlighted by Diamond Head

public areas. Air conditioning, TV, balconies. Ice machine on every floor. Laundromat. Organized children's activities over Christmas. Double: $44–$70 (penthouse); $9 each additional person; children under twelve free in parents' room. Maximum three adults per room. Hyatt reservations system, 800-228-9000; or Hyatt Regency Waikiki, Honolulu, HI 96815.

Pacific Beach—349 rooms with *lanai*. Across street from ocean. Toward end of Waikiki. TV, air conditioning, kitchenette. Restaurants, pool area accessible. Mini grocery store on lobby level. Little discotheque. Car parking for disabled possible but roundabout. 280 rooms can be made accessible. Bathrooms accessible to standard chair. No grab bars. Connecting rooms available. Double: $26–$38 Apr. 1–June 18 and Sept. 1–Dec. 20; otherwise $30–$42; $6 each additional person; children under twelve free in parents' room. Pacific Beach, 2490 Kalakaua Ave., Honolulu, HI 96815, 808-922-1233.

Hilton Hawaiian Village—1,604-room hotel complex covering twenty acres away from Waikiki center (a brisk fifteen-minute walk). Has best beach of any Waikiki area hotel. Total resort with six nightclubs, eight restaurants, within a semi-accessible shopping center (over a hundred shops). No specially modified rooms for the disabled. Bathrooms small but standard wheelchair can manage. Management will not remove bathroom doors. Very casual. Public areas barrier-free. Laundromat. Ice machines. Balconies, color TV, refrigerators. Wheelchair rentals at $10.40 plus tax a week. Supervised children's program in summer and December at minimal cost. Double: $33–$57; $5 additional person; children any age free in parents' room. Reservations: New York, 594-4500; Chicago, 346-2772; Los Angeles, 628-6231; San Francisco, 771-1200; Toronto, Canada, 362-3771. Hilton Hotels in Hawaii, 2005 Kalia Rd., Honolulu, HI 96815.

(*Waikiki*) *Holiday Inn*—636 rooms with *lanai.* Familiar Holiday Inn architecture. At outskirts of Waikiki, across street from ocean and zoo. Two rooms for paraplegics on twenty-fifth floor, complete with over-the-bed trapeze, grab bars at tub and toilet. Other standard rooms with bathroom doors clearing at twenty-four inches. Some connecting rooms. Air conditioning, TV, laundromat, soft drink and ice machines. Most public areas, including pool sunning area, accessible. Free parking. Standard double: $39–$42 Dec. 20–Apr. 15, $35–$38 otherwise. Children under twelve free in parents' room. Reservations: Los Angeles, San Francisco, Seattle, 800-453-5555; New York, 212-736-4800; Boston, 800-243-2350; Chicago, 654-2700. Waikiki Holiday Inn, 2570 Kalakaua Ave., Honolulu, HI 96815.

Sheraton-Waikiki—1,900 rooms right on beach at Waikiki. Central location. Popular convention hotel. Barrier-free design in public areas where levels change by gradual slopes. Padded smooth carpet somewhat hard to push on; elevators close quickly. Rooms large, and standard wheelchair can maneuver in bathroom. Management will also remove doors if required. No grab bars. Some balconies. Connecting rooms. Color TV and closed-circuit movies. Refrigerators available at $10 a week. Braille menus. Parking garage accessible. Full range of shops and services. Five restaurants include Hanohano Room on thirty-first floor reached by outside glass cage elevator. Supervised children's activities in summer. Guests can dine around at other

Sheratons (Surfrider, Princess Kaiulani, and Moana; Royal Hawaiian inaccessible to wheelchairs) and charge to bill. Double: $35–$56 July 1–Dec. 20; then $41–$60; $7 for a third adult; children under eighteen free in parents' room. (Three-person-per-room maximum). Sheraton reservations: 800-325-3535; in Canada, 800-261-9393 eastern or 800-261-9330 western. Sheraton Hotels, P.O. Box 8559, Honolulu, HI 96815.

BEYOND WAIKIKI

Kahala Hilton—372 rooms. Right on Kahala Beach in residential/country club neighborhood opposite side of Diamond Head from Waikiki. Away from action. Enjoys star-studded clientele of movie stars, diplomats, and royalty. High occupancy rate. Staff will assist at entrance step. Public areas accessible via elevators. Bathroom doors are twenty-eight inches wide. Some rooms with refrigerator. Air conditioning, TV. Supervised children's program at school holiday periods. $56–$90 for a double. Children free in their parents' room. Hilton reservation system, see Hilton Hawaiian Village, above. Kahala Hilton, Honolulu, HI 96815.

Kuilima Hyatt—500 rooms on beach at Kuilima Point on north shore, fifty-five-minute drive from Waikiki. Features golf, tennis, other outdoor sports. Public areas (including restrooms with stall door open) accessible to standard wheelchair. Two rooms accommodating disabled are No. 207 with ocean view and No. 208 overlooking bay and pool. Large bathrooms. No grab bars. Refrigerators. Balconies. Ping-pong, tandem bicycles, buggy rides, theater. Arts and crafts classes teach *lei* making, shell crafts. Organized children's programs year-round at $10/day. Limousines for local sightseeing. Double: $33–$50; $5 each additional person; children under twelve free in parents' room. (Four-persons-per-room maximum.) Hyatt reservations 800-228-9000. Kuilima Hyatt Resort Hotel, Kahuku, Oahu, HI 96731.

OUTER ISLANDS

Accessible hotels include the Surf Resorts on Maui and Kauai (InterIsland Resorts, Box 8539, Honolulu, HI 96815); and Sheraton Molokai (see Sheraton above for booking information). Also Mauna

Kea, built by Laurance Rockefeller on the Big Island. Generally considered one of the world's greatest hotels, with a golf course around ancient lava flows. (Mauna Kea Beach Hotel, Kamuela, HI 96743).

PRACTICAL INFORMATION

WEATHER AND SEASONS

High and low seasons in Hawaii are determined not by the weather, but rather by mainland and Japanese vacation patterns, meaning that July to early September and December 20 to mid-April are peak months. October, with a weeklong Aloha cultural festival (third week on Oahu, and later or earlier on other islands), is also popular. The weather is just about ideal year-round, although rainstorms do occur during winter. Little rain falls in spring and summer and "days with rain" on the weather chart may mean intoxicating sunny-day showers—that proverbial liquid sunshine—accompanied by many rainbows. According to a local saying, "When heaven cries the earth lives." The chart below indicates weather at the conventional seaside resorts. The high mountains can be cool or cold. It snows on the Big Island, where there is skiing.

Average Weather in Hawaii

	Average Low		Average High		Days with Rain
	°C	°F	°C	°F	
Jan.	20	68	23	73	14
Feb.	20	68	23	73	10
Mar.	21	70	23	73	13
Apr.	21	70	24	75	12
May	22	72	26	79	11
June	23	73	27	81	11
July	23	73	28	82	13
Aug.	23	73	29	84	13
Sept.	23	73	28	82	13
Oct.	22	72	28	82	13
Nov.	21	70	27	81	14
Dec.	21	70	25	77	15

WARDROBE

Your favorite informal summer and spring weight clothes are suitable.

Women—Daytime: slacks, T-shirts, blouses, dresses, sundresses, any resort wear, bathing suit, beach coverup, sunhat or scarf, comfortable shoes (sandals, sneakers, walking shoes), large pocketbook, tote bag, or saddlebag. *Muumuus* (Mother Hubbards introduced by the New England missionaries) in neon prints are uniforms here, many tourists buy them on the spot. Evening: for swank hotel dining rooms or nightclubs, summer dress clothes or best patio wear (long or short skirts, patio pants, halterbacks). Shawl, sweater, or raincoat (a good idea, even at a tropical resort).

Men—Daytime: short-sleeved sports or knit polo shirts, slacks or walking shorts, sandals or sneakers or other comfortable shoes, swim trunks, weatherproof windbreaker, visor cap or sporty hat. Evening: conservative sports jacket and tie and closed shoes for nightclubs and the better restaurants. The flowered aloha (Hawaiian) shirt is a man's answer to the *muumuu.*

Laundromats—For special laundry requirements, consider booking a hotel with a self-service laundromat (see Hotels, *above*).

FOOD

Luau, a barbecue which traditionally centers around a pig just roasted in a pit, is Hawaii's gastronomical claim to fame. The pig is served with island fruits, raw fish, *poi* (slightly fermented taro root—definitely an acquired taste), and dozens of other dishes. (Hotel *luaus* usually include many American mainland dishes.) Papayas, mangoes, pineapples, and bananas are on every island menu. (Good health tip: Eat fruit in moderation.) The ubiquitous macadamia nuts and coconuts turn up in brownies, cakes, and pies. World renowned Kona coffee, with a rich mocha aroma and taste, is grown on the Big Island. Fish are served with continental or island sauces. Japanese and Chinese restaurants abound. But most hotel menus lean toward the international favorites (steaks, hamburgers, french fries, chef salads, and the like). Fantasy cocktails begin and end with the *mai tai* (a powerful fruit punch and rum concoction), often served with *pupus* (hors d'oeuvres). Dinner at hotel coffee shops runs about five dollars and up. Better restaurants can be ten to twenty dollars, or more. Allow two to five dollars for breakfast or lunch at a coffee shop. Food possibilities also include the take-out meals from hamburger and pizza restaurants, or the delis and grocery stores tucked into side streets.

SHOPPING

Island souvenirs made of coral, shells (especially the tiny pukas that are all the rage and command high prices at mainland department stores, compared to six dollars or less for a necklace here), and monkeypod wood, as well as macadamia nuts, can be purchased at specialty shops or at five-and-ten or department stores at lower prices. Film may be up to one-third higher here, so stock up at home. Cartons of pineapples and papayas can be ordered at hotel shops for delivery to the airport in your name, or they can be purchased right at the airport. Avocados, bananas, litchis, and papayas must be treated to U.S. Department of Agriculture specifications before shipment to the mainland, however, so buy them at an export shop (not the supermarket). Birds-of-paradise and anthuriums are among the popular cut flowers to take home. You cannot bring into the mainland fruits not mentioned above or *mauna loa*, gardenia, or jade vine flowers; coffee berries or other berries or certain pulpy seeds; sugar cane; cactus; and potted plants (except for certain preinspected orchids). Leis of plumeria, orchids, carnations, ginger, *pikake*, tuberoses, and crown flowers can be worn home.

GUIDE DOGS

All dogs entering Hawaii are subject to 120 days of quarantine at the owner's expense of five dollars a day. Dogs entering from Australia, who undergo a three-day inspection, are the exception.

OBTAINING INFORMATION

HAWAII VISITORS BUREAU

General tourist information, as well as the *Hotel Guide* listing 162 hotels that accommodate wheelchairs. Headquarters is 2270 Kalakaua Ave., Honolulu, HI 96815 (across street from Sheraton-Waikiki), telephone 808-923-1811. Branches are at 3440 Wilshire Blvd., Los Angeles, CA 90010, 213-385-5301; 209 Post St., San Francisco, CA 94108, 415-392-8173; 410 N. Michigan Ave., Chicago, IL 60611, 312-944-6694; 609 Fifth Ave., New York, NY 10017, 212-759-3655; and 1100 Seventeenth St., N.W., Washington, DC 20036, 202-872-0118.

ORGANIZATIONS

The following organizations may be able to answer specific questions related to a particular disability or to accessibility in general:

Multiple Sclerosis Society—Hawaiian Islands Chapter, 245 N. Kukui St., Honolulu, telephone 531-4127.

Muscular Dystrophy Association—68 Ala Moana, Suite 414, Honolulu, telephone 533-6641 or 536-8844.

Veterans Administration—Prince Jonah Kuhio Kalanianaole Federal Building, 300 Ala Moana, Honolulu, telephone 546-2150.

Easter Seal Society—In Honolulu call Bruce Mitchell or Kathy Bogowitz (536-1015) to find out what athletic events are scheduled or to use the ESS swimming pool.

ACCESS GUIDE

Maui—*Guide for the Handicapped*, available from the Easter Seal Society of Maui County, P.O. Box 935, Kahului, Maui, HI 96793.

NATIONAL PARKS

Hawaii Group, National Park Service—At Pacific International Building, 677 Ala Moana Blvd., Honolulu, HI 96813.

Access/National Parks: A Guide for Handicapped Visitors details accessibility of Volcanoes and City of Refuge parks on the Big Island and Haleakala park on Maui. It is $3.50 from Superintendent of Documents, U.S. Government Printing Office, Washington, DC 20402. The stock number is 024-005-00691-5.

THE ANSWER MAN

Handi-Cabs of the Pacific—Offers to answer specific questions regarding accessibility of attractions on Oahu. See Local Tours and Transportation, above.

2

ALL OUTDOORS

When man becomes integrated with his environment in a physical way; when he hikes, skis, runs or pulls himself in a pulk [Norwegian sled] through it, he comes in contact with hidden resources he never knew existed.

—BRECKENRIDGE

This section is dedicated to Lily Tomlin's Crystal, who wanted to soar.

The thirty-five-year-old quadriplegic, whose slogans were "Paraplegic Power" and "Keep on Rolling," was last seen strapped chair and all to pink and green Rogallo wings, as she lifted high into the California sky.

Crystal is the creation of Lily Tomlin, whose portrayal of her in the 1977 Broadway hit *Appearing Nitely* won the applause of many earthbound wheelies who also long to soar. And while hang gliding may not be the ideal sport for you, many other adventures you may not have dreamed possible are.

If you do have limited mobility, the sudden fluid movement of gliding or floating could produce an all-time high. Freedom of movement you never knew was possible is yours when you slide over the snow on skis or by sled, according to Hal O'Leary, director of the Winter Park (Colorado) Handicap Skiing Program. Through that program about 350 amputees, hemiplegics, blind or mentally retarded persons, as well as those with cerebral palsy, multiple sclerosis, postpolio, spina bifida, aneurysms, or traumatic congenital defects, learn to ski each year.

In addition, Winter Park runs a summer edition, with hiking, backpacking, float trips on the Colorado River, fishing, sailing, canoeing, arts and crafts, overnight camping at Devil's Thumb Ranch, chairlift rides, and nature hikes.

Another example of the many outdoor sports and adventure programs offered throughout the United States is the Outward Bound School (OBS) course in wilderness survival where ablebodied and physically disabled adventurers combine exploring the possibilities of outdoor adventures and broadening perceptions of capability. Activities may include canoeing, rock climbing, navigation with map and compass, time alone in the woods with minimal equipment. Summer programs are conducted in the Minnesota wilderness for individuals whose disabilities range from deafness to paraplegia; similar programs are conducted for deaf and hearing-impaired persons by OBS in North Carolina both summer and winter.

In describing a trip in which a group of ten (equal numbers of ablebodied and disabled men and women) paddled canoes twenty miles, slept on the trail for four nights, climbed, and crossed a swamp in a makeshift raft, the Minnesota OBS project director said, "We learned that disabled people aren't as fragile as we thought. The primary difference was that things took a little longer. Their mobility was limited, so group problems like the swamp crossing were more complex. . . ."

According to that report, which appeared in the *OBA News* (Fall 1976), everyone shared, carrying Duluth packs weighing seventy to a hundred pounds. One wheelie slung his pack over the back of his chair on the portage.

Your best overall bet in accessible outdoor vacations at this point may be the state and national parks and recreational areas. Look through U.S. Sources in the following section for suggestions. (The accessibility guidebooks also detail barrier-free out-of-doors facilities.) Here are some examples.

• Apalachicola National Forest, Florida, where Trout Pond recreational area twelve miles from Tallahassee has a ramped swimming pool, a water-play area with jets of water, fishing pier, Braille signs, and other modifications.

• Will-A-Way recreational area in Fort Yargo Park, Georgia, with cottages and campgrounds, fishing, and nature trails.

• Michigan's forty-three parks are being assessed in an effort to open them up to everybody and to foster their use.

• A Fish and Game Department project in Montana is making parks and campsites possible through designs that also provide docks for disabled fishermen.

• The modified parks in Ohio, where the Mohican, Salt Fork, and Shawnee State Park lodges have ramps throughout as well as elevators. Mohican and Shawnee have several rooms especially modified for handicapped guests, and Salt Fork has paved trails and a modified showerhouse in one area of the campsite. Barkcamp Park has a paved walk to the fishing area.

• Button Bay State Park in Vermont, with a sixty-foot fishing pier.

Details for obtaining information on these and other sites are given in the U.S. Sources section that follows.

Also consider nongovernmental offerings, such as the White Oak Village in the West Virginia mountains, with cottages, trailer camping, picnic grounds, and more, spread over 2,600 acres that include a large lake. To open fall 1978.

Ask locally about smaller operations, typified by the two wheelchair gillies working out of Marv Koep's Nisswa Bait & Tackle Shop in Nisswa, Minnesota. They know the beats where the bass, northern pike, walleyes, and panfish run.

Peruse the *Access/National Parks* guide for the handicapped (see index) for arrangements as diverse as accessible camping at Cinnamon Bay Campground at Virgin Islands National Park on St. John in the U.S. Virgin Islands, where tents and cottages are for rent, to the campground at the Catoctin Mountain Park in Maryland, where trails lead to some attractive overlooks and group camping, hiking, and fishing are arranged. This book is not limited only to full-fledged national parks, for this is also an excellent reference book to hundreds

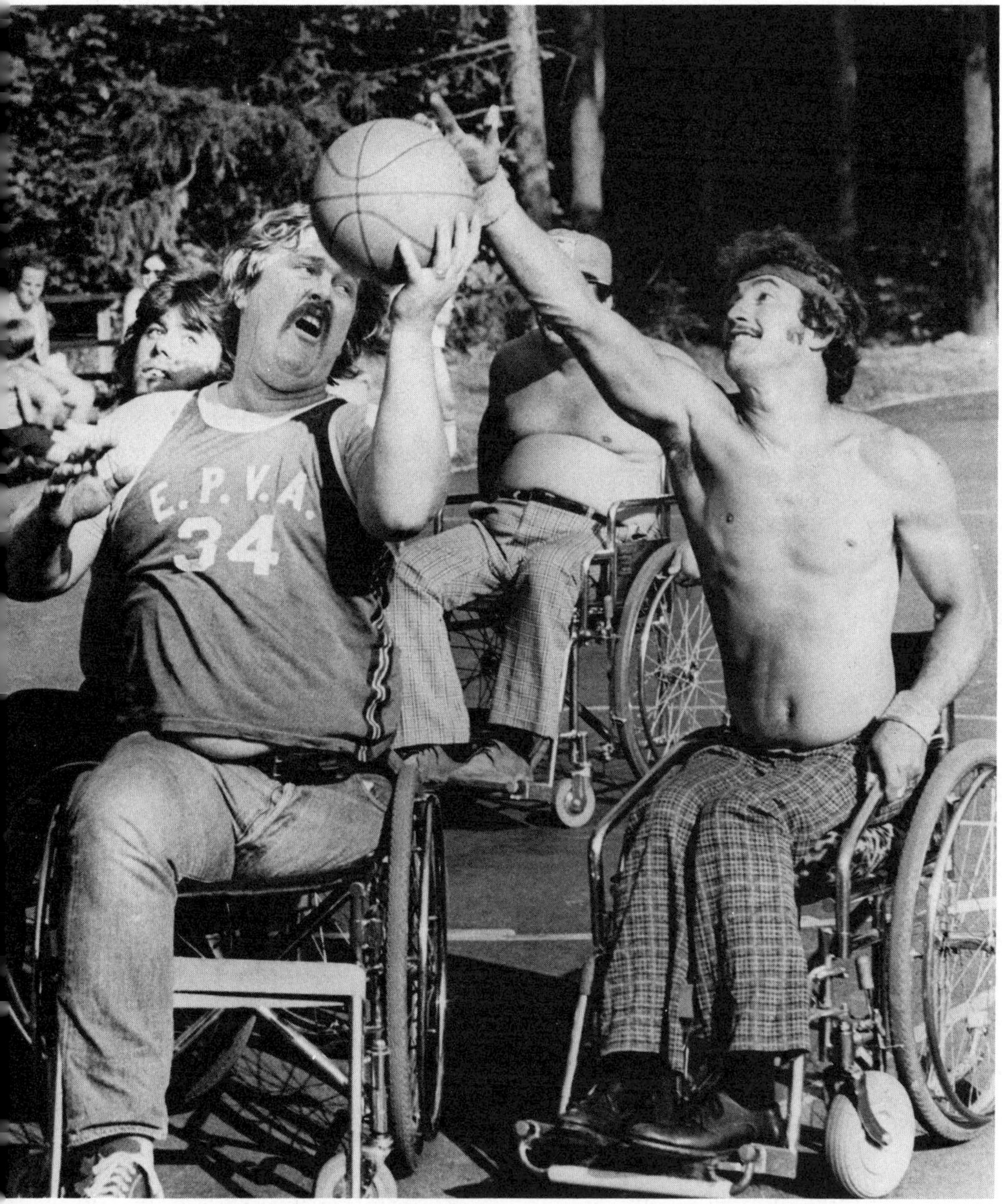

Courtesy The 52 Association

Disabled vets at a 52 Association meet

of sites such as presidents' birthplaces and U.S. battlefields and monuments; there's even an Indian trading post described.

If you aren't the rugged outdoor type, consider the national parks for little sorties, returning to comfortable park lodges and inns or nearby motels at night.

As stated, your best bet in campsites is likely to be the state and national parks. Before you take off, however, contact the state or site where you plan to camp to see if you'll need a permit or reservation to stay there. Because of overflow crowds in national parks, the *National Parks* guide might well be used in conjunction with *Doorways to Adventure—Visit a Less-used Park* (described below).

While recreational vehicles (RV) lend extraordinary freedom—no more searching for hotels, motels, restaurants, and restrooms when you carry them with you—they do present the problems of finding accessible sites where you can hook up for the night. Despite the growing number of assorted campers being driven by disabled drivers, there are few accessible commercial campground facilities. If an ablebodied person is along to help with the "land arrangements," the problem is lessened. Kampgrounds of America (KOA), one of the largest commercial networks, with 800 locations where you might pay an average of $5.50 a night for two, does have an occasional accessible site, but such sites are not indicated in the KOA directory.

Another problem with RVs is the steep cost of buying one, possibly $13,000 for a twenty-three-foot Class A Winnebago, plus modification costs. Other makes and models could run less or even up to $40,000 for a custom job. *Buyer's Guide* (see General Information in Part IV) is a source of adapted RVs and vans.

Many innovative persons have found ways to modify vans, cars, VW buses, and trailers to their own purposes at a price they can afford. One postpolio nature lover bought a secondhand British Sprite trailer for $500 and has devised a ramp that slides up and under the body. (In younger years when he was on crutches and used to pitch a tent he used very long stakes that he could pound into the ground without bending. He preferred state parks with lakes and owned a lightweight canoe that he could swim from in deep water.)

A most rewarding book, and probably the definitive word on motor-camping, is *Wheelchair Vagabond* by John G. Nelson, who hit the road in a variety of rigged-up vehicles after multiple sclerosis hit him. A kind of *Travels with Charley* for disabled vagabonds, the author intertwines his shopping lists and wardrobe suggestions with reveries, and his sources of factual information with accounts of his adventures and misadventures as he explores the country. (Unlike John Steinbeck's venerable poodle Charley, Nelson's mutt Lobo doesn't take to touring and has to be returned home after only two weeks.) Recommended reading for armchair travelers, and a *must* if you are going traveling in a camper.

The examples touched upon here are only points of departure for countless fresh-air vacations. Listed below are sources of information for the above prospects and others. Also see Cars, Section 1, Part II for rental RVs; and Children, under General Information, Section 1, Part IV.

SOURCES

Breckenridge Outdoor Education Center—Rustic accommodations in the Colorado mountains. Programs offered to schools, agencies, church groups, and private organizations at about $20 per student per day, including meals, lodging, and specialized gear. Winter: skiing, mountaineering, skating, sledding. Summer: backpacking, climbing, mountaineering, horseback riding, initiative games, rock climbing, environmental studies, minimal impact living and travel, folksinging, and stargazing. Especially for mentally disabled adults and children. Breckenridge Outdoor Education Center, P.O. Box 168, Breckenridge, CO 80424.

Doorways to Adventure—Visit a Less-used Park—A guide for avoiding the crowds in the national parks; item 024-005-00589-7, $.70 from the Superintendent of Documents, Government Printing Office, Washington, DC 20402.

The Easter Seal Directory of Resident Camps for Persons with Special Health Needs—A state-by-state listing of camps classified according to the disabilities they are geared to. Stock No. E-41, $1.50 from National Easter Seal Society, 2023 W. Ogden Ave., Chicago, IL 60612.

52 Association—This association runs a forty-one-acre recreational rehabilitation center for severely disabled U.S. servicemen in Ossining, New York, providing facilities for wheelchair basketball, paddleboats for leg and arm amputees, swimming and diving pools, archery, track and field, tennis, golf driving ranges, a ramped swimming pool, and tandem bikes for blinded vets and their sighted companions. Campsites for overnight stays. 52 Association, 147 E. 50th St., New York, NY 10022, 212-752-1855.

Marv Koep's Nisswa Bait & Tackle Shop—Two wheelchair gillies assist fishermen throughout the summer on most of the area lakes. For fishing regulations and guides' rates, contact Marv Koep's Nisswa Bait & Tackle Shop, Nisswa, MN 56468, 218-963-2547.

National Inconvenienced Sportsmen Association—Fifteen chapters throughout the country arrange sports, such as skiing, golf, waterskiing, sailing. $10 annual dues for handicapped members; $15 for nonhandicapped. For nearest chapter, write to the headquarters: Fred T. Nichol, National Inconvenienced Sportsmen Association, Penn Mutual Building, Third Floor, 4105 E. Florida Ave., Denver, CO 80222, 303-757-3381.

New England Handicapped Sportsmen's Association—Adaptive sports instruction for ambulatory amputees and postpolios, as well as for persons with cerebral palsy, and certain spinal cord injuries (and at Haystack and Mount Sunapee, the blind). Winter weekends. Downhill skiing at Haystack, Vermont, and Mount Sunapee State Park, Wildcat and Cannon Mountain, New Hampshire. Summer outings to Cape Cod for waterskiing and tennis. Membership $15 a year. New England Handicapped Sportsmen's Association, P.O. Box 2150, Boston, MA 02106, 617-262-0440.

North American Riding for the Handicapped Association (NARHA)—An organization of medical professionals and expert horsemen and women devoted to teaching riding to handicapped individuals for therapy and pleasure. For the name of an NARHA member near you, write to the association in care of Diana F. Seacord, Thistle Croft, Mendon, MA 01756. Please enclose a self-addressed stamped envelope. Allow as much time as possible if you wish information on riding vacations in another state or part of the country.

Outward Bound School (OBS)—A respected international program in coping with nature, it teaches you to discover "in the uncertainty of wilderness travel... not only what you are, but what you can be," according to the OBS literature. The school is so successful that many major corporations send their executives there to develop certain life skills. The Minnesota OBS in 1976 initiated ten-day courses for persons with such disabilities as multiple sclerosis, cerebral palsy, muscular dystrophy, paraplegia, and limb defects. Also for hearing-impaired and deaf persons. In fact, for almost anyone over eighteen who can manage his or her own bowel and bladder programs, personal hygiene and dressing. Outdoor skills not a prerequisite but you must pass a basic physical. See discussion in the text. The Minnesota program is $300 (tuition grants are available). A similar program for deaf participants is run by the North Carolina OBS. Contact: Disabled Program, Minnesota Outward Bound School, 308 Walker Ave. South, Wayzata, MN 55391; 612-473-5476; North Carolina Outward Bound School, P.O. Box 817, Morgantown, NC 28655, 704-437-6112.

Rand McNally Campground and Trailer Park Guide—National edition at $7.95 covers 20,000 campgrounds in the United States, Canada, and Mexico. A Western edition is $3.95; Eastern edition, $5.95. Rand McNally Map Store, 10 E. 53rd St., New York, NY 10022.

Wheelchair Vagabond—By John G. Nelson. Camping in a rigged-up car. Hardcover copies at $7.95 and two or more paperbound copies at $4.95 each (single paperbacks not available). California residents add 6 percent sales tax. From Project Press, 710 Wilshire Blvd., P.O. Box 1796, Santa Monica, CA 90406.

Winter Park Handicap Skiing (WPHS)—See description in body text. Nine-year-old program. Winter Park is sixty-seven miles from Denver and best reached by car. WPHS will help you locate barrier-free rooms. Winter Park Handicap Skiing, Box 313, Winter Park, CO 80482, 800-525-3424.

HINTS

• On rugged holidays, take along spare wheelchair spokes.

• Make reservations early for national and state park accommodations and campsites.

• Take *Access/National Parks: A Guide for Handicapped Visitors.* Often not available at the parks themselves. Furthermore, park personnel may not know the location of accessible facilities, which are carefully spelled out in this newly revised book. 197 pages. Maps.

3

U.S. SOURCES: A GUIDE TO BARRIER-FREE VACATIONS

Is it or isn't it accessible?

That question comes up whenever you contemplate an outing or a vacation. To provide detailed information on the endless things to see and do in the United States is impossible in a book of this size. Instead, contacts are listed who can provide general information and others who can answer specific questions, such as "Is it or isn't it . . . ?"

Even this concise listing touches upon the amazing variety of vacation possibilities that are accessible: for example, do you know about the Islands of Peace nature resort for disabled nature lovers on the Mississippi River in Minnesota, where you can ride on pontoon boats, fish, or hike on paved trails? or the outstanding prehistoric Indian site in Chillicothe, Ohio? or that Atlantic City, New Jersey oceanside resort with the famed boardwalk—great for wheelies—is making a comeback with legalized gambling casinos?

Any booklets or leaflets described herein have been verified recently as to their availability. Order them to use in planning your trip.

Included under their state listings and identified by a star ★ are twenty-two of the country's stellar attractions with clues to *doing* them.

Likewise, thirteen theme parks that are accessible have been keyed with a diamond ♦. Theme parks, because they are a new concept, are usually built barrier-free, with all the ramps, smooth paths, large toilet stalls, and special parking zones you could wish for. A streamlined version of old-fashioned amusement parks, the theme parks offer X number of "themes" (usually six), which, for example, could be different European villages—the most popular theme.

The information compiled herein has been provided for the most part by state government agencies or rehabilitation organizations of the various states.

ALABAMA

GENERAL TOURIST INFORMATION: *Alabama Has It All*, a booklet on attractions, includes a chart showing sixty-nine state parks that accommodate the handicapped. State of Alabama, Bureau of Publicity and Information, Montgomery, AL 36130, 800-633-5761.

ALASKA

GENERAL: Alaska Department of Commerce and Economic Development, Tourism Division, Pouch E, Juneau, AK 99811. SPECIFIC ACCESSIBILITY INFORMATION: Easter Seal Society, Box 2432, Anchorage, AK 99510. LITERATURE: *Anchorage—A Guide for the Physically Handicapped*, from Easter Seal Society, above. LOCAL TOURS: Robert E. Stravens, Manager, Juneau Travel, has conducted tours for small groups in wheelchairs. Juneau Travel, 14 Marine Way, Juneau, AK 99801, 907-586-6031. COMMENT: "Tourism beyond the major urban areas of Anchorage, Fairbanks, or Juneau poses rather severe difficulties for a handicapped person," according to a spokesman for the state. "If all other conditions were favorable in this large area of unpredictable weather, much strictly visual satisfaction might be derived from our natural scenic features of mountains, trees, seacoast. Long distances and minimal terminal facilities—practically none with appropriate sanitary accommodations or 'handicapped' hardware, do not lend themselves to [the disabled traveler]. I do not know of any common carriers—rail, ship, air, or bus—which are appropriately equipped to insure maximum convenience or comfort . . . over long travel times and distances encountered here." (Alaska might be best on a special group tour or by car with companions.)

★ MOUNT MCKINLEY. Towering 20,300 feet, the highest mountain in North America is a shimmering mass of granite, glacier ice, and snow. The views—especially at sunrise—are breathtaking, a photographer's dream. The accessible new McKinley Village hotel could be your base for this excursion. The *Access/National Parks* guide (see index) has precise notes on the park's accessibility.

ARIZONA

GENERAL: Arizona Office of Tourism, 1700 W. Washington, Rm. 501, Phoenix, AZ 85007, 602-271-3618. Phoenix and the Valley of the Sun Convention & Visitors Bureau, 2701 E. Camelback Rd., Phoenix, AZ 85012, 602-957-0070. SPECIFIC: Community Council Information & Referral Service, Arizona Easter Seal Society, 702-706 N. First St., Phoenix, AZ 85004, 602-263-8856; for Tucson, 602-991-1794. LITERATURE: *Directory of Barrier-Free Buildings, Phoenix.* At press time an accessibility guide to Phoenix, Tucson, Yuma, Kingman, and Prescott is being prepared. Available from Easter Seal Society (above). TRANSPORTATION: Modified taxis that transport wheelchair passengers are Yellow Cab Co. (telephone 252-5071) in Phoenix, $4.85/pickup plus $.80 a mile; and Handi-Car (telephone 325-2222) in Tucson, $2.50/pickup and $.50 a mile.

★ GRAND CANYON. America's undisputed number one scenic attraction, this brilliant 217-mile slash in the earth's surface offers spectacular panoramas from the canyon rim (7,000 feet). Hotels that accommodate wheelchairs include the Yavapai Lodge and El Tovar, and budget priced rooms at the Motor Lodge are due to open in 1979 or 1980. Mule pack trips to the floor of the canyon, available in summer, should be booked six to nine months in advance. Contact: Grand Canyon National Park Lodges, Grand Canyon National Park, Grand Canyon, AZ 86023, 602-638-2631. Flightseeing tours (1 hour, 15 minutes) dip into the canyon for a bouncy but spectacular roller-dip ride in small airplanes (such as the nine-passenger Cessna 402). Not recommended if you lack strong arms enabling you to hang on, or if you get airsick easily. Flights via Scenic, Nevada, and Las Vegas Airlines originate in Las Vegas. The *Access/National Parks* guide (see index) has detailed notes on accessibility.

ARKANSAS

GENERAL: Arkansas Department of Parks and Tourism, State Capitol, Little Rock, AR 72201, 501-371-1511. SPECIFIC: Easter Seal Society, 2801 Lee, Little Rock, AR 72205, 501-663-8331; Arkansas State Spinal Cord Commission, 4120 W. Markham, Little Rock, AR 72205, 501-661-9494; Enterprises for the Blind, 2811 Fair Park Blvd., Little Rock, AR 72204, 501-664-7100; Veterans Administration, 1200 W. Third St., Little Rock, AR 72201, 501-378-5571. LITERATURE: Accessibility guide is being prepared at press time by the Arkansas Environmental Barriers Council, P.O. Box 4610, Central Baptist Hospital, Rm. 350, 12th and Marshall Sts., Little Rock, AR 72202. SERVICES: Dial-A-Ride, operated by Our Way, 2500 McCain Pl., North Little Rock, AR 72116, 501-758-8032. Babysitting with disabled children available from Easter Seal Society (number above). Visiting nurse service, Homemakers Upjohn, 4120 W. Markham, Little Rock, 501-661-1170. NOTES: A minibus equipped with lifts for wheelchairs transports disabled visitors around the State Capitol grounds and to the parking lot. Ouachita National Forest and Greers Ferry Lake parks have trails for the blind and wheelchair-bound, respectively. Also see Hot Springs, listed under Spas, in Part III.

CALIFORNIA

GENERAL: For Los Angeles, Southern California Visitors Council, 705 W. Seventh St., Los Angeles, CA 90017, 213-628-3101; San Diego Convention and Visitors Bureau, 1200 Third Ave., San Diego, 92101, 714-232-3101; San Francisco Convention & Visitors Bureau, 1390 Market St., San Francisco, 94102, 415-626-5500 (wheelchair visitors should use Hayes St. entrance when going in person). GENERAL AND SPECIFIC: Redwood Empire Association represents nine counties that include San Francisco and the Napa wine and redwood country, and offers a list of accessible attractions. Redwood Empire Association, 476 Post St., San Francisco, 94102, 415-GA 1-6554. LITERATURE: Los Angeles, *Around the Town With Ease*, Junior League of Los

Angeles, Farmer's Market, Third and Fairfax, Los Angeles, 90036, 213-937-5566 (postage free or enclose $.46 in stamps to expedite first-class mailing). San Diego guide for the handicapped, *A Step in Time*, Community Service Center for the Disabled, 4961 University Ave., #5, San Diego, 92105, 714-283-5901 (enclose a stamped, self-addressed six-by-nine-inch envelope). *Guide to San Francisco for the Disabled*, Easter Seal Society, 6221 Geary Blvd., San Francisco, 94121, 415-752-4888. *Wheeling Your Way Through San Jose*, Easter Seal Society, 1245 S. Winchester Blvd., San Jose, 95128. *Open Doors*, Easter Seal Society, 31 E. Canon Perdido, Santa Barbara, 93101. Noteworthy developments toward a barrier-free society have taken place in California, especially in Berkeley and in the southern part of the state. For example, the Center for Independent Living (2539 Telegraph Ave., Berkeley, 94704, 415–841–4776) is a model organization providing services to disabled, blind, deaf, and elderly people that range from job development, medical services, and wheelchair repair to providing door-to-door transportation. Tours of the Center are available. Copies of the "CIL Program Overview" are available from the above address. A $.50 donation is requested. PUBLIC TRANSPORTATION: Note that the BART subway system in San Francisco is accessible to wheelchair passengers and that buses with lifts have begun to appear on certain public bus routes in Los Angeles, San Diego, San Mateo, and San Jose. PRIVATE TRANSPORTATION: Ambulettes or vans with ramps taking up to fourteen chairs. Pinetree Service Corp., 320 E. Bixby Rd., Long Beach, 90807, 213-595-6472.

TOURS/SAN FRANCISCO: Company of same name at 375 O'Farrell, San Francisco, 415-928-1000, operates minibuses and will assist anyone who can stand enough to pivot into a seat. Also tours for the blind. ATTRACTIONS: In addition to the more publicized items is Skunk Railroad on the Mendocino coast, where you can ride for forty miles on a storybook train through spectacular scenery. Accessible if you can transfer from a wheelchair to a train seat. Contact Redwood Empire Association, above.

★ **GOLDEN GATE BRIDGE.** Here is a manmade wonder to behold from a car window or from countless vistas. The lyrical 4,200-foot suspension bridge, painted orange, appears golden at sunset and is the most charming attraction of this most charming city. (Hard put to describe it, Frank Lloyd Wright once said, "What I like most about San Francisco, is San Francisco.")

★ GIANT TREES. The sequoias and redwoods, the world's largest trees in girth and height respectively, can best be observed from Redwood National Park along the Pacific Coast, and Sequoia and Kings Canyon national parks in the High Sierras. The *Access/National Parks* guide (see index) details park facilities for the disabled.

★ ♦ DISNEYLAND. Accessible adventures and attractions are listed on a printed card. Disneyland, Anaheim, CA 92803 (also see index).

COLORADO

GENERAL: State of Colorado, Division of Commerce and Development, 500 State Centennial Building, Denver, CO 80203, 303-839-3045. PUBLIC TRANSPORTATION: Buses with lifts or ramps in Denver. NOTES: A number of sports and outdoors and adventure vacations are offered in this state. Check the index for those subjects. Roaring Fork Braille Trail in White River National Forest, at 10,400 feet, offers the blind and sighted alike a "micro-wilderness" experience. Pueblo, the state's third largest city and a center of industry, is a model of accessibility and recipient of the Carolyn Keane Memorial Award for providing opportunities for handicapped citizens. It is awarded by the International City Management Association. Pueblo's accessible features include a shopping center, all pay phones, some pay phones you can use without leaving your car, four indoor swimming pools, and hand rails at many of the 573 ramped sidewalk curbs.

CONNECTICUT

GENERAL: Connecticut Department of Commerce, Division of Tourism, 210 Washington St., Hartford, CT 06106, 203-566-3385. LITERATURE: Accessibility guides to Stamford and Hartford (under revision at press time) available from Easter Seal Society of Connecticut, P.O. Box 1013, Amston, CT 06231. ATTRACTIONS: Mystic Seaport forty-acre museum village of American maritime history hands out a sheet on accessible attractions to be used in conjunction with a map. Mystic Seaport, Mystic, CT 06355, 203-536-2631. Mystic Marinelife Aquarium, almost totally barrier-free. Mystic Marinelife Aquarium, Mystic, CT 06355, 203-536-9631.

DELAWARE

GENERAL: Delaware State Visitors Service, 630 State College Rd., Dover, DE 19901, 302-678-4254. LITERATURE: *A Guide to Northern Delaware for the Disabled*, Easter Seal Society, 2705 Baynard Blvd., Wilmington, 19802, 302-658-6417. Rehoboth Beach, *Welcome Handicapped Visitors!*, Delmarva Easter Seal Rehabilitation Center, 204 E. North St., Georgetown, DE 19947, 302-856-7364.

DISTRICT OF COLUMBIA

GENERAL: Washington Area Convention and Visitors Bureau, 1129 Twentieth St., N.W., Washington, DC 20036, 202-659-6400. SPECIFIC: Information Center for Handicapped Individuals operates the Handicapped Visitor Services booth in the National Visitors Center, Union Station, 50 Massachusetts Ave., N.E., daily 8 A.M. to 10 P.M. LITERATURE: *Access Washington*, available from Information Center for Handicapped Individuals, 1413 K St., N.W., Washington, DC 20005, 202-347-4986 or 347-5667. "For Your Information," a fact sheet for obtaining half-price tickets for the handicapped and elderly plus an accessibility map and notes on reserving a wheelchair, available from the John F. Kennedy Center for the Performing Arts, Washington, DC 20566. TRANSPORTATION: The Metro (subway) is wheelchair accessible. Daylong ticket permits boarding and reboarding Tourmobile bus, which shuttles past sightseeing attractions. Wheelchairs can board with assistance. Tourmobile, 900 Ohio Dr., S.W., Washington, DC 20024, 202-554-7950. TOURS: Washington and Williamsburg, Virginia, for the physically disabled, deaf, blind, mentally retarded, or elderly. Buses and vans can accommodate wheelchairs. Ability Tours, 729 Delaware Ave., S.W., Washington, DC 20024, 202-554-9104.

★ THE CAPITAL CITY. Most landmarks and museums are accessible. A noteworthy new attraction is the National Air and Space Museum that is even futuristic (specially designed clamp-on mirrors for wheelchairs aid persons with limited head mobility). For White House tour, request VIP tickets from your representative or senator and inform him or her if you use a wheelchair. Use the sources and literature listed above to plan your strategy.

FLORIDA

GENERAL: State of Florida Department of Commerce, Division of Tourism, Collins Building, Tallahassee, FL 32304. Also available, two lists of accessible state attractions. SPECIFIC: *A Directory of Special Services and Rehabilitation Facilities for the Handicapped & Disabled in Florida* lists local Easter Seal Societies, which might be approached with specific questions. Available from Florida Easter Seal Society, Rt. 1, Box 350, Sorrento, FL 32776. LITERATURE: *Access to Gainesville*, Chamber of Commerce, 300 E. University, Gainesville, FL 32602; *Guide for the Handicapped—Jacksonville*, Easter Seal Society, 904-355-2631; *Guide to Manatee & Sarasota Counties*, Happiness House Rehabilitation Center, 401 Braden Ave., Sarasota, FL 33580; *Orlando Guide for the Handicapped*, Orlando Area Tourist Trade Association, P.O. Box 15492, Orlando, FL 32809. *Accessibility Lower Pinellas Co.* (includes St. Petersburg and Treasure Island), Easter Seal Rehabilitation Center, 7671 U.S. Highway 19, Pinellas Park, FL 33565, 813-527-5793; *Tampa Area for the Physically Handicapped*, Easter Seal Society, Rt. 1, Box 350, Sorrento, FL 32776, 904-383-6186. ATTRACTION: Apalachicola National Forest, with fishing pier, ramp into pond for water play, and other barrier-free features. Contact District Ranger, P.O. Box 68, Crawfordville, FL 32327.

★ ♦ WALT DISNEY WORLD. The home of Mickey Mouse and Snow White, the world's most popular vacation resort (with 13 million visitors annually) was designed from its inception with wheelchair travelers, both large and small, in mind. Thus, it is properly done: even the ferryboat is accessible. Printed cards list precisely which of the Magic Kingdom attractions are accessible. Wheelchairs can be rented for $1. Of the two hotels on the grounds, the Polynesian Village connects with the amusements via a monorail, and the Contemporary is served by a bus with hydraulic lift or a limousine. Contact Walt Disney World, P.O. Box 40, Lake Buena Vista, FL 32830.

★ **THE EVERGLADES.** Home of the Seminole Indians and 1.4 million acres of subtropical swamps inhabited by alligators and a brilliant array of birds. This national park on the edge of Miami includes several short paved nature trails and offers audiovisual shows and interpretive talks. Accessibility is detailed in the *Access/National Parks* guide (see index).

♦ **BUSCH GARDENS.** The Dark Continent. African themes and animals. Busch Gardens, 3000 Busch Blvd., Tampa, FL 33612.

GEORGIA

GENERAL: Tourist Division, Georgia Department of Industry & Trade, 1400 N. Omni International, P.O. Box 1776, Atlanta, GA 30301, 404-656-3545. LITERATURE: *Getting About Atlanta*, Easter Seal Society, 1211 Spring St., N.W., Atlanta, GA 30309, 404-873-1391. ATTRACTION: Will-A-Way recreation area in Fort Yargo Park, with family cottages and a group camp, fishing, playground, nature trail devoted solely to disabled. Contact Recreation Coordinator, Will-A-Way Recreation Area, Winder, GA 30680, 404-867-5313. Jekyll Island, a coastal island, with accessible convention center. Contact Promotional Association, 329 Riverview Dr., Jekyll Island, GA 31520, 912-635-2545. PUBLIC TRANSPORTATION: Buses with lifts or ramps in Atlanta.

♦ **SIX FLAGS OVER GEORGIA.** Wheelchairs available. Six Flags, P. O. Box 43187, Atlanta, GA 30336, 404-948-9290.

HAWAII

See destination feature. ★ The two volcanoes on the Big Island are considered one of the natural wonders of the United States.

IDAHO

GENERAL: Division of Tourism & Industrial Development, Capitol, Boise, ID 83720, 208-384-2470. SPECIFIC: Dick Schaaf, Idaho Vocational Rehabilitation, 1365 N. Orchard, Boise, ID 83704. Bill Kincaid, c/o Brownfields, 122 N. Fifth, Boise, ID 83702. For blind individuals: Howard H. Barton, Jr., Administrator, Idaho Commission for the Blind, 341 W. Washington St., Boise, ID 83702, 208-384-3220. PUBLIC TRANSPORTATION: Urban Specials has a small fleet of vans, one with lift and tie-downs, and offers twenty-four-hour reservation door-to-door service. WHEELCHAIR REPAIR: Valley Porta-Sales, 4299 Chinden Blvd., Boise, ID 83704, 208-376-7575. Tony Schulhauser, Parts Consultant, Intermountain Surgical Supply Co., 1115 Grove St., Boise, ID 83702, 208-344-8651. ATTRACTION: Veterans Memorial State Park in Boise features asphalt trails into the natural areas by a lake and river.

ILLINOIS

GENERAL: Office of Tourism, Department of Business & Economic Development, 205 W. Wacker Dr., Chicago, IL 60606, 312-793-4732. Chicago Convention and Tourism Bureau, 332 S. Michigan Ave., Chicago, IL 60603, 312-922-2530. LITERATURE: *Access Chicago* includes list of local tours for wheelchairees, $1 from Rehabilitation Institute of Chicago, 345 E. Superior St., Chicago, IL 60611. *Access North Suburban Chicago*, $1 from League of Women Voters of the Deerfield Area—write Access, P.O. Box 124, Deerfield, IL 60015. The Chicago Council on Fine Arts is preparing a resource book with architectural accessibility, art classes, exhibits, performances. For availability information contact Joyce Walsh, Rm. 1101, 123 W. Madison St., Chicago, IL 60602, 312-744-6630. *What'll We Do Today?* includes under "Senior Citizens" and "Handicapped" possible activities and attractions, available from Chicago Department of Human Resources, 640 N. LaSalle St., Chicago, IL 60610. AIRPORT GUIDE: An annotated map of O'Hare Airport (the world's busiest) for the elderly and disabled is available from Department of Aviation, Rm. 1111, City Hall, Chicago 60602.

★ SKYSCRAPERS. The real monuments of twentieth-century architecture are primarily here (not in New York). They are the buildings designed by Louis H. Sullivan, Frank Lloyd Wright, Mies van der Rohe, and Eero Saarinen, to name a few. The skyscrapers in Chicago's Loop are best seen from the sidewalk. The area is congested. The ArchiCenter of the Chicago School of Architecture Foundation is in a semi-barrier-free building, where anyone can attend its lecture slide shows on architecture. The ArchiCenter is at 310 S. Michigan Ave., Chicago, IL 60604, 312-782-1776.

♦ MARRIOTT'S GREAT AMERICA. *Welcome to Great America* folder details the park's accessibility and includes a map. Great America, 1 Great America Parkway, P.O. Box 1976, Gurnee, IL 60031, 312-249-2000.

INDIANA

GENERAL: Indiana Department of Commerce, Tourist Division, 336 State House, Indianapolis, IN 46204, 317-633-5423. SPECIFIC: Agencies listed in *Directory of Services for the Handicapped*, available from the Division for the Handicapped, Indiana State Board of Health, 1300 W. Michigan St., Indianapolis, IN 46202. LITERATURE: *Navigation Unlimited in Indianapolis*, Marion County Muscular Dystrophy Foundation, 615 N. Alabama St., Indianapolis, IN 46204, 317-632-8255. TRANSPORTATION: Dial-a-ride taxis with lifts include Yellow Medi-Car in Indianapolis, telephone 637-5421. ATTRACTIONS: Copies of a list of barrier-free facilities in state parks are available from Herbert R. Hill, Director, Public Information and Education, Department of Natural Resources, 608 State Office Building, 100 N. Senate Ave., Indianapolis, IN 46204.

IOWA

GENERAL: Development Commission, 250 Jewett Building, Des Moines, IA 50309, 515-281-3251.

KANSAS

GENERAL AND SPECIFIC: Department of Economic Development, 503 Kansas, Topeka, KS 66603, 913-296-3481. SPECIFIC: Division of Disabled, Human Relations Commission, City Hall, 215 E. 7th St., Topeka, KS 66603, 913-295-3800. LITERATURE: *A Guide for the Disabled of Wichita*, Easter Seal Society, 3701 Plaza Dr., White Lakes Plaza, W., Topeka, KS 66609. *Facilities Directory* for Topeka, from Human Relations Commission, above. TRANSPORTATION: Topeka public buses are wheelchair accessible.

KENTUCKY

INFORMATION: Both general and specific information on accessible hotels, motels, and attractions throughout the state are available from L. B. Harper, Travel for the Handicapped, Department of Public Information, Capitol Annex, Frankfort, KY 40601, 502-564-4930. The department has assessed the state for group facilities and will work with persons planning group tours. PUBLIC TRANSPORTATION: Buses with lifts or ramps in Lexington. ATTRACTION: Kentucky Derby. Churchill Downs can seat wheelchairs on the first floor only. The dining room with a view of the whole race track is available only to groups by reservations.

LOUISIANA

GENERAL: Tourist Development Commission, Box 44291, Capitol Station, Baton Rouge, LA 70804, 504-389-5981. Greater New Orleans Tourist & Convention Commission, 334 Royal St., New Orleans, LA 70130, 504-522-8772. LITERATURE: *Baton Rouge, a Guide for the Handicapped*, Junior League of Baton Rouge, 4950-C Government St., Baton Rouge, LA 70806. *Guide to New Orleans for the Physically Disabled* (work in progress, 1978), Easter Seal Society, P.O. Box 8425, Metarie, LA 70011. *A Guide to Facilities in Shreveport and Bossier City for the Handicapped*, Convention and Tourist Bureau, P.O. Box 1761, Shreveport, LA 71166, 318-222-9391. ATTRACTION: Mississippi Queen riverboat between New Orleans and Vicksburg or St. Louis is for the most part accessible. Stateroom doors are twenty-four inches wide but doors to verandahs and bathrooms are only twenty-two inches. Dining room seating no problem with advance notice. Doorway risers are three-quarters of an inch. Views from the boat include wooded shoreline, old plantations, and river traffic, but ground sightseeing is questionable due to the levees and big hills. Contact the Delta Queen Steamboat Co., 511 Main St., Cincinnati, OH 45202.

★ **NEW ORLEANS AND ALL THAT JAZZ.** America's most original art form —jazz—was born here, and to this day it permeates the city with joyful or soulful sounds. To hear jazz you have only to wander at night through the French Quarter, where streets are lined with jazz bars, many of them virtually barrier-free (sometimes there are one or two steps). People tend to drop in for a drink and then move on to the next. Cars are banned in this quarter at night, allowing wheelchair visitors to sail right up the middle of Bourbon Street.

MAINE

GENERAL: State Development Office, State House, Augusta, ME 04333, 207-289-2656. SPECIFIC: Stanley A. Jones, Executive Secretary, Governor's Committee on Employment of the Handicapped, 32 Winthrop St., Augusta, ME 04330, 207-289-3056.

MARYLAND

GENERAL: Division of Tourist Development, Department of Economic and Community Development, 1748 Forest Dr., Annapolis, MD 21401, 301-269-2686. LITERATURE: *Ready/Set/Go*, Baltimore guidebook for the physically disabled, The Baltimore-Central Maryland League for Crippled Children and Adults, 1111 E. Cold Spring Lane, Baltimore, MD 21239, 301-323-0500. *Bawlamer! an informal guide to a livelier Baltimore*, $2.95, a general guide to the city, keys restaurants for accessibility. Available from Baltimore Promotion Council, Baltimore Convention & Visitors Bureau, 22 Light St., Baltimore, MD 21202, 301-727-5688. A list of accessible attractions is also available from that address.

MASSACHUSETTS

GENERAL: Department of Commerce and Development, Division of Tourism, 100 Cambridge St., Boston, MA 02202, 617-727-3201. SPECIFIC: Easter Seal Society, 37 Harvard St., Worcester, MA 01608, 617-757-2756. LITERATURE: *Access to Boston* and *Wheeling Through Worcester* both available from Easter Seal Society address above. TOURS: Para Tours, 698 Beacon St., Boston, MA 02116, conducts sightseeing tours for paraplegics, 617-247-2532.

MICHIGAN

GENERAL: Travel Bureau, Department of Commerce, 300 S. Capitol Ave., Lansing, MI 48913, 517-373-0670. SPECIFIC: Above agency, attention of Addie Burroughs. LITERATURE: *Access Michigan*, Michigan Center for a Barrier Free Environment, 22646 Woodward, Ferndale, MI 48220. ATTRACTIONS: *Handicapped Facilities/Michigan State Parks* assesses forty-three parks. Folder from the Travel Bureau. *Guide to Detroit for the Handicapped*, Easter Seal Society, P.O. Box 101, Westland, MI 48185, 517-722-3065. *Grand Rapids for the Handicapped*, Easter Seal Society, 4065 Saladin Dr., S.E., Grand Rapids, MI 49506, 616-942-2081. *A Guide for the Handicapped, Flint*, Easter Seal Society, 1420 W. Third Ave., Flint, MI 48504. PUBLIC TRANSPORTATION: Buses with lifts or ramps in Detroit and Grand Rapids.

MINNESOTA

GENERAL INFORMATION: Tourism Information, Department of Economic Development, 480 Cedar St., St. Paul, MN 55101, 612-296-5025. SPECIFIC: Access Minesota, State Council for the Handicapped, Metro Sq., 7th & Robert St., St. Paul, MN 55101, 612-296-6785 (TTY 612-296-8205). Currently conducting a statewide accessibility survey. A list of contacts in various communities is available from the council. LITERATURE: *List of Building Accessibility* (Minneapolis) available from the State Council. *Easy Wheelin' in Minnesota* by Robert R. Peters, Education Services Department, The Minneapolis

Star/Tribune, 425 Portland Ave., Minneapolis, MN 55488. NATURE VACATIONS: Program underway to make state parks accessible and to foster enjoyment of the parks. Contact Department of Natural Resources, Centennial Office Building, St. Paul, MN 55101, 612-296-6157. Islands of Peace, on Mississippi River islands near Fridley, have been set up by a foundation as a nature resort for the disabled, who can ride in a pontoon boat, fish, or "hike" on paved trails. TRANSPORTATION: Project Mobility dial-a-ride pilot project in parts of Minneapolis at $.35 (must be a registered rider). Buses with hydraulic lifts. Call 827-2531.

MISSISSIPPI

GENERAL: Travel Department, Agricultural & Industrial Board, P.O. Box 849, Jackson, MS 39205, 601-354-6715. LITERATURE: *A Key to Jackson for the Physically Limited*, Easter Seal Society, P.O. Box 4958, Jackson, MS 39216.

MISSOURI

GENERAL: Division of Tourism, P.O. Box 1055, Jefferson City, MO 65101, 314-751-4133. LITERATURE: *St. Louis has it A to Z for the handicapped*, Easter Seal Society, 4108 Lindell Blvd., St. Louis, MO 63108. A brand new accessibility guide (available from the Tourism Division) includes full notes on attractions ranging from museums, monuments, and parks, to the state fair, the Shepherd of the Hills farm, and Hannibal, Mark Twain's hometown. PUBLIC TRANSPORTATION: Buses with lifts or ramps in St. Louis.

★ **GATEWAY ARCH.** Rising 750 feet on the Mississippi riverfront, this huge arch is called the Gateway to the West. It is visible from many vantage points, but wheelchair sightseers cannot ride to the observation deck at the top because the elevators are too small. (There are also steps at the entrance.)

♦ **WORLDS OF FUN.** Wheelchairs available. Worlds of Fun, 4545 Worlds of Fun Ave., Kansas City, MO 64161, 816-454-4545.

♦ SIX FLAGS OVER MID-AMERICA. Complimentary wheelchairs. Six Flags, Box 666, Eureka, MO 63025, 314-938-5300.

MONTANA

GENERAL: Travel Promotion Unit, Department of Highways, Sixth and Roberts, Helena, MT 59601. Chamber of Commerce, 110 Neill Ave., Helena, MT 59601. SPECIFIC: Association for Rehabilitation, P.O. Box 636, Miles City, MT 59301; United Cerebral Palsy Association, 2626 2nd Ave. S., Great Falls, MT 59405; Association for the Deaf, 5309 7th Ave. S., Great Falls, MT 59405; Coalition of Handicapped Individuals, 910 Judy Dr., Missoula, MT 59801; Association for the Blind, P.O. Box 1268, Great Falls, MT 59403; Easter Seal Society, 4400 Central Ave., Great Falls, MT 59401; Association for Retarded Citizens, 27 Grand Ave., Billings, MT 59101. FISH AND GAME: Program underway to make parks and campsites accessible through barrier-free design of docks, loading ramps, outdoor theaters, and the like. All state parks and most fishing sites can accommodate wheelchairs.

NEBRASKA

GENERAL: Department of Economic Development, Box 94666—301 Centennial Mall S., Lincoln, NE 69509, 402-471-3111. SPECIFIC: League of Human Dignity Chapter of the Paralyzed Veterans of America, 518 S. 86th St., Omaha, NE 68114, 402-393-1656. Also Mayor's Committee on Employment of the Handicapped in any city. LITERATURE: Newly revised accessibility guide to the Lincoln area, from League of Human Dignity. *A Guide Book to Omaha for the Handicapped*, Easter Seal Society, P.O. Box 14204, Omaha, NE 68114. TRANSPORTATION: Dial-a-ride in Lincoln at $.35 cents. Call the LTS office listed in phone book for information. Mobility Inc., in Omaha, call 342-3992, at rates comparable with taxis. NOTE: Lincoln has a network of curb cuts which make getting to the museums, parks, and theaters easier.

NEVADA

GENERAL: Nevada Department of Economic Development, Dept. 3, Carson City, NV 89701, 702-882-7478. SPECIFIC INFORMATION: Governor's Committee on Employment of the Handicapped, State Mail Rm., Las Vegas, NV 89158. LITERATURE: A printed sheet for disabled tourists, and *Access Las Vegas*, including the surrounding area, available from the Department of Economic Development.

★ **LAS VEGAS.** The dazzle of "The Strip" of flashy hotels and casinos must be seen to be believed. There is twenty-four-hour gambling and two dozen cabarets where the superstars entertain. *Access Las Vegas* (above) is your best guide to how, where, and what. The Riviera Hotel is among the barrier-free hotels. Circus-Circus, among others, has accessible game tables and shows. (And yes, you can play a slot machine sitting in a wheelchair.)

★ **HOOVER DAM.** (Nevada-Arizona border) A pleasant half-day outing from Vegas. The interior of the 726-foot-high and 1,244-foot-wide dam on the Colorado River can be toured in a wheelchair.

NEW HAMPSHIRE

GENERAL: Office of Vacation Travel, Box 856, Concord, NH 03301, 603-271-2666. SPECIFIC: Michael Jenkins, Governor's Commission for the Handicapped, 6 Loudon Rd., Concord, NH 03301, 603-271-2773. SPORTS: See section All Outdoors.

NEW JERSEY

GENERAL AND SPECIFIC: Division of Travel and Tourism, P.O. Box 400, Trenton, NJ 08625, 609-292-2470 or 71. ATTRACTIONS: Fully accessible are the Meadowlands Race Track and Giants Stadium in East Rutherford, and Smithville historic village. Quite accessible are these seaside resorts with boardwalks: Asbury Park (long popular with senior citizens), Ocean City, Wildwoods-by-the-Sea, and Atlantic City. The last is undergoing vast renovations and construction due to the recent legalization of gambling. New hotels are built barrier-free and old ones are remodeled to be so. Resorts International Hotel already has an accessible casino, but the Ramada Inn next door is probably a better bet in lodging. Contact the state office, above, for a list of contacts at these attractions.

♦ **GREAT ADVENTURE.** Features a wildlife park you can drive through in your car. *Let Us Make You Smile* folder details accessible rides, restaurants, and restrooms. Great Adventure, P.O. Box 120, Jackson, NJ 08527, 201-928-2000.

NEW MEXICO

GENERAL: Tourist Division, Department of Development, Bataan Memorial Building, Santa Fe, NM 87503, 505-982-4231 and 800-545-9876. SPECIFIC: Bill Whalin, Division of Vocational Rehabilitation (DVR), Architectural Barriers Specialist, 122 La Veta, N.E., Albuquerque, NM 87108. During business hours, call the local branch of the DVR in larger towns. Also, Easter Seal Society, 4805 Menaul Blvd., N.E. Albuquerque, NM 87110, 505-256-9824. TRANSPORTATION: In Albuquerque, Easter Seal dial-a-ride and Thunderbird Taxi Service. ATTRACTIONS: Accessible are all university campuses, the whole state museum system in Santa Fe, the Sandia Peak Tramway, for aerial views of the scenery year-round (third longest tram in the United States, it climbs to the crest at 10,378 feet). Also, the Santa Fe Opera (July and Aug.) where wheelchairees get the standing-room rate of about $3.

NEW YORK

GENERAL: State Department of Commerce, Travel Bureau, 99 Washington Ave., Albany, NY 12245, 518-474-4116. New York (City) Convention and Visitors Bureau, 90 E. 42nd St., New York, NY 10017, 212-687-1300 (can also answer some specific questions on accessibility). LITERATURE: *Vacationlands New York State Supplement for Handicapped and Senior Citizens* for Adirondacks-Champlain area, Central areas, the Catskills, Niagara frontier, Finger Lakes, Capital-Saratoga, Hudson Valley, Southwest Gateway, Thousand

Islands-St. Lawrence, and New York City. Please specify area. Available from Easter Seal Society, 2 Park Ave., New York, NY 10016. *Tri City Directory* (Buffalo, Lockport, Niagara Falls), Building Barriers Committee, Rehabilitation Association of Western New York, P.O. Box 74, Buffalo, N.Y. 14205. *Access New York* (for east midtown Manhattan) includes accessible hotels, Institute of Rehabilitation Medicine, New York University Medical Center, 400 E. 34th St., New York, NY 10016. *Consumer Rights for Disabled Citizens* (contains travel notes for NYC), $2 from Department of Consumer Affairs, 80 Lafayette St., New York, NY 10013. *Tips for the Physically Handicapped Accessibility Guide*, Lincoln Center for the Performing Arts, 1865 Broadway, New York, NY 10023, 212-765-5100. *NYS Thruway Facilities for the Handicapped*, maps out seventeen accessible rest stops (useful because the book of rest stops nationwide, offered by the President's Committee, may not always be exact in the case of New York), New York State Thruway Authority, Albany, NY, 12201. *See Syracuse*, Easter Seal Society, 109 S. Warren St., Syracuse, NY 13202, 315-471-7873. NYC INFORMATION: Call 472-1003 for the day's free recreational and cultural events for the disabled. NYC TRANSPORTATION: 100 minibuses with level-changing capabilities to operate on modified scheduled public bus routes are being ordered. About 400 kneeling buses are already in circulation. Both Jiffy Cabs (214-03 36th St., Bayside, New York, 212-HA 8-5832) and Ding-a-Ling (534 Hudson St., New York, NY 10014, 212-691-9191) operate conventional taxis and ambulettes. NYC TOURS: New Freedom Adventures (2684 Nostrand Ave., Brooklyn, NY 11210, 212-951-6666) will custom-design tours for individuals or groups (and work with retail travel agents). Itineraries are planned by a registered and certified occupational therapist/travel agent who takes interests and ability into account.

★ STATUE OF LIBERTY. An elevator in the patina-green symbol of liberty in New York Harbor (a gift of the French people to America) takes you to an observation terrace.

★ THE EMPIRE STATE BUILDING. Offers fairyland views of midtown Manhattan from the eighty-seventh floor, but there are a total of eight steps between the elevator and the observation deck and no attendants to assist. (The World Trade Center Twin Towers, at 110 stories [from which *King Kong* made his swan dive], is readily accessible for wide views over New York Harbor and beyond.) For accessibility details of the attractions just described, see the Easter Seal Society's New York City section. See the Niagara Falls frontier section for the attraction that follows.

★ NIAGARA FALLS. Counted among the Seven Natural Wonders of the World, can best be seen from Goat Island or Prospect Point on the U.S. side (the falls span the border with Canada). At times as much as an awesome 100,000 cubic feet of water per second crashes down the falls.

NORTH CAROLINA

GENERAL: Division of Travel and Tourism, 430 N. Salisbury St., Raleigh, NC 27611. PUBLIC TRANSPORTATION: Buses with lifts or ramps in High Point.

NORTH DAKOTA

GENERAL AND SPECIFIC: North Dakota State Highway Department, Capitol Grounds, Bismarck, ND 58505, can provide lists of accessible attractions and hotels/motels, places that care for a handicapped child, wheelchair repair services, and state social services, including special camps. LITERATURE: *A Guidebook to Jamestown* ($.25) and *A Guidebook to Valley City*, both for the handicapped, Easter Seal Society, Box 490, Bismarck, ND 58501. ACCESSIBLE ATTRACTIONS: The reconstructed towns of Frontier Village at Jamestown and Bonanzaville at West Fargo, the sixty-ton concrete Buffalo Monument; Medora, a restored cowboy town in the Badlands; the state capitol and zoo in Bismarck; and Ft. Lincoln State Park.

OHIO

GENERAL: Department of Economic and Community Development, P.O. Box 1001, Columbus, OH 43216, 614-466-8844. Chillicothe Ross Chamber of Commerce, 85 W. Main St., Chillicothe, OH 45601, 614-772-4530. GENERAL OR SPECIFIC: Zanesville Area Chamber of Commerce, 47 N. Fourth St., Zanesville, OH 43701. Akron Regional Development Bd., 1 Cascade Plaza, Akron, OH 44308, call 376-6660 locally. SPECIFIC: For Chillicothe, Mrs. Don McHenry, Ross County Society for Crippled Children and Adults, 9 Kearsley Pl., Chillicothe, OH 45601. LITERATURE: *Seeing Ohio by Wheelchair*, $1.25, Fairlawn Junior Women's Club, Box 5225, Akron, OH 44313. *Greater Cincinnati Guidebook for the Handicapped*, The Hamilton County Easter Seal Society, 7505 Reading Rd., Cincinnati, OH 45237, 513-948-1615. *A Guide to Toledo for the Handicapped*, Chamber of Commerce, 218 Huron St., Toledo, OH 43604. *Direction: Akron Area Guide for the Handicapped*, Junior League of Akron, 929 W. Market St., Akron, OH 44313. *Dayton facilities for the handicapped*, Chamber of Commerce, One Eleven W. First St., Dayton, 45402. ACCESSIBLE ATTRACTIONS: At Chillicothe, Mound City Group, an outstanding prehistoric Indian site, and "Tecumseh!" outdoor drama. At Zanesville, the *Lorena* sternwheeler, 133 passengers, operating May through Sept. Crew will assist persons over small risers. STATE PARKS: Shawnee, Salt Fork, and Mohican lodges are designed with ramps and elevators. Salt Fork park has eighteen modified campsites and special picnic areas. The Golden Buckeye Card and the Therapeutic Passport Discounts are available to Ohioans who are over 65 years of age or persons who are permanently and totally disabled, respectively. Holders are entitled to discounts at state parks, such as 50 percent off on camping and golf, and 30 percent off lodge rooms and cabins on specified days. Permanently disabled Ohio veterans may camp free in state parks and receive the same discounts offered senior citizens. A folder detailing the programs is available from the Department of Natural Resources, Ohio Department of Natural Resources, Division of Parks & Recreation, Fountain Sq., Columbus, OH 43224.

♦ **KINGS ISLAND.** *Wheelchair Admittance Facilities* folder lists possible amusements. Kings Island, P.O. Box 400, Kings Mills, OH 45034.

OKLAHOMA

GENERAL: Tourism and Recreation, 500 Will Rogers Building, Oklahoma City, OK 73105, 405-521-2406. SPECIFIC: Executive Secretary of the Governor's Committee on Employment of the Handicapped, 301 Will Rogers Building, Oklahoma City, OK 73105, 405-521-3756. Also Mayor's Commission, at the same address. TRANSPORTATION: Yellow Cab Co. of Oklahoma City offers a "Handi-Van" service, 405-236-5551. WHEELCHAIR SERVICE: Best Rents in Oklahoma City has rental, sales, and repair. A-Able in Tulsa does repairs. CONVENTION CENTERS: Both Myriad in Oklahoma City and the Tulsa convention centers are accessible.

OREGON

GENERAL: Travel Information, Oregon Department of Transportation, 101 Highway Building, Salem, OR 97310, 503-378-6309. SPECIFIC: Aid, Easter Seal Society, 4343 S.W. Corbett Ave., Portland, OR 97201, 503-228-5108. Oregon Architectural Barriers Council, 4060 Stewart Rd., Eugene, OR 97402.

PENNSYLVANIA

GENERAL: Bureau of Travel Development, Rm. 206 S. Office Building, Harrisburg, PA 17102, 717-787-5453. GENERAL AND SPECIFIC: Philadelphia Convention & Visitors Bureau, 1525 John F. Kennedy Blvd., Philadelphia, PA 19102, 215-864-1976. SPECIFIC: For Philadelphia, Bonnie Gellman, Director, Mayor's Office for the Handicapped (MOH), Rm. 427, City Hall Annex, Philadelphia, PA 19107, 215-MU 6-7120. LITERATURE: *Guide to Philadelphia for the Handicapped*, from MOH, above. *Bucks County Guide for the Physically Limited*, Bucks County Easter Seal Center, 2400 Trenton Rd., Levittown, PA 19056. OUTDOOR RECREATION: George Burns, Project Coordinator, Office of State Planning and Development, Recreation Planning Section, Finance Building, Harrisburg, PA 17120. ATTRACTION: National Gettysburg Battlefield Tower, a vantage point at 300 feet that is fully accessible, with views over the Civil War battlefields.

Contact National Gettysburg Battlefield Tower, Gettysburg, PA 17325, 717-334-6754.

★ **LIBERTY BELL.** If you slept through the Bicentennial, don't worry, it's always 1976 (or 1776) in Philadelphia. The building and improvements that were done for the celebrations—including a new ground level pavilion for the Liberty Bell—are accessible. The Philadelphia accessibility guide (above) tells how.

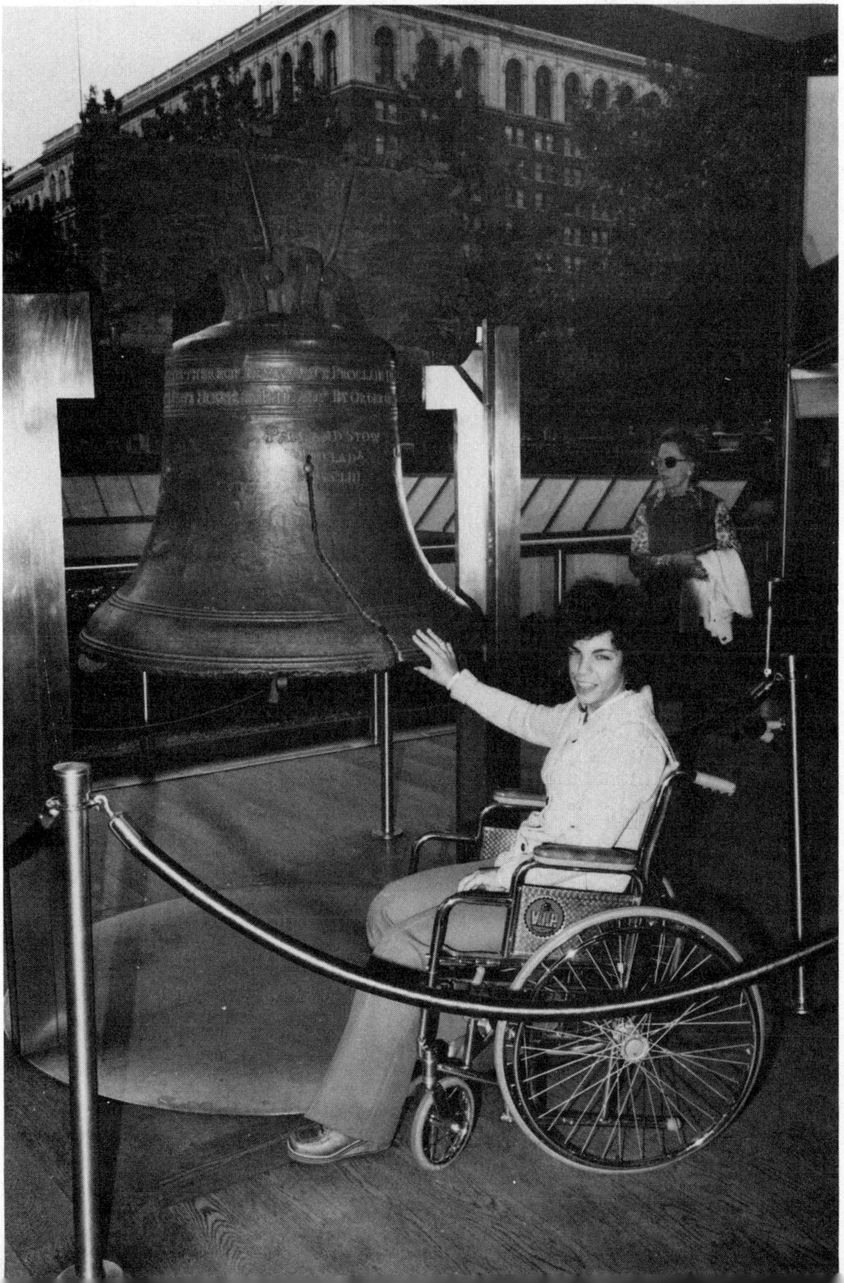

♦ HERSHEYPARK. Personified chocolate bars walk around here. Wheelchair rental at $1, plus $1 deposit, Hersheypark, Hershey, PA. 17033, 717-534-3977.

RHODE ISLAND

GENERAL AND SPECIFIC: Robert E. Wilcox, Rhode Island Department of Economic Development, One Weybosset Hill, Providence, RI 02903, 401-277-2601. LITERATURE: Statewide accessibility guide being prepared at press time. Available from Mr. Wilcox, above. *A Survey of Building Accessibility to the Handicapped* for Barrington, Cranston, East Providence, Providence, and Warwick, available from Nancy D'Wolf, Easter Seal Society, 667 Waterman Ave., East Providence, RI 02914.

SOUTH CAROLINA

GENERAL: Department of Parks, Recreation and Tourism, Edgar Brown Building, 1205 Pendleton St., Columbia, SC 29201, 803-758-2536. Charleston Park, Recreation and Tourism Commission, P.O. Box 634, Charleston, SC 29402, 803-722-1681. ATTRACTIONS: Charles Towne Landing in Charleston, a park designed for both mentally and physically handicapped with seven miles of paths through eighty acres of gardens that can be toured by wheelchair or the touring tram. Site of early settlement. Park and museum depict Colonial life. Group visits can be arranged. Contact the Landing at 1500 Old Town Rd., Charleston, SC 29407, 803-556-4450. Note that in historic Charleston there are some ramped curbs and designated parking areas for the disabled. The Association for the Blind's fragrance garden is at 41 Pitt St., and the renovated Calhoun Mansion, a private residence at 16 Meeting St., will arrange for the blind to examine the carved woodwork, which has exceptionally fine relief. The renowned Festival of Two Worlds, begun in Spoleto, Italy, in 1958, now has an annual U.S. counterpart in late spring in Charleston. Called the Spoleto Festival U.S.A., it brings together the world's top performing artists, painters, and sculptors. A list of restaurants, lodging places and recreational facilities suitable for disabled festival-goers has been prepared especially with the festival in mind by Advocacy for Handicapped Citizens, 111 Church St., P.O. Box 1254, Charleston, SC 29404, 803-723-2518. This list should be used in conjunction with the festival program and ticket information folder available from Spoleto Festival U.S.A., P.O. Box 704, Charleston, SC 29402.

SOUTH DAKOTA

GENERAL: Division of Tourism, Joe Foss Building, Pierre, SD 57501, 605-224-3301. A list of community agencies concerned with the disabled is also available. LITERATURE: *Wheelchair Vacationing in South Dakota*, from above address.

★ **MOUNT RUSHMORE NATIONAL MEMORIAL.** The heads of Presidents Washington, Jefferson, Lincoln, and Theodore Roosevelt carved on a mountainside measure 600 feet from chin to top. Best views are in the morning and most dramatic views are under floodlight from June 1 to Labor Day. Visitor Center accessible. The lighting can be observed through a large window at the center.

TENNESSEE

GENERAL: Tourist Development, 505 Fesslers Lane, Nashville, TN 37210, 615-741-2158. SPECIFIC: Governor's Committee on Employment of the Handicapped, 1808 West End Building, Nashville, TN 37203, 615-741-2051. Rev. Robert Stanhart, National Paraplegia Foundation, The Upper Room, 1908 Grand Ave., Nashville TN 37212, 615-327-2700. Disabled American Veterans, War Memorial Building, Nashville, TN 37219, 615-242-7134. Multiple Sclerosis Society, 116 20th Ave. S., Nashville, TN 37203, 615-327-0545. Muscular Dystrophy Association, Parkview Towers, Nashville, TN 37219, 615-329-9460. Contact Dale Wiley, state director, White House Conference on Handicapped Individuals, for specific information on hotels and restaurants in state's four largest cities. He is at 660 Capitol Hill Building, Nashville, TN 37219, 615-741-1676. LITERATURE: An accessibility guide including the state parks and their lodges and motels is slated for 1978 publication. Available from the Governor's Committee. TRANSPORTATION: Nashville Metropolitan Transit Authority has two special public conveyance vehicles on order for an expected 1978 delivery. WHEELCHAIR REPAIRS: Mid-South Brace Shop, 1921 Church St., Nashville, TN 37203, 615-329-3585. Wheelchair Repairs & Rentals, Williams Surgical Supply Co., 1816 Church St., Nashville, TN 37203, 615-327-4931.

♦ **OPRYLAND.** Centers around country music. Free wheelchairs available. Special wheelchair section designated in the Grand Ole Opry House. Opryland, P.O. Box 2138, Nashville, TN 37214, 615-889-6600.

TEXAS

GENERAL: Travel & Information Division, Department of Highways, Austin, TX 78701. LITERATURE: *Access Dallas* (includes accessibility maps of Dallas/Ft. Worth Airport, downtown Dallas showing curb cuts, and the State Fairgrounds), Easter Seal Society, 4429 N. Central Expressway, Dallas, TX 75205, 214-526-3811. *A Guide to Houston for the Handicapped*, Coalition for Barrier Free Living, P.O. Box 20803, Houston, TX 77025, 713-526-1651. Accessibility guide to San Antonio, Easter Seal Society, 2203 Babcock Rd., San Antonio, TX 78229, 512-699-3911. NOTE: Virtually all of the state's thousand highway rest stops are accessible.

★ **ASTRODOME.** This Houston sports and convention complex is so vast that an eighteen-story skyscraper could be built within.

♦ **ASTROWORLD.** Star Spangled Nights, the nightly fireworks, are a summer attraction. Astroworld, P.O. Box 1400, Houston, TX 77001, 713-748-1234.

UTAH

GENERAL: Utah Travel Council, Council Hall, Capitol Hill, Salt Lake City, UT 84114, 801-533-5681. SPECIFIC: Barbara Murphy, Executive Secretary, Governor's Committee on Employment of the Handicapped, Utah Division of Rehabilitation Services, 330 E. 500 S., Salt Lake City, UT 84111, 801-533-5991. LITERATURE: Accessibility guide for Salt Lake area available from Utah Rehabilitation Association, 638 Wilmington Ave., Salt Lake City, UT 84106, 801-533-5975.

VERMONT

GENERAL: Travel Division, 61 Elm St., Montpelier, VT 05602, 802-828-3236. List of accessible hotels and organizations that deal with the disabled available. SPECIFIC: Peter Grassadonia, Executive Secretary, Governor's Committee for Employment of the Handicapped, 81 River St., Montpelier, VT 05602, 802-828-2861. PUBLIC TRANSPORTATION: Chittenden County Transportation Authority in Burlington, 802-864-0211, by special arrangement. WHEELCHAIR SERVICES: Roy's Orthopedic and Vermont Surgical Equipment, both in Burlington. ATTRACTIONS: The Department of Forest and Parks has revamped Coolidge State Park to include ramps to restrooms. A sixty-foot fishing pier for wheelchairs is at Button Bay State Park.

VIRGINIA

GENERAL: State Travel Service, 6 N. Sixth St., Richmond, VA 23219, 804-786-2051. SPECIFIC: Faye K. Straub, Department of Vocational Rehabilitation, 4615 W. Broad St., Box 11045, Richmond, VA 23230. Mary Ann Cashett, National Paraplegia Foundation, Fisherville, VA. Mobility on Wheels, 1712 Glendon Ave., Norfolk, VA 23518, 804-587-8346. LITERATURE: *Tidewater Access Guide*, for Norfolk, Portsmouth, Chesapeake, and Virginia Beach, from Mobility on Wheels, above. PARKS: Among the barrier-free parks are Bayville, designed for the disabled, in Virginia Beach, Prince William Forest, Pocahontas, and Chincoteague National Wildlife Refuge. A pilot project of the U.S. Department of Agriculture is the Outdoor Patterns for People Project, in George Washington National Forest (Harrisburg, VA 22801). Trails have been laid out to open the forest for everyone. Visitors are encouraged to walk in the cool water of a safe wading stream, to smell the sassafras or wintergreen, or to drive, walk, or hike to lookout points over the Shenandoah Valley. The visitors' center and restrooms of Stratford Hall, Robert E. Lee's birthplace in Westmoreland County, are barrier free. The ground floor of this handsome eighteenth-century brick mansion is also accessible, but the second-story parlor floor is at the top of seventeen steps.

★ **COLONIAL WILLIAMSBURG.** The pretty pink brick buildings of this reconstructed eighteenth-century Colonial capital of Virginia are often impassable (what did the founding fathers know from barrier-free architecture?). Even so, a remarkable number of the buildings and gardens are passable. Wheelchairs can be rented on the spot. *A Guide for the Handicapped* (available from the Colonial Williamsburg Foundation, Williamsburg, VA 23185) tells precisely which attractions, restaurants, and hotels are accessible. Because the paths may be hard to push on, one enterprising couple hired two high school boys (recruited locally through a docent) to push them.

♦ **BUSCH GARDENS.** The Old Country. Just what the name implies. The only inaccessible attraction is a cruise on the Rhine River. Busch Gardens, P.O. Drawer F-C, Williamsburg, VA 23185.

WASHINGTON

GENERAL: Travel Development Division, Department of Commerce & Economic Development, General Administration Building, Olympia, WA 98504, 206-753-5630. Seattle/King County Convention and Visitors Bureau, 206-447-7273. SPECIFIC: Barbara Allan, Barrier Free Design, Easter Seal Society, 521 Second Ave. W., Seattle, WA 98119, 206-284-5706. Easter Seal Community Aid Directory, Eastern Washington Office, W. 510 Second Ave., Spokane, WA 99204, 509-838-8353. The United Way Crisis Clinic, 206-323-2100. Dept. of Veterans Affairs, P.O. Box 9778, Olympia, WA 98504. LITERATURE: *Access Seattle*, from Easter Seal Seattle address, above. *Guide to Spokane Area for the Handicapped*, Easter Seal Society, W. 510 Second Ave., Spokane, WA 99204. TOURS: Gray Line Sightseeing can accommodate wheelchair passengers on tours of the Seattle waterfront, on city bus tours, and on Mount Rainier tours, by storing wheelchairs in the baggage compartment and assisting the occupants aboard. TRANSPORTATION: Public buses in Seattle with lifts or ramps. Also the "Cabulance" ambulette service run by Shepard Ambulance. TRAVEL NOTES: Seattle is built on hills and it rains a great deal. The Seattle landscape of mountains and evergreens surrounded by large bodies of fresh and salt water is often shrouded in clouds.

WEST VIRGINIA

GENERAL: West Virginia Department of Commerce, Travel Development Division, State Capitol, Charleston, WV 25305, 304-348-2286. LITERATURE: *West Virginia Travel Guide for the Handicapped*, State Board of Vocational Education, Division of Vocational Rehabilitation, State Capitol, Charleston, WV 25305, 304-348-2375. LIST: "Accessibility Study of Recreation Facilities in the Charleston Area," Recreation Director, West Virginia Rehabilitation Center Institute, Charleston, WV 25112. TRANSPORTATION: Multicap Service in Charleston. By appointment. 304-343-4324. WHEELCHAIR REPAIR: Boll Rental Service, 717 Bigley Ave., Charleston, WV 25302, 304-345-2944. ATTRACTIONS: List of facilities in state parks available from Governor's Office of Economic and Community Development, Charleston, WV 25305 (attention of Lana Meadows). White Oak Village, a model fresh-air camp with barrier-free cabins and cottages is to be used especially by people from West Virginia, Virginia, the District of Columbia, Maryland, Delaware, and Pennsylvania. Includes trailer campsites, a nature center, and a fifty-acre lake. Target opening date is Fall 1978. Contact Wood County Parks and Recreation Commission, Box 208, Parkersburg, WV 26101.

WISCONSIN

GENERAL: Division of Tourism, Department of Business Development, 123 W. Washington Ave., Madison, WI 53702, 608-266-3222. SPECIFIC: Wisconsin Easter Seal Society, 2702 Monroe St., Madison, WI 53711, 608-231-3411. MOBIL (Madison Organization Behind Independent Living) 608-222-3737. LITERATURE: *Wisconsin's Capital With Ease*, Dane County Easter Seal Society, 21 E. Gorham St., Madison, WI 53703, 608-255-9489. *Accessibility Now!* for the Fond du Lac area. Fond du Lac Convention Bureau, 207 N. Main St., Fond du Lac, WI 54935, 414-923-3010. TRANSPORTATION: Public bus in Madison available on a dial-a-ride basis is identified as the E.H. (Elderly and Handicapped) service, 608-241-4695.

WYOMING

GENERAL: Travel Commission, I-25 at Etchepare Circle, Cheyenne, WY 82002, 307-777-7777. SPECIFIC: Norma Hill, Governor's Committee for the Employment of the Handicapped, 307-777-7657. TRAVEL NOTES: Many of the major attractions including Yellowstone and Grand Teton National Parks, and most museums provide handicapped visitor service.

★ YELLOWSTONE. The largest national park, covering 2.2 million acres; the thermal attractions, with 3,000 geysers including the famous Old Faithful that erupts at sixty-five-minute intervals, are the park's highlights. But there is also inspiring scenery and abundant wildlife. Pathways to view Old Faithful are accessible. The *Access/National Parks* guide (see index) lists barrier-free features at Yellowstone as well as at Grand Teton.

COMMONWEALTH OF PUERTO RICO

GENERAL: The Puerto Rico Tourism Development Co. has offices at: 2531 Briarcliff Rd., Atlanta, GA 30329, 404-633-1475; 11 E. Adams St., Chicago, IL 60603, 312-922-9701; 10100 Santa Monica Blvd., Los Angeles, CA 90067, 213-555-4482; 1290 Ave. of the Americas, New York, NY 10019, 212-541-6630; 1625 Massachusetts Ave., NW, Washington, DC 20036, 202-387-1837. NOTES: Puerto Rico and the U.S. Virgin Islands, below, offer Caribbean charms with many of the advantages of home; that is, English is spoken, the U.S. dollar is the currency, your health insurance plan *may* be honored, and you'll find familiar brands of everything. The capital city of San Juan is hard to negotiate in a wheelchair (see notes under Cruises, Part II). There are accessible hotels (most with a casino) including the Condado Holiday Inn, Howard Johnson's, and Sheraton; also the semiaccessible El San Juan (two-inch step to the bathroom) and Dutch Inn, a small independent hotel, where the public areas are fine for wheelchairs and the staff is kindly disposed, but the bathroom doors are too narrow for a chair. MEDICAL EMERGENCIES: An "Assist" program is operated on a twenty-four-hour basis for tourists with medical emergencies. Call the Presbyterian Hospital at 724-2160 (and if you have trouble getting through the notoriously busy Puerto Rican phone system, call your hotel desk for help).

U.S. VIRGIN ISLANDS

GENERAL: U.S. Virgin Islands Government Information Center, 10 Rockefeller Plaza, New York, NY 10020, 212-582-4520. SPECIFIC: Locally, call Marjorie Foley, Regional Library for the Blind, on St. Thomas, 774-6770; and Elroy George at the Veterans Administration, 774-5380. On St. Croix call Eryle Rohlsen, at the VA, 773-0471. NOTES: The three U.S. territories are St. Thomas, St. John, and St. Croix. When flying into Charlotte Amalie on St. Thomas, capital of the islands, bear in mind that Eastern's Boeing 727s, carrying 103 passengers from Miami, are currently offering the only direct service from the States. While the Harry S. Truman Airport runways there are being extended, American Airlines' 707s are flying to St. Croix, where passengers transfer to smaller Convair 440s for the flight in. To board and deplane handicapped passengers here, a "walking chair" device that climbs stairs might be used or you might be lifted bodily. St. John is primarily a nature preserve. For further notes see Hotels and Motels, Cruises, and General Information for the subhead Children. Also see comment under Puerto Rico, above.

NATIONWIDE INFORMATION

The United States Travel Service (USTS) operates a toll-free telephone information service. It can provide general or specific information on all the states, including the names of barrier-free hotels or accessible facilities in the U.S. national parks. It will also mail out a number of books and booklets on such aspects of travel as the outdoors or holiday planning. Call Monday through Friday from 9 A.M. to 8 P.M. (Eastern time): 800-323-4180. In Illinois call 800-942-4833.

ACCESS UPDATE

The National Easter Seal Society has prepared a list of city access guides produced by the local societies, which it plans to keep up-to-date. Available from Information Center, National Easter Seal Society, 2023 W. Ogden Ave., Chicago, IL 60612.

Reported to be in the works are guides to Little Rock, Arkansas; Santa Cruz, California; Vallejo, California; Carbondale, Illinois; Columbus, Ohio; and Lancaster, Pennsylvania.

4

HOTELS AND MOTELS

You could use the letter on page 218 as the prototype whenever you wish to inquire about the accessibility of a particular hotel. Of course everyone has his own requirements, and you should amend the letter to fit yours. If you use a custom-built motorized chair you might need doors wider than twenty-eight inches. If you require a special diet ask if the kitchen can oblige. Mrs. A. does not need grab bars in the bathroom or over the bed, but if you do, inquire. Questions such as those cited in the letter should also be asked when you telephone for a reservation. Get confirmation as to the accessibility in writing unless you are confident about a hotel. For example, if a Holiday Inn is said to be accessible it is almost certain to be so. A hotel staff member will be more careful to verify facts if he must sign his name to them. And should you receive misinformation a letter helps you register a complaint. (If a hotel is billed as barrier-free and it is not, by all means report it to the management, and if it is a chain hotel, report it to the corporate level. See the section Why Plan a

11-71 Stone Avenue
Forest Hills, New York 11375
September 1, 1978

Manager
Marriott's Essex House
160 Central Park South
New York, New York 10019

Sir:

My wife and I are planning to spend a few days at your hotel. She is totally confined to a wheelchair (she does not require any special attention of the hotel staff, however), and we would like you to answer the following questions regarding the hotel to be absolutely sure that it will be fully accessible.

Your cooperation in replying to the questions will be most sincerely appreciated:

1. Is there a curb where the cars pull up for the guests to enter the hotel, or is the front ramped? Can wheelchairs use the main entrance or must they use a side door, service entrance, or other route?
2. Are there any steps at all going from the street into the lobby? If so, how many, and is there a ramp?
3. Are hotel ramps graded no steeper than a one-inch rise in every twelve inches?
4. Are there any steps to reach the elevators in the lobby?
5. Are there any steps in the lobby that my wife would have to use in order to get to (a) the coffee shop, (b) the dining room, (c) the nightclub, or (d) other public areas?
6. Is the door to the elevator (lift) at least twenty-eight inches wide and is the elevator large enough to accommodate a wheelchair?
7. Are the bathroom doors in the guest rooms at least twenty-eight inches wide? How wide are they? Do they open out, or in such a way as not to block the plumbing?
8. Is the hotel a high-rise?
9. Are the guest rooms in the main building where all of the other facilities are? How wide are their doors?
10. My wife drives a car with hand controls. Can she park her car and enter the hotel without encountering architectural barriers (steps, steep ramps, the like)? Because of the hand controls, she usually prefers to park it herself rather than have a valet car-parking service do it.

Please enclose a hotel brochure and rate sheet with your letter.

Thank you for your prompt attention, cooperation, and consideration. We await your kind reply.

Yours truly,

Robert A.

Trip? When Rosemarie's room billed as barrier-free was inaccessible, her travel agent wrote to the management and sent a copy of the letter to the president of the chain.)

When you telephone the central reservations system of a hotel chain, keep in mind that the reservations agents are equipped only with general computerized information about their properties: yes, they can usually tell you if accessible rooms (sometimes called "ambulatory rooms") are available. But if you have a personalized question, they may not have the answer and may not be able to get it. In many cases they cannot make outgoing calls and may advise you to call the individual hotel.

Keeping in mind a quadriplegic friend who uses a lift for transfer into bed and cannot sleep in a platform bed (he can use a rollaway bed) the author called the major chains listed immediately below to inquire about their bed design. All but two said to call the hotel in question. Only the TraveLodge and Hyatt central reservations agents said they would check with the hotel and call back. If you have anything other than routine questions (such as the width of the doors, or whether there are ramps and grab bars and the like) be prepared to call the hotel itself.

A number of the leading hotel and motel chains are becoming known for their facilities and services designed for disabled guests. Among them are Best Western, Hilton, Holiday Inns, Howard Johnson's, Hyatt, Marriott, Quality Inns, Ramada Inns, TraveLodge, and Sheraton. (See Reservations and Information below.)

As examples of the many hotel companies with actual policies concerning facilities for disabled guests, we cite those of Holiday Inns, TraveLodge, and Sheraton.

Holiday Inns has the goal of one barrier-free room per one hundred rooms, a policy that was established twelve years ago. At last count, 625 of their 1,700 locations had such rooms. TraveLodge aims for two rooms per location. And Sheraton—in addition to modifying some old properties and building all new ones with special facilities—is especially service oriented, with corporate directives issued on the care of handicapped guests.

While each chain's definition of "barrier-free hotel" varies somewhat, Holiday Inns' is a typical example: entrance doors are at least thirty-two inches wide and rooms have space enough for a wheelchair to navigate; a lift bar is hung above the bed to permit swinging into bed; the bathroom has a "drive under" sink, faucets and water glass within easy reach, as well as grab bars by the tub, shower, and toilet, which is wheelchair height; light and TV switches are conveniently located; the parking slot is extra wide; and the entrance is ramped.

A Holiday Inns spokesman remarks that while they do not experience heavy demand for the barrier-free rooms, they feel it is important to have them available. Note that architectural guidelines for such things as how to construct a ramp and the ideal height for drinking fountains and telephones for use by persons in wheelchairs have been established by the American National Standards Institute (item A117.1) and are available from the Architectural and Transportation Barriers Compliance Board, Room 1004, 330 C Street, SW, Washington, D.C. 20201. The American Hotel & Motel Association (AHMA), which for some years has fostered barrier-free architecture and special services for disabled guests, has information available for its members who wish to make their hotels accessible. (AHMA, 888 Seventh Ave., New York, NY 10019).

No two persons have the same requirements. As stated, Mrs. A. does not need grab bars. Somebody else does. Mrs. A. cannot get out of her chair. Someone else might be able to walk a few steps, in which case the width of the bathroom door is not a factor. At some hotels, the entrance to a dining room might have to be ramped, or perhaps only one of two dining rooms is accessible.

Some hotels were built accessible. The Hyatt Regency on Waikiki beach in Honolulu, described elsewhere, is an example of that. Some hotels have added ramps or widened doors as a postscript. The Pineapple Beach Resort on St. Thomas in the U.S. Virgin Islands epitomizes this. It was not consciously designed for wheelies, but it is on flat ground and most of the rooms are on one level. Handicapped guests *discovered* the Pineapple a few years ago, and since that time the management has added additional features to make it even more accessible. Many rooms at the Pineapple open right onto the beach banded by an indescribably blue sea. (Pineapple Beach Resort, P.O. Box 2516, St. Thomas, VI 00801, 809-775-1510).

A neighboring hotel, The Pavilions, might not suit everyone, but for a person able to step down into the slightly sunken tub or shower,

Courtesy The Pavilions

You can have your own private pool at The Pavilions on St. Thomas

this hotel could be a find. Every unit has a living room, kitchen, bed, bath, patio, and pool—all on one level (except for the sunken bath). Each is completely enclosed by walls or tall hedges of thick island foliage to offer you complete privacy for sunning or swimming in your pool. If you shy away from public beaches and pools and have some flexibility, this might be for you. Note that winter is the high season with higher rates in the Caribbean. For example, winter 1977/78 daily rates at The Pavilions were $76 to $86 for two ($12 each for a third or fourth person), while a recent three-night summer package (April 11–December 19) was $73.50 to $88.55 per person in a double. (For booking or information contact Robert F. Warner, Inc., 630 Fifth Ave., New York, NY 10020, 212-JU6-4500. Offices also in Boston, Washington, and Chicago.)

Some wheelchair travelers have discovered their own favorite resort hotels. Consider the ocean resorts of New Jersey: the boardwalks are fine for ramblers, and persons with limited mobility have long known this. The current renovation of Atlantic City, prompted by the advent of legalized gambling earlier this year (1978), has already resulted in one additional barrier-free hotel, Resorts International.

Mr. A., a seasoned traveler, always asks if a hotel is a high-rise, because he generally finds the newer hotels to be easier to negotiate. Likewise he tends to be suspicious of anything described as "quaint" or "charming," just another way of saying "inaccessible," he says. But this is not always the case.

If the chalet style of architecture has kept you away from ski resorts but you'd like to experience one, consider the barrier-free Hilton at Vail, Colorado.

If rambling New England inns conjure up visions of rustic stairways and outmoded plumbing, look into the characteristic old Woodstock Inn, in Woodstock, Vermont, where the management will ramp one small curb. The rest is pretty much accessible to wheelchairs, although baths don't have grab bars and the public restrooms are inaccessible. In the past this hotel has hosted Ski for Light, a one-to-one cross-country skiing event of sighted and blind skiers. (Woodstock Inn, 14 The Green, Woodstock, VT 05091, 802-457-1100, or call 800-555-1212 for the Rockresorts reservation office in your region.)

You may have to look a little harder to find your ideal hotel, but it does exist. Once you have figured out your maximum and minimum standards at a hotel, make up a form letter, and whenever you see an ad for a hotel that strikes your fancy, send a letter to find out if it is accessible. You can build up a file of suitable hotels.

A number of the so-called "budget motels" feature barrier-free architecture, and there is an occasional hotel that's accessible in a chain not usually identified as "accessible." The Americana Inn in Albany, New York (800-228-3278), has twelve special rooms, ramps, reserved parking, and an elevator panel in Braille. A number of independent hotels are equipped for disabled guests. One is the Metropolitan Hotel that's conveniently located near many of the attractions in Washington, D.C. (Metropolitan Hotel, 1143 New Hampshire Ave., N.W., Washington, DC 20037, 202-467-5830).

Then there are *the* hotels, some of those famous old dowager hotels such as The Homestead in Virginia, and The Greenbrier in West Virginia, included on lists of the finest hotels in America. Built originally as spas for persons suffering from arthritis and rheumatism, they often did—and do—cater to the carriage trade and to this day continue to provide the very best in the way of food and service as well as hydrotherapy and often physiotherapy administered by professional staffs.

AT THE HOTEL

Although the Marriott's Essex House, which Mr. A wrote to, was not accessible in every way, Bob and June A. decided to stay there anyway because of its superb location overlooking Central Park. Among the features that kept it from being strictly barrier-free were the three steps leading to the dining room (the staff will assist here) and the bathrooms that were spacious but lacked grab bars. Hotel renovations underway at press time, however, call for a number of modified units on the second floor for handicapped guests.

Here Bob and June are pictured arriving at the hotel. (June had turned her car over to the valet parking attendant at the entrance when he assured her that he had driven cars with hand controls before.) Here the doorman gives them a hand with their luggage and shows them into the lobby, where the bellman takes over. If the doorman helps with your wheelchair or luggage or does anything more than show you in, you may wish to tip him up to a dollar at this time.

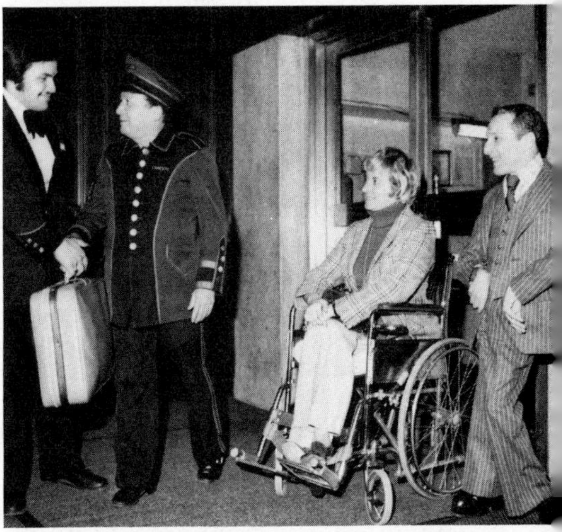

Bob's reservation is in order and he signs in. He shows a credit card to secure his account—otherwise, depending on the hotel, he might be asked to pay cash in advance. (If a travel agent had booked the hotel, Bob would now present vouchers from the agency.) The desk clerk gives them the key to their room.

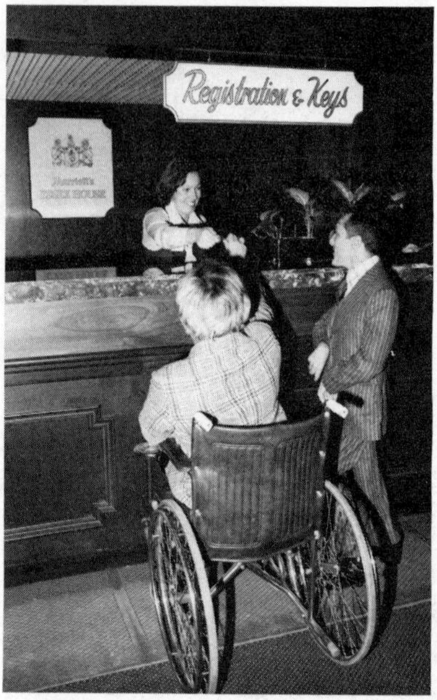

Their bellman takes them up.

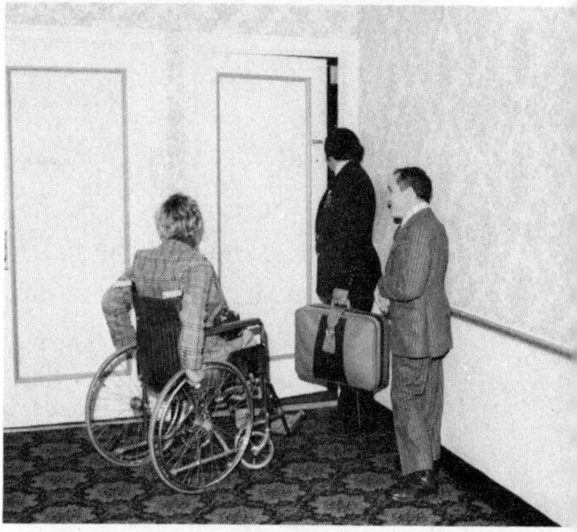

He points out the various features, such as how to adjust the heat.

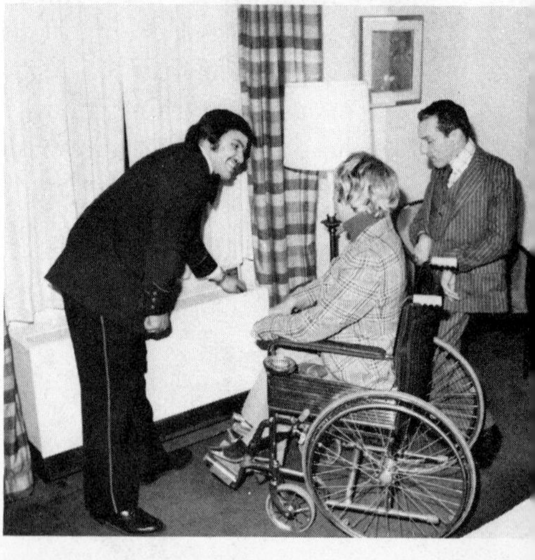

June tips him a dollar.

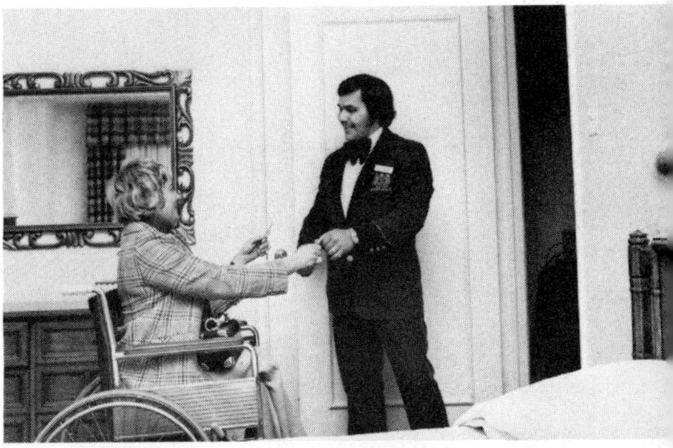

Bob had chosen a "full service" hotel because sometimes it is nice to have meals or a snack in your room, to have your clothes pressed or other services. Breakfast in their room—a real luxury—and June tips the waiter 15 percent of the bill.

An hour or so before you plan to leave, you can call the desk and tell them you'll be checking out and ask them to put your bill in order. This may expedite check-out. When you are ready to leave, call the bell captain and ask him to send someone for your bags.

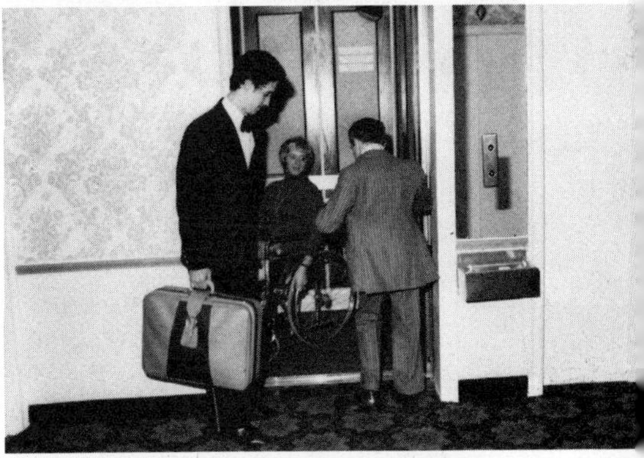

Checking out takes place at the cashier's desk.

RESERVATIONS AND INFORMATION

City hotels usually keep the same rate structure year-round, while resort hotels often have high and low seasons and the seasonal rate changes. Some of your best buys come at transitional periods. The weather is probably the same, give or take a degree or two, and you can have the high-season advantages at low-season rates.

Learn to take advantage of regular packages that entitle you to lower hotel rates. All you have to do is to determine if the hotels that figure into the package are barrier-free (which you can often do through a simple letter or phone call placed by yourself or your travel agent). For example, the Marriott's Essex House is one of several fashionable New York hotels that are filled with businessmen during the week and offer weekend packages to induce business. Whereas a standard room at the Essex House runs from $70 to $90, a weekend package rate of $79.90 covers one night's accommodation for two persons, dinner, and breakfast (and an additional night is $40). (Book through the Marriott reservations system, see below.) Also see discussion of packages under Hawaii and Trains elsewhere, and check the index for other hotel references.

MAJOR CHAINS

Call or write the following hotels, motels, or motor hotels for information on facilities for disabled guests, reservations, or copies of their directories, which designate their barrier-free locations.

Best Western—Nationwide and Canada. Said to have more than 350 accessible locations, but some properties listed in the directory as accessible may not meet Best Western's barrier-free requirements. A company spokesman has explained that because all Best Westerns are independently owned and operated, the directory listings were based on information provided by the individual managements, which was not exact in every case. According to the spokesman, "Next year the handicapped listings in the *Travel Guide* [directory] will be awarded only to those properties which comply with Best Western's standards." Those standards include 32-inch-wide doorways and halls, hand rails in the bathroom, convenient bedside switches, Braille-dial telephones, special menus, and other points. Inquire: Best Western, Dept. PB, P.O. Box 20, Phoenix, AZ 85001, 800-528-1234 or in Arizona dial 800-352-1222.

Holiday Inns—Nationwide and international; 625 accessible locations. Offers the Inner Circle courtesy card entitling the holder to a number of courtesies including the best available room, express check-in, check-cashing of up to $50 per stay (to bearers of a backup credit card such as American Express or Diners), a free weekday morning newspaper. Inner Circle application form available by calling 901-362-4827, or write Customer Relations, Holiday Inns, 3781 Lamar Ave., Memphis, TN 38118. The hotel directory is available from that address. Holiday Inns has no nationwide toll-free number for individuals to use. Check your local telephone directory, and book through the local listing.

Howard Johnson's—Nationwide except for the northwestern states. 300 accessible locations. 222 Forbes Rd., Braintree, MA 02184, 800-654-2000.

Hyatt—Mainly in the South and Southeast and on the West Coast. Write to Donna Barron, Director of Public Relations, Hyatt Corporation, 1338 Bayshore Highway, P.O. Box 945, Burlingame, CA 94010, for a list of accessible properties. 800-228-9000 for reservations.

Quality Inns—Nationwide. 100 accessible properties. Quality Inns, 10750 Columbia Pike, Silver Spring, MD 20901, 800-228-5151.

Ramada Inns—Nationwide and international. 455 accessible locations. P.O. Box 590, Phoenix, AZ 85001, 800-228-2828.

TraveLodge—Nationwide and international. TraveLodge, El Cajon, CA 92020, 800-255-3050.

The following chains *do* have accessible rooms, and they are known to the computer reservations system. Their directories, however, do not indicate them.

Marriott—Nationwide and international. Advertising Department, 5161 River Rd., Bethesda, MD 20016, 800-228-9290.

Hilton—Nationwide. Hilton's Preferential Card accords certain VIP courtesies to holders. Hilton Hotels, 9080 Wilshire Blvd., Los Angeles, CA 90210, 213-278-4321. Also check your telephone directory for a local Hilton listing.

Sheraton—Nationwide and international. Has an especially well developed program of courtesies for blind guests, including Braille menus. Sheraton Corporation, 470 Atlantic Ave., Boston, MA 02210, 800-325-3535.

BUDGET MOTELS

Budget motels are the fastest growing segment of the U.S. lodging industry, with more than 170,000 rooms now available in a trend that really got underway about 1970. These are the no-frills motels, the so-called VWs of the lodging industry. Rooms are basic but comfortable. One of the frills that is often missing is the restaurant. If this matters to you, be sure to ask. At budgets you usually pay 25 to 40 percent less than you would at a local standard motel. (Standards are estimated to average about $21.50 nowadays.) Some budgets start as low as $9. Like Econo-Travel, they bid you to "spend a night, not a fortune."® The following have reported that they have facilities for persons who are wheelchair-bound or have limited mobility. Some are indicated in their directories.

California 6 and Western 6—West Coast, Nevada, and Arizona. All locations with one or two accessible rooms. California 6 and Western 6, P.O. Box 5348, Hacienda Heights, CA 91745.

Days Inns—South, Southeast, and expanding nationwide and into Canada. Days Inns, 2751 Buford Highway N.E., Atlanta, GA 30324, 800-241-7111.

Econo-Travel—From Vermont to Florida and as far west as Missouri. Directory identifies one accessible property (near Civil War battlefield in Fredericksburg, Virginia). Econo-Travel, P.O. Box 12188, Norfolk, VA 23502, 800-446-6900 (1-800-582-5882 for Virginia only; 461-6000, Norfolk area).

Koala Inns—Northeast. Newest location at Hyannis, Massachusetts (on Cape Cod), has five rooms for disabled guests, and all future inns will be so designed. Koala Inns, 170 Forbes Rd., Braintree, MA 02184, 617-848-6750.

Marcus Hotel Corporation—Midwest. Facilities including single levels or ramps for the physically handicapped traveler at all locations. Contact Spectrumedia Communications, 212 W. Wisconsin Ave., Milwaukee, WI 53203, 414-272-6020, for list of properties.

Mini-Price Motor Inns—Las Vegas and Milwaukee. Both locations designed for wheelchair travelers. Mini-Price, 105 Michigan St., Milwaukee, WI 53203.

Motel 6—Nationwide. Accessible rooms in all units built after 1972 (earlier ones have no grab bars but can usually accommodate chairs). Over fifty post-1972 buildings include one special unit per fifty rooms, with wider doors, ramps, lower TV set, grab bars, special commode and sink, and a specially constructed shower with seat and handheld shower nozzle. One of the largest budget chains with 300 locations. List of accessible locations available from Motel 6, 1888 Century Park East, Los Angeles, CA 90067, 213-277-6666.

Regal 8—Mostly in the Midwest. Almost all locations are suitable for wheelchair travelers. Regal 8, P.O. Box 1268, Mt. Vernon, IL 62864, 618-242-7240.

Thr-rift Inns—Virginia and Maryland. Annapolis Inn is barrier-free. Thr-rift Inns, P.O. Box 2699, Newport News, VA 23602.

SPAS

Hot Springs, Arkansas—Hot Springs National Park regulates concessioners of bathing establishments. There are more than forty mineral springs. Persons unable to afford the cost of the baths may use them at government expense, with a doctor's recommendation. Mild year-round climate and recreation including horseback riding, scenic drives, fishing, and boating. See the *Access/National Parks* guide (check index). For a list of accessible hotels, which includes a Holiday Inn, Ramada Inn, and at least a dozen others, contact the Arkansas Department of Parks and Tourism (see state listings).

Hot Springs, Virginia—Socialites of bygone days used to luxuriate in the baths as mint juleps were floated out to them on cork trays. That's the way it was. Today at The Homestead in this beautiful mountain setting, other "cures" are administered by physicians and physiotherapists, including hydrotherapy, infrared, and sunlamp treatments. Most resort amenities, European cuisine, golf, tennis, and skiing. The Homestead, Hot Springs, VA 24445, 800-336-5771, (800-542-5734 for Virginia only).

Marlin, Texas—Falls Motor Hotel health spa and hot mineral baths are complete with registered masseurs and masseuses. Marlin attractions include golf, fishing in the Brazos River, and a restored Gay Nineties mansion. Falls Motor Hotel, 226 Coleman, Marlin, TX 76661.

White Sulphur Springs, WV—The Greenbrier is in a class with The Homestead for style and tradition. One of America's legendary grand resort hotels, it offers a fine program of physiotherapy. See Children, listed under General Information, Part IV, Section 1. The Greenbrier, White Sulphur Springs, WV 24986, 800-624-6070.

Thermopolis, Wyoming—It means "hot city," and at least fourteen hotels, including a Holiday Inn, dot the area. The Gottsche Rehabilitation Center is here. Wild, scenic country said to be a geologist's showcase, beautiful canyons, and great trout fishing. For information and a hotel list contact Wyoming State Travel Commission (see state listings) or Gottsche Rehabilitation Center, P.O. Box 790, Thermopolis, WY 82443.

CONVENTIONS

SMALL GROUPS—John C. Bechtel, director, General Services, United Cerebral Palsy Association, 66 E. 34th St., New York, NY 10016, 212-481-6306, keeps a log of U.S. hotels that have rooms for up to thirty wheelchairs and barrier-free meeting rooms. His notes include the newest properties. As a special service for handicapped travelers, Mr. Bechtel will share his information with small-meeting planners or others who need such group arrangements.

MEETING PLANNER—*Barrier Free Meetings* is a meeting planner's manual for assessing conference sites and following through in every way. 73 pages, AAAS No. 76-7, $4 from American Association for the Advancement of Science, Sales Office, 1515 Massachusetts Ave., N.W., Washington, DC 20005. Allow six to eight weeks for delivery.

PRACTICAL INFORMATION

MEAL PLANS

Abbreviations that commonly appear with a hotel's rates refer to the meal plan. They are:

- EP—European Plan (room only)
- CP—Continental Plan (room and a continental breakfast of coffee and rolls or toast)
- AP—American Plan (three meals)
- MAP—Modified American Plan (breakfast and dinner)

When not indicated, the rate is EP—room only.

PER PERSON DOUBLE OCCUPANCY

Hotel rates are often stated as "$X per person double occupancy." This means that when two persons share the room each one pays X dollars. Single occupancy rate could be twice X, or otherwise determined.

TIPS ON TIPPING

There are no hard and fast rules on tipping, but there are some guidelines for how much to give whom:

- The doorman, twenty-five or thirty-five cents each time he hails a cab for you. Nothing if he simply holds the door, but if he helps you out, sets up your chair, and takes your baggage in, tip him up to a dollar.
- Bellman, about fifty cents per bag and fifty cents for opening the room.
- Room service waiter, 15 percent of the bill, with a fifty-cent minimum.
- Bellman or valet who delivers special requests—let's say you call down for a newspaper—fifty cents.
- Chambermaid, nothing for one or two nights; thereafter, if it is a luxury hotel, check with the management on the custom.
- Valet parking attendant, fifty cents each time he handles your car.
- When staying at a resort hotel where you have all meals at an assigned table in the dining room, at the end of your stay you may tip your waiters at the rate of two dollars a day (to be divided among them), the dining room captain fifty cents per day; wine steward and bar waiters 15 percent of your wine or bar bill.
- Never tip the hotel management.
- As a rule, motels are pretty much self-service, but if someone other than the man behind the desk should assist you, you could tip as you might at a hotel in the area.

MISCELLANEOUS

- "Lower outer" is sometimes used to describe a ground-floor room at the outer edge of a unit at a motel or motor inn. Do ask for a convenient, accessible room when booking.
- Airlines will make reservations for you with hotels they work with. United, for example, through its computer reservations system can book rooms at Holiday Inns, Howard Johnson's, Hyatt, Ramada Inns, Sheraton, Del Webb, Western International, Interisland Resorts, and Outrigger.

• If you are staying at a hotel or motel that offers no room service, check with the staff or use the Yellow Pages for local restaurants that deliver.

• Check-out time usually is from 12 noon to 2 P.M., but if your plane, bus, or train does not leave for several hours, you may ask the desk for permission to stay in your room a while longer (they will often let you, unless space is tight); or you may speak with the chambermaid, who may be willing to make up your room last. Sometimes the hotel management will assign one common room for use by a number of guests with late departures.

• You often find a weekly guide to local events, entertainment, and restaurants in your room. Use the phone numbers listed therein and call to see if places are barrier-free.

• Pack a flashlight to use in case the light switch cannot be reached from bed.

• A cordless gadget that allows you to turn off the TV or lamp from bed can easily be attached to the television in many hotels. (In some cases, however, the sets have been rigged up to impede theft and the device cannot be attached.) The Invento sonic switch model is available from Hammacher Schlemmer, 147 E. 57th St., New York, NY 10022, 212-937-8181 or 914-946-7725, catalog item N5000, $19.95 plus handling. The Whistle Switch, activated by a whistle, is a similar device. Available from Joan Cook, Inc., 3200 S.E. 14th Ave., Fort Lauderdale, FL 33316, catalog item 1404-X, $17.95.

• A folding "bed board" is also available from Hammacher Schlemmer (immediately above). Offers support for persons with back troubles. Item Z72R, it weighs 12 pounds and is $17.95. The two-pound carrying case, ZNCC, is $10. Some hotels supply boards on request.

• The American Automobile Association is making a thorough survey of hotels and motels to determine their accessibility, to be included in the AAA guidebooks, which already list some accessible lodgings. See AAA in index.

• *The Wheelchair Traveler*, by Douglass R. Annand, is a directory of more than 3,500 hotels and motels (accessible in varying degrees) in the United States, Canada, Mexico, and Puerto Rico. Available at $4.95 (plus $.65 third-class postage or $1 first-class) from *The Wheelchair Traveler*, Ball Hill Road, Milford, NH 03055.

Any rates or prices quoted above are subject to change.

"You've been extremely helpful and I'm certainly looking forward to the trip," a well-prepared traveler tells her agent (page 20).

PART IV

GETTING READY TO GO

1

GENERAL INFORMATION

A MAGIC NUMBER

Dial (1-) 800-555-1212 to find out if a hotel, tour operator, or motorcoach company has a toll-free number before making that long distance call. Operations that now have them range from the expected (large hotel chains and the like) to the unexpected (individual hotels, budget motels, travel agencies, state tourist offices, and resort areas).

Traveler's Toll-Free Telephone Directory, with 10,000 airline, campground, honeymoon resort, and state-by-state hotel listings, is available from Landmark Publishing, Box 3287 R, Burlington, VT 05401, at $2.50.

ARTS

Information on accessible museums, exhibitions, and theaters is included in material available from ARTS, Box 2040, Grand Central Station, New York, NY 10017.

CHILDREN

General—When traveling with children, be sure to inquire if there are special children's fares or any family plans for which you qualify. Also study hotel room rates carefully. Some hotels charge the full rate for any child other than an infant. Others have a lower children's rate or allow children up to a certain age—usually twelve—to stay free in their parents' room. Ramada Inns has an eighteen-year-old cutoff and Hilton allows children of any age to stay free with their parents.

Active kids/inactive parents—If you are the disabled parent of able-bodied youngsters, consider vacationing at a resort hotel that is barrier-free and also offers supervised play programs for the children. Write to the hotel of your choice to see if it has this double feature. Also check with the local tourist board for information on children's activities. Are there day camps or tours for kids? For example, if you were staying at any of the fully accessible hotels on St. Thomas in the Virgin Islands (including Frenchman's Reef Holiday Inn, where supervised children's activities are seasonal, or the Pineapple Beach Resort or The Pavilions), you might arrange for Kidpower in Charlotte Amalie to fetch your child, take him to the beach or St. John island or elsewhere for a day (at $20) and return him to the hotel. (Kidpower, Box 3865, St. Thomas, VI 00801, 809-774-6159.)

When investigating kid stuff, compare prices. Some hotels offer gratis programs, others charge up to ten dollars or more a day. Supervised children's activities range from hula lessons at Mauna Kea in Hawaii to Spanish lessons at the Dorado Beach in Puerto Rico and golf, tennis, and target-shooting for older children at The Greenbrier in White Sulphur Springs, West Virginia. (Above hotels are accessible.) Dozens of other hotels offer similar programs. Also see Hawaii in the index.

Disabled kids/able parents—Any child who is responsive to his environment benefits just like anybody else from a vacation. If a child is physically up to it, he can make trips ranging from a visit to a zoo,

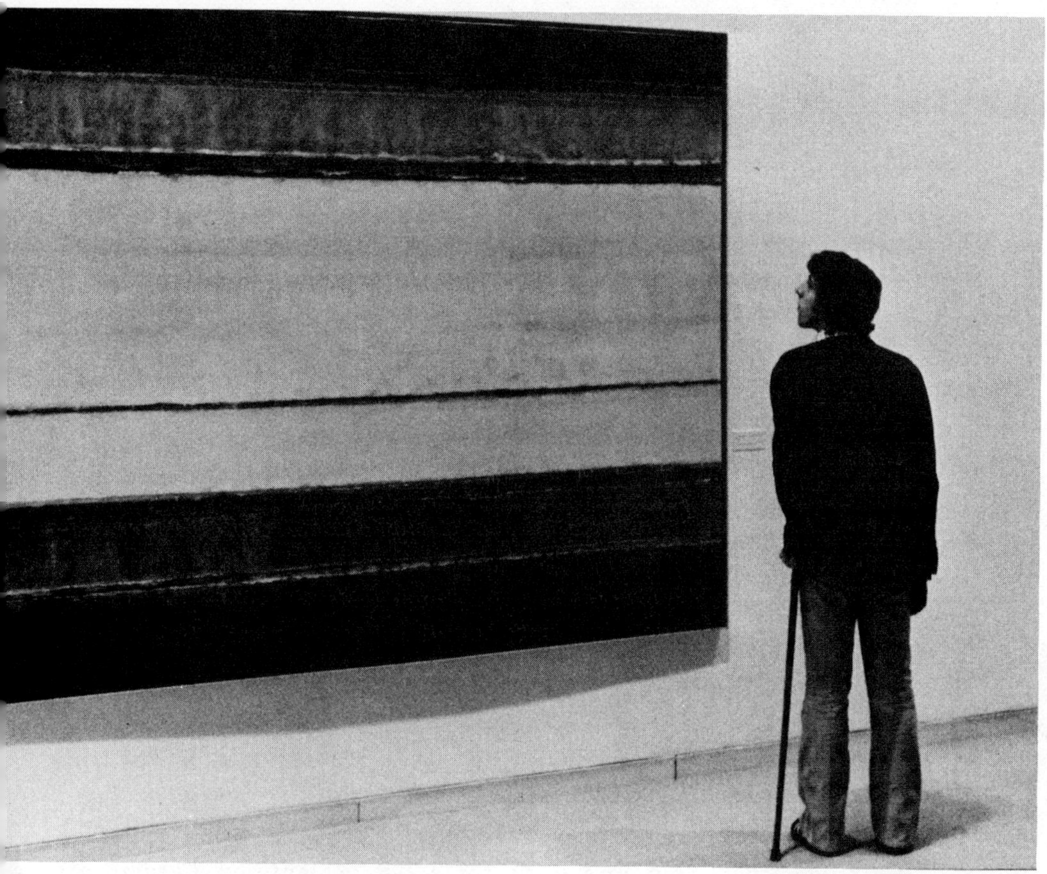

Courtesy *ARTS*

Many U.S. galleries are barrier-free

such as Good's Zoo at Oglebay Park in Wheeling, West Virginia, to a long car trip or a flight to Disney World, which after all was designed for children of all ages. Small fries who can be lifted by their parents overcome any barriers. For example, there is virtually nothing a kid could not see at Disney World, although a number of attractions are inaccessible to grown-ups confined to chairs.

According to one therapist at a children's hospital, parents tend to overprotect the disabled child. She would encourage you to take your children on vacation unless they are very severely disabled. One Alabama pediatrician who specializes in handicapped youngsters suggests that such severely disabled children be left at a respite center when the parents travel.

If you have misgivings about leaving your child with the baby-sitter secured by the hotel where you are staying, you might call the local Easter Seal Society (ESS) or a foundation identified with your child's disability for recommended sitters. The ESS of Little Rock, Arkansas, itself offers baby-sitting with such children.

When traveling by various modes of transportation, the same procedures would apply to disabled children as to adults. For example, the child (unless a babe in arms) would be expected to have his or her seat belt fastened for airplane departures or landings.

The Boy Scouts of America has developed programs for handicapped boys, with special troops for the visually handicapped, mentally retarded, deaf, physically handicapped, or socially maladjusted. They learn the scout skills of camping, hiking, swimming, and cooking. Contact the Boy Scouts of America, North Brunswick, NJ 08902. A manual, *Scouting for the Physically Handicapped*, is available.

"Membership in Girl Scouting is open to *all* girls." This philosophy brings disabled girls into troops with nondisabled children whenever possible. The *Leader's Guide, Handicapped Girls and Girl Scouting*, catalog number 26-108, is available from National Equipment Service, Girl Scouts of the United States of America, 830 Third Avenue, New York, NY 10022.

Contact the Camp Fire Girls for a booklet entitled *Leaders of Handicapped Girls* for information on group leaders who wish to work with girls who have physical, emotional, or mental limitations. Code number D-94, one dollar from Camp Fire Girls, 450 Avenue of the Americas, New York, NY 10011.

INSURANCE

Trip cancellation insurance, with premiums from $2.50 to $4 per $100 coverage, insures you against loss should you have to interrupt a prearranged trip. For example, if you are traveling on a low airfare with the condition that you stay no fewer than fourteen days but no more than twenty-one days and you become ill after one week and must return home, you will have to augment your ticket to the full one-way fare. If you have trip insurance, the difference in fare will be covered. If you are traveling with a charter group on one of the nonscheduled charter airlines, you stand to lose the entire

Disney World will delight children of all ages

fare if you are unable to fly home with your group. Hotels, package tours, ships, and often trains and other prearranged services may be covered. In order to collect you must have medical proof (get a doctor's letter on the spot) that you or a family member with whom you are traveling is too ill to continue the trip. This would hold true if the trip were called off for the same reasons. Insurance covers you should you be required to alter your trip due to the critical illness or death of an immediate family member in North America. You can buy insurance from an insurance agent, but most travel agents sell it and can answer your questions. Be sure to ask what the ceiling to the coverage is, and if it covers an illness related to an existing condition. As with any insurance policy, there is a lot of fine print and the policies do vary. The four principal companies with trip cancellation insurance are Continental Casualty, National Union Fire Insurance Company of Pittsburgh, Omaha Indemnity (Mutual of Omaha), and Travelers.

Available travel insurance policies, such as those offered by the above companies, may also include accident and/or sickness insurance. A typical policy might offer $1,000 to $5,000 accident medical expenses and daily sickness hospital indemnity at $30 a day for rates ranging from $2.95 to $11.10 for one week (lower rates for shorter periods). Residents of New York are not eligible for the travel accident insurance.

No one ever expects to curtail a trip for unfortunate reasons, but it can and does happen. Trip cancellation insurance is a great investment. Also see discussion of insurance in the transcript under Why Plan a Trip?

Emergency Evacuation Service—International SOS Assistance, an organization with medical assistance worldwide, includes among its services to members providing the most effective transportation (be it surface ambulance, stretcher on a commercial airliner, or air ambulance) to the nearest adequate hospital, and if advisable after the patient's condition has stabilized, transportation to a hospital nearer home. All inclusive. You must have your accident or illness while traveling at least 100 miles from home to benefit. Sample membership rate structure: $22 a month or $1 a day with a ten-day minimum.

SOS keeps vital medical information on members on file for emergency use.

International SOS Assistance is at 1420 Walnut St., Philadelphia, PA 19102, 215-732-9091.

Note that a basic health insurance policy such as that of Blue Cross and Blue Shield probably will not pay for an air ambulance or stretcher. Medicare probably will pay for such transportation only to the nearest hospital.

Also see the discussions of health insurance under Medical Questions and Answers and air ambulances and stretchers under Airlines.

MISCELLANEOUS TIPS

• Always look up friends of friends in new places. If possible, have your friends write them in advance, or give you a letter of introduction. Also have names of other persons—perhaps a name of someone at the United Cerebral Palsy Association or Easter Seal Society or other association–to call upon in an emergency.

• Don't hesitate to ask strangers if they know where there's an accessible restroom, to give you a hand with your chair, or to help you cross a busy street. Strangers are usually glad to help out, although you might wish to size up the person you ask, i.e., don't stop the little guy rushing along with the brief case who looks like he's late for an appointment, but do stop the husky college student who is walking slowly.

• Keep snack food with you. Fruit, cheese, and crackers, energy bars from the health food store, packets of instant soup. A hotel or motel may not have a restaurant and you might prefer to eat in.

• Buy stamps at your local post office for the post cards you will mail on vacation in the United States (including the U.S. Virgin Islands and Puerto Rico). Take addressed gummed labels for the cards.

• Get a secondhand secretary's posture chair to substitute for your wheelchair at times. The man who offers this suggestion says that the seat screws all the way down and the backrest can be removed and strapped to the seat, so that it goes through as regular airline baggage.

The chair enables him to enter the bathroom of motels with narrow doors, and even scoot about inside his small camper. He notes that small "inaccessible" rooms are often less expensive.

• When buying seats for theater, festival, or arena events, ask if you will be seated in standing room, thus qualifying for a lower rate in some instances.

• Take little packets of paper liners for toilet seats in your pocket or handbag. They are made by Celebrity and cost about two dollars for a twelve-pack with twenty liners per pack. Sold at many department store notions counters, including Sears and J C Penney stores. If you have difficulty in locating them inquire from B. Altman & Company, Mail Order Department, 316 Fifth Ave., New York, NY 10016.

• *Traveler's Checklist* is an illustrated folder of mail-order items ranging from a therma-pack cordless heating pad and a neat makeup or shaving extension mirror to lightweight suitcases. *Traveler's Checklist* is at Cornwall Bridge Rd., Sharon, CT 06069, 203-364-0144.

• A tripod chair of lightweight aluminum folds to resemble a walking cane and opens to let you sit when there's a wait or you are tired. $12.95 (plus $1.10 shipping and handling) from Hammacher Schlemmer, 147 E. 57th St., New York, NY 10022, 212-937-8181 or 914-946-7725.

• Keep a log of your trip for future reference. Note such details as the type of aircraft, your seat number and location and whether it was convenient (you may request it on future flights), car routes if driving, and mark your map for accessible reststops and hotel discoveries. Also keep track of actual trip costs. This enables you to estimate the budgets for future trips.

MONEY MATTERS

Credit cards—Even if you operate on a pay-as-you-go basis, a credit card is almost indispensable to today's traveler.

A credit card verifies your credit rating with travel suppliers. A hotel, for example, may require a cash customer to pay his bill in advance. Car rental companies probably will not turn a car over to a non-card carrying traveler until they run their own credit check on him, which could take days. (See discussion under Rental Cars.)

In some cases, information on the holder is stored with a computer memory bank, obviating his need to spell out any special requirements every time he calls to reserve. This holds true with certain car rental operations and airlines. (See index.)

Do not assume that a card will be accepted everywhere. Always check in advance. Some restaurants and hotels—especially small hotels and budget motels—may not accept them.

Dozens of cards are issued, including those of hotels, airlines, car rental companies, and gasoline and oil companies. But when an ad for a travel product refers to "major credit cards," it probably refers to the bank cards or to the "travel and entertainment" ("t-and-e") cards of American Express, Diners Club, and Carte Blanche. You pay a twenty-dollar annual membership fee for these t-and-e cards, which have built-in travel accident and/or life insurance policies of up to $30,000. The major bank cards, MasterCharge and especially Visa, are also becoming more widely accepted by hotels and restaurants, and while you do pay interest on accounts not paid within fifteen days, these cards may be sufficient for someone who travels or entertains too infrequently to warrant a twenty-dollar yearly t-and-e card fee.

If you are deciding among the three t-and-e cards, compare their membership advantages. Booklets on them are available from American Express Card Division, American Express Plaza, New York, NY 10004, 212-480-2000, and Diners Club, 10 Columbus Circle, New York, NY 10019. You can call Carte Blanche headquarters in Los Angeles to discuss services—they have no booklets—at 213-480-3210.

Examples of membership benefits you will find are machines at major airports that produce traveler's checks when the American Express card is introduced, and a payment plan with a number of hospitals who will accept the American Express card in payment for treatment.

If you plan to charge your airline ticket, you might consider using a t-and-e card that offers an automatic insurance benefit. You could still use your airline credit card number initially when booking the flight.

Some establishments, especially shops, grant cash customers a slight discount. Inquire.

Traveler's checks—The major ones—American Express, First National City, Thomas Cook, and Barclay's Bank—are accepted almost everywhere. You can cash them easily and can recoup your loss in most cases if they are lost or stolen. A service charge of fifty cents to a dollar per $100 may be charged. Barclay's Bank checks carry no service charge, and certain savings and loan banks or other banks where you have a specified type of account may charge no fee. You do have to go in person to the bank, travel agency, or airport booth and personally sign each check you buy. Likewise you must sign in person to cash them.

Tip—Always buy some checks in small denominations—tens and twenties. There are many times when you may wish to make a small transaction. (Small denominations are especially useful when traveling in foreign countries where you may not wish to have a lot of "change" in the local currency.)

Cash—Carrying a large amount of cash is not generally advisable. If you should, keep it on your person or in a handbag that is always in hand, or in a hotel's vault. There is probably no insurance covering theft from a vault, however, unless the hotel is found negligent, in which case the coverage might be in the vicinity of $500, depending on the hotel. Even so, valuables might well be left in the vault.

Do not plan to cash personal checks in strange places unless you have prearranged it through your home bank or know that your credit card will serve as security. For example, American Express will cash a card holder's personal checks for up to $500 (giving you $50 in cash and $450 in traveler's checks) at AmExCo branches worldwide.

Tip—Get a stack of dollar bills at the bank (new money is nice) to simplify tipping, taxi fares, and the like when you travel.

PACKING

Wardrobe—At least two weeks before your trip decide what clothes to take, allowing time to try on what you have and do any necessary repairs, alterations, laundry, or dry cleaning. This also allows you to shop. Bear in mind that clothes bought for one particular occasion are often a bad investment, so choose things you will subsequently wear at home.

The keys to your wardrobe are (1) the weather and (2) your itinerary. If you are going to stay at one Caribbean resort, for example, a wardrobe similar to that described elsewhere for Hawaii is fine. While evening dress is informal for gentlemen at most Caribbean resorts now, double-check with your vacation resort on that point.

For a progressive journey, such as a group tour by motorcoach, match wardrobe to itinerary and pack systematically. For a fall tour of New England with a number of one-night stands, one knowledgeable couple packed everything they expected to wear on a particular day in plastic bags, and that included everything from the skin out. (Zipper sweater bags, available at five-and-tens, are useful in packing.)

For a day of museum-going in Boston, the couple packed tailored shirts and blazers, while they had organized tweed slacks and sweaters to wear for a day's drive to look at the autumn foliage. Since a day of sightseeing often runs behind schedule, they also dressed in the morning with a view toward dinner. The gentleman does not trust an itinerary that reads, "Arrive hotel at 5 P.M., dinner at 7," and even so, he says, it is often six o'clock before your suitcases are delivered. He lacks good muscle coordination and dresses slowly. Thus in the morning he would put on the trousers he intended to wear to dinner. In the evening he would freshen up and change his shirt, tie, and jacket for dinner.

Another suggestion for days on the road: Pack most of your wardrobe in a master suitcase and whenever you land for several days at one hotel, pack what you will need for the next few days in a smaller bag. Collapsible canvas bags that lie flat in your suitcase are great for that purpose.

While you want to be covered for every eventuality, climate, and occasion, you do not need to be laden down. Once you have decided what to take, try to weed it out by one-third. Eliminate extra items of the same genre. If your trip is lengthy or if you have special laundry requirements you might look for a hotel with a self-service laundry. Hotel laundry service often takes several days and can be expensive.

Be sure to pack anything special that you need. Examples are a reacher (available at hardware or medical/surgical supply companies), bent straws, plastic drinking cups, a plastic "pottie" or urinal or whatever for emergency use.

What not to pack—Carry the following in your handbag or hand luggage: any medication you depend upon; essentials to last twenty-four hours (in case your bags arrive late); your airline, train, or bus tickets and hotel vouchers (and passport if going abroad); wheelchair narrowing device.

Some packing suggestions—Entire books have been written on this subject. Here are a few suggestions:

- Turn untailored clothes inside out to fold. Creases less apparent.
- Use toothpaste to polish metal jewelry (but not gems).
- Dermassage body lotion doubles as a cream for fine leather.
- Rubber gloves will protect your manicure if you plan to do hand laundry. Pack cold-water soap.
- Leave home dressed for your destination if you are flying. In mid-January wear summer clothes plus warm tights or thermal underwear, a cardigan, and a lightweight raincoat if traveling from a cold to a hot climate. On the plane, peel off the warm layers if practical and stick them in your flight bag. The system works in reverse. If you are especially sensitive to extreme cold, disregard this suggestion.
- Women who are comfortable in pantsuits or trousers often find them preferable to skirts for traveling when their chairs or themselves are handled a great deal.

Luggage—If you carry your own bags, consider the popular lightweight canvas bags. Consider suitcases with wheels or buy caddy attachments available at most luggage or department stores.

When choosing luggage for a trip, keep in mind the allotments of the various carriers, discussed under Airlines, Part II, Section 4.

If you are packing in two bags, take one flat bag for clothes and one large satchel for shoes, shaving kit, hair dryer, and other bulky items.

How not to lose your luggage—You may have heard that old traveler's adage, a fool and his *luggage* are soon parted, but it is possible to reduce the risk of loss. For instance:

- Personalize your cases with bright hotel stickers, stripes of tape, or other original marks. A great deal of elephant gray, blue, and red fiberglass luggage appears on an airport carousel after any given flight, and personal marking prevents someone with look-alike bags grabbing yours by mistake.
- Put your name (and/or address) on the outside. Also put both your name *and* address on the inside.
- Lock your bags.
- Remove the tags from previous trips.
- Watch your bag being tagged when you check in. If you are traveling by air and do not recognize the airport code, ask. JFK, PHL, and BOS are easy enough, but ORD? That's Chicago O'Hare. Keep your baggage claim stub.

Check the index for wardrobe and baggage as they relate to airlines, trains, destination, and the like.

PHOTOGRAPHY

These notes for novice photographers are from Todd Weinstein, who photographed the picture stories in this book.

If you are buying a camera, go to a large camera store that offers many models. Pick them up. How do they feel? Look for one that is easy to load and easy to handle. Examples of this are the Polaroid SX-70 series and the Instant Kodak, as well as the Instamatics. Any camera that takes film cartridges, of course, will be easier to load than those which must be threaded.

Decide how much film you will need for the trip. Buy twice that amount. Film is probably cheaper and better stored in a hometown camera store than at a resort. If you need to buy film at a tourist haunt, look for a regular camera supply place (not a souvenir shop). In hot, damp climates it is particularly important that film be kept cool and dry during prolonged storage.

Professional photographers generally do not allow their film to be X-rayed by the airport security system, although security officials maintain that such X-raying will not affect the film. Rather than take chances, you might have your film bag hand-checked like the professionals do.

For best color results, use Kodak film and request Kodak processing.

If you have problem vision or trouble handling a camera, but you can switch a tape recorder on and off, consider recording your trip in sound rather than picture. Possibilities are endless: the traffic sounds of a big city, regional accents of the people, music at a folk evening, even the remarks made by your tour guide.

REFERENCES

American Foundation for the Blind—Travel Concessions for Blind Persons details discount fares available to blind persons and their travelmates under certain circumstances, on buses, trains, and some steamships. American Foundation for the Blind, 15 W. 16th St., New York, NY 10011.

American Alliance for Health—A bibliography of recent publications entitled *Travel and Tourism Opportunities for Impaired, Disabled and Handicapped Individuals* is available from IRUC/American Alliance for Health, Physical Education, and Recreation, 1201 6th St., N.W., Washington, DC 20036.

Accent on Information—A computerized information system retrieves recent articles published in *Accent* (a quarterly magazine for disabled persons, at $3.50 a year), on a number of subjects including travel, automobile travel, and public transportation. There is a $6 charge for the computer search for the twenty-five most recent citations, and photocopies of the articles are available at twenty-five cents each. Accent's *Buyer's Guide*, a classified directory that includes recreation and travel products and services, is an annual at $10. Accent is at P.O. Box 700, Bloomington, IL 61701.

Moss Rehabilitation Hospital—The Travel Information Center at Moss answers trip planning questions of a medical or tourism nature, often providing very general tourism information, which Moss suggests taking to a travel agent who can put your trip together. Travel Information Center, Moss Rehabilitation Hospital, 12th St. and Tabor Rd., Philadelphia, PA 19141, 215-329-5715.

SATH—Society for the Advancement of Travel for the Handicapped can provide general information, such as a bibliography, to consumers, as well as a list of member travel agents nationwide. This organization works primarily on a travel industry level. SATH, 26 Court St., Brooklyn, NY 11242, 212-858-5483.

RIGHTS

If in a travel situation you believe you have been discriminated against or humiliated, or have suffered a violation of your human rights because you are disabled, you should determine what your rights are. (You might need to seek the advice of an attorney.)

You may (1) complain to an administrative agency, such as a state civil rights commission or other agency or department of state, city, county, or federal government that is empowered to protect the rights of individuals. Or (2) depending on the circumstances of the situation, you may initiate a lawsuit. Or both.

Routine complaints—If you have the bothersome problems that every traveler encounters sooner or later (the airline loses your luggage and doesn't make good or a package tour does not live up to the contract, and the like), you may ask your travel agent to look into it, report it to your city or state consumer protection agency, or go to the government regulatory agency in the case of transportation companies. For example, if your complaint is against an airline, you should first try to negotiate with the carrier. If this is not satisfactory, you may then go to the Civil Aeronautics Board, which can go to the carrier. The CAB cannot adjudicate claims, but often it can get the carrier to take a second look at the problem. If your grievance results from a matter of aviation safety (and that would include the security check on the ground), you should contact the Federal Aviation Administration, Community and Consumer Liaison Division, Public Affairs, Department of Transportation, Washington, DC

20591. The Civil Aeronautics Board Office of the Consumer Advocate is at 1825 Connecticut Ave., N.W., Washington, DC 20428.

Architectural barriers—If you come upon any post-1968 buildings financed with federal funds that are not barrier-free to persons with disabilities, you should report them to the Executive Director, Architectural and Transportation Barriers Compliance Board, Washington, DC 20201. A folder entitled *Access America: The Architectural Barriers Act and You*, available from the above address, outlines the complaint process and enforcement rules.

SENIOR CITIZENS

Discounts—Always ask if you qualify for a senior citizen discount. A number of attractions, hotels (including Sheraton), and the like offer them, as well as some airlines.

The Golden Age Passport available free from the U.S. National Park Service entitles U.S. citizens or permanent residents who are sixty-two or older to a 50 percent discount for federally administered sites or services, such as camping in a national park. The Passport is available at ranger stations of the national park or forest services throughout the country, and you must apply in person.

Gomer's Guides (from the Atlantic to the Mississippi) lists hotels that offer senior citizens discounts. Also discount coupons for attractions. In large type. Available at $3.95 from *Gomer's Guides*, Box 310, Maplewood, NJ 07040.

Now It's Your Turn to Travel, by Rosalind Massow (Macmillan Publishing Company, 1976; $4.95 at bookstores), was written expressly for "mature people" and includes helpful information as well as notes on thirty-five countries.

Organizations—Of the associations of older persons whose programs include tours, one of the largest is the American Association of Retired Persons (AARP). Members must be fifty-five or older. The AARP Travel Service (555 Madison Ave., New York, NY 10022) offers slow-paced vacations in the United States and abroad. The tours are not designed for the nonambulatory, but hotels are selected with few steps and low bathtubs, motorcoaches have low steps, and a number of holidays are called "extended vacations," with never a change of hotel. AARP offers domestic and foreign itineraries.

Assistance—Even though you normally get around pretty well on your own two feet, don't hesitate to ask for a wheelchair or other services to help diminish those hopelessly long corridors at the airport, train station, or wherever. The airlines, Amtrak, and theme parks have chairs for just that purpose.

TAXIS

You may have to rely on taxis for local transportation once you get to your destination. As a prospective passenger you may be vulnerable: you cannot easily dash into the street to hail an oncoming cab, or the driver may not spot you easily due to your seated position if you are in a chair. Your best bet is to telephone for a radio cab and have it come to you. Some companies have become known as being particularly responsive to disabled passengers. In New York, for example, Ding-a-Ling, which operates both radio cabs and ambulettes, has such a reputation. See the state listings in this book, or ask locally.

To hold a New York City taxi franchise, a company may not discriminate among passengers (the only grounds for refusing a fare are disorderly conduct or that the driver is returning to the garage). Other cities' franchises may have similar stipulations. Drivers, however, often tend to avoid problem situations, and a driver who has never assisted a wheelchair traveler may not realize that the chair probably folds and slips into the trunk. Some companies do not have insurance that would cover the passenger or driver if either were injured in transferring a nonambulatory traveler into the cab. If a driver refuses you on the grounds that you are handicapped, you may take his license number and report him to the city agency that regulates taxicabs.

WEATHER

One good thing about the United States: it is always in season. Somewhere you will always find sunshine and somewhere you will always find snow (skiing at Mammoth, California, runs until June or July, and the glaciers of Alaska are eternal).

The local tourist office may exaggerate about its 100-percent perfect weather, so read weather charts in an atlas or newspaper. (*The New York Times*, for example, prints the weather from representative cities worldwide as a daily fixture.) Try to get the monthly average daily high and the average daily low. "Average" temperature is not an accurate indication. For example, deserts are hot by day and cold by night and a desert "average" might be a balmy 75° F (24° C), instead of the blistering 115° F and chilling 45° it is in reality. Also check for days with rain or snow, or inches of rainfall.

WHEELCHAIRS

For travel in general:

• Have the brakes, spokes, and tires checked before departure, and if you are headed for a remote place, take spare parts, such as extra spokes.

• Never travel without a wheelchair narrowing device. This one tool can enable you to gain as much as four precious inches that could mean entering or not entering a narrow passageway. Stalls in public restrooms, unless modified, are rarely as wide as twenty-four inches, for example. Keep the narrower with you at all times when you travel. Don't leave it back at the hotel when you take off for a day of sightseeing. Narrowers can be ordered through your wheelchair dealer. The Everest & Jennings (E&J) narrower is called "Reduce-A-Width" and is available from E&J, 1803 Pontius Ave., Los Angeles, CA 90025. Note: A man's belt or strong string can sometimes be used to narrow a chair. Other useful accessories are a baggage rack, also available from E&J, and a saddle bag, which you might improvise from a canvas or leather carryall or small satchel.

Average High and Low Temperatures for Various Cities, in degrees Fahrenheit

CITY	Jan.	Feb.	Mar.	Apr.	May	June	July	Aug.	Sept.	Oct.	Nov.	Dec.
United States												
Atlanta	52/37	53/38	60/42	70/50	79/59	86/67	87/70	87/69	81/64	72/53	61/42	52/37
Boston	37/22	37/22	45/30	55/39	66/49	76/58	80/64	79/64	73/56	63/47	52/37	40/26
Chicago	33/19	35/21	43/29	57/40	69/51	79/61	84/67	82/66	75/57	63/47	47/33	36/11
Denver	42/16	45/19	51/25	61/34	69/43	81/52	87/58	85/57	77/48	66/37	53/26	45/18
Honolulu	77/67	77/67	77/68	78/69	80/71	81/72	82/74	83/74	83/74	82/73	80/71	78/69
Kansas City	39/21	44/25	54/34	66/46	75/56	85/66	91/71	89/69	81/60	70/49	54/35	43/25
Las Vegas	55/33	62/39	69/44	79/53	88/60	99/68	105/76	103/74	96/65	82/53	67/41	58/36
Los Angeles	65/45	66/47	69/49	71/52	74/55	77/58	83/62	84/62	82/60	77/56	73/51	67/48
New Orleans	64/48	67/50	71/55	78/62	84/66	89/77	90/76	91/76	87/73	80/65	70/55	65/50
New York	40/26	40/25	49/33	58/42	69/53	78/62	82/67	80/66	75/60	65/50	53/40	42/29
Memphis	51/32	54/34	61/41	72/51	80/60	88/68	91/72	91/70	86/62	76/51	62/39	53/33
Miami	78/59	79/58	81/61	85/65	87/69	90/73	91/74	91/75	90/74	86/70	81/64	79/60
Minneapolis	22/2	26/5	37/18	58/33	69/45	78/55	84/61	81/59	72/48	61/37	40/22	27/9
Philadelphia	42/28	42/28	52/35	62/44	73/55	81/64	85/69	83/67	77/61	67/50	55/41	44/31
Reno	45/16	50/21	57/26	65/30	71/36	80/40	89/46	88/43	81/36	69/29	56/21	47/16
San Francisco	55/45	59/47	61/49	62/49	63/51	65/53	64/53	65/54	68/55	68/54	64/51	57/47
San Diego	64/46	65/48	67/50	68/53	70/57	72/60	76/63	77/64	76/62	73/57	71/51	66/47
Seattle	44/33	47/34	51/36	58/40	66/45	70/50	76/54	75/54	69/50	60/44	50/38	46/36
Toronto	30/18	31/19	39/27	53/38	64/47	76/57	80/62	79/61	71/54	60/45	46/35	34/23
Washington, D.C.	44/29	45/29	55/36	65/44	75/55	83/64	86/68	84/67	78/61	67/49	56/39	45/31
International												
Acapulco	85/70	87/70	87/70	87/71	89/74	89/76	89/75	89/75	88/75	88/74	88/72	87/70
Bahamas	76/67	77/67	78/68	80/69	83/72	86/75	88/76	88/76	87/76	85/75	80/71	78/69
Bermuda	68/58	68/57	68/57	71/59	76/64	81/69	85/73	86/74	84/72	79/69	74/63	70/60
Jamaica	86/67	86/76	86/68	87/70	87/72	89/74	90/73	90/73	89/73	88/73	87/71	87/69
Mexico City	66/42	69/43	75/47	77/51	78/54	76/55	73/53	73/54	74/53	70/50	68/46	66/43
Puerto Rico	80/70	80/70	81/71	82/72	84/74	84/75	84/76	85/75	86/75	85/75	83/74	81/72

Courtesy: United Airlines

• Mark your chair with your name. This can be done with tape. You might also include your address, although some people do not like to advertise that they are away from home.

• If traveling by car, or if otherwise feasible, carry two strips of wood two by four by thirty inches to ramp a slight incline.

Wheelchair block?—If you do not own a wheelchair and do not always need one, do not hesitate to request those offered by transportation companies or theme parks. They may be available in unexpected places. Many shopping malls now have them, courtesy of the Easter Seal Society. Note under the state listings in Part III, Section 3, and the various accessibility guides that you can order that many attractions are now equipped with house wheelchairs.

Perfect present—A wheelchair might be the perfect present for someone with limited mobility, Virginia Marshall writes in *Wheelchair Sightseeing in Missouri*. "Happiness can be a wheelchair," she says and notes that it need not be new, shiny, or beautiful but can be secondhand or borrowed or rented from pharmacies or firms listed in the Yellow Pages, with five dollars a week the current average rental rate in Missouri (probably more in large East and West Coast cities). "Gramps or Auntie may not be bedridden . . . but there's the chronically bad back, the stiff knees, the arthritic hip. . . . For them, a wheelchair could . . . open a whole new world of places to go, things to do and see and enjoy." If you could benefit by a chair why not come right out and say so the next time someone asks if there is a present you would like? Or if someone in your family could use it, you could all chip in and buy one.

"Call Auntie's wheelchair her Happy Chair, since using it will make it possible for her to see such happy spectacles as Fall foliage, Spring redbud and dogwood, antiques shops and craft displays. Call her chair her Glee Wheels, her Sunshine Express or her Jolly Rover."

Booklet—Tips for how the ablebodied can best assist someone in a wheelchair, as well as developments in the field of wheelchair travel, are included in the booklet *Assisting the Wheelchair Traveler*. It is being revised by the George Washington University Medical Center, Division of Rehabilitation Medicine, Suite 714, 2300 Eye St., N.W., Washington, DC 20037. Upon request, they will send you ordering information as soon as it is available.

Check the index for wheelchair references related to specific modes of travel and the like.

Any rates or prices quoted above are subject to change.

2

MEDICAL QUESTIONS AND ANSWERS

These are actual questions that have been asked by prospective travelers who are disabled. The answers and opening remarks are by Dr. Arthur S. Abramson.

To travel in good health, you must take several things into account: proper sleep and rest, motion, cleanliness, and food and drink.

People who are disabled, even at their peak of fitness, tend to have somewhat lower energy reserves because the disability has taken something away from them. Therefore, it is the better part of wisdom not to act as if you were an ablebodied athlete. When you are traveling you are usually more active than you are at home during the day. New sights and sounds are stimulating if you keep moving, but you will enjoy them much better if you take a break during the day. When traveling, you require more rest. In the heat of the day it is almost international practice to take a little siesta, and of course you should get a normal night's sleep. Also try to rest for at least one hour lying down before dinner. From personal experience I know that dinner cannot be enjoyable if you are totally exhausted. And dinner is one of the times you should enjoy when you are traveling. After all, one of the reasons why people travel is to experience new food. Be prepared to enjoy it.

Another consideration is movement. If you are traveling by car, there is no reason to sit folded up for eight hours at a time, seeing all the sights through the car window. You need to stretch, to get out of that folded position. And if you can do no more than get into a wheelchair, even that is a change. It is important to get out and get fresh air.

In hot climates a nice cold, bracing shower in the morning provides a real stimulus to getting up. Make time for a shower in the evening, as well, to provide the kind of muscular relaxation needed for good sleep.

When you are traveling in the United States, you will have to assume, generally correctly, that foods will be similar, the standards of hygiene uniform, and the tap water, by and large, pure. But these are factors that you would have to take into account if traveling outside this country, especially in Asia, Africa, and certain other parts of the world. In order to be absolutely certain that you are not taking any unnecessary chances in those circumstances, there are things you can do. For example, do not drink tap water. If you do require water, especially if you have a condition that requires you to force fluids, you will be safe to drink sealed soda water bottled by a reputable firm, usually under franchise, such as Coca-Cola. That franchise requires the use of pure water, and Coca-Cola beverages are available everywhere in the world. Do be sure that it is the genuine article, however, and not, for example, Coca-Cola bottles refilled with some mysterious local liquid. Of course, boiled water is acceptable, but you don't always know if water advertised as "boiled" is indeed boiled.

In terms of foods, avoid milk products, including ice cream, iced drinks (because the ice may be made with impure water), and uncooked leafy vegetables or those grown in the ground: rather, eat cooked vegetables and hot foods. Stay away from custards, mayonnaise, and all other foods that form excellent culture media for bacteria. This latter rule also applies to the United States, especially in the offbeat restaurants during the summer. For dessert, eat fruit that you can peel yourself.

Those are good rules-of-thumb as far as food and water are concerned. I have traveled all over the world, and I have followed those rules and have never had any Delhi Belly, Montezuma's Revenge, or Turkish Delight.

Anyone with a special medical consideration, such as diabetes, medication allergy, contact lenses, and the like, to whom a crisis could occur, should register with the Medic Alert Foundation International. Members wear a wristlet identifying their condition and bearing the phone number of Medic Alert, where emergency treatment information is registered. The Medic Alert emblem is recognized worldwide and there are branches of the foundation in fifteen countries. Medic Alert is at P.O. Box 1009, Turlock, CA 95380, 209-632-2371. Registration is ten dollars for lifetime membership.

Answers to the questions below are generalized and may not apply in all cases. It is therefore recommended that you discuss your own requirements with your physician.

GENERAL

Will my health insurance be honored away from home?

Certain policies, including Blue Cross and Blue Shield, and Aetna—as well as Medicare—are honored anywhere in the United States, Puerto Rico, the U.S. Virgin Islands, American Samoa, Guam, Canada if you are en route to/from Alaska, or any foreign country if the nearest hospital to your U.S. location happens to be there.

Outside the United States, the traveler must pay his medical bills and can present them for possible reimbursement to Blue Cross and Blue Shield or Aetna when he has the receipted bills showing the name of the patient, when the services were rendered, what services were rendered and for what condition, and an itemization of charges.

Medicaid is administered on a state-by-state basis and usually covers only local medical services. Check with your local office to see if its coverage is more extensive.

See the discussion of credit cards under General Information, Part IV, Section 1. Note that American Express credit cards are now being accepted as payment for treatment at some hospitals.

Suppose I lose medicine or run out?

Carry with you about one-third more than you or your doctor estimates you will need for a trip of reasonable duration. (If traveling outside the United States, keep in mind that since narcotics and dangerous drugs are prohibited entry by U.S. law, even your own medicines containing them which are *reentering* the country are subject to this law. Such medicines might be diuretics, heart drugs, tranquilizers, sleeping pills, depressants, stimulants, and cough medicines, among others. Therefore, you should have all drugs, medicinals and the like properly identified; carry only the amount that might be carried normally by someone with a health problem; and carry a statement from your physician that the medicines are being used under a doctor's prescription and are necessary to your well-being. These suggestions and other Customs hints for U.S. residents reentering the country are spelled out in a booklet *Know Before You Go*, available from the Department of the Treasury, U.S. Customs Service, Washington, DC 20229.

As a guard against loss, always keep at least half of your medicine with you (in your pocketbook, flight bag, pocket, or wherever). You may wish to pack half in your suitcase. An exception might be insulin, which you would not want to risk getting into an unpressurized hold of an airplane, where it might freeze. Modern aircraft have pressurized and temperature-controlled cargo holds. Carry corrective lens prescriptions also. Take a copy of prescriptions with you, in case you lose your medicine, or for practicality on extended trips. While a prescription written by a doctor in one state cannot be filled at a pharmacy in another, you can always have your prescription rewritten by a doctor in the state you are visiting.

How do I find a nurse or companion to accompany someone on a trip?

You might ask the airline, Amtrak, or other carrier if it can recommend someone. If the trip is by air, you could ask Air Medic (see the air ambulance section under Airlines in Part II) to provide a qualified attendant as well as other medical services and equipment. Or you can make direct arrangements with a nursing service. Examples of these are:

(1) Homemakers Upjohn (HU), which has more than 220 branches in the United States. HU can provide attendants ranging from RNs and LPNs to aides, companions, and homemakers. Aero-

nurses (often former Air Force nurses) are also available. All HU personnel have been screened and insured and are actual HU employees (as compared with nurse registries). They can accompany you on a trip and/or remain with you at your destination. There is local on-site supervision and twenty-four-hour backup. Rates are on an hourly, daily, or weekly basis. Check the telephone Yellow Pages or contact Homemakers Upjohn, Kalamazoo, MI 49001, 800-253-8600.

(2) Guardian Angels, an L.A.-based service that has ten registered nurses, trained in flight medicine with refresher courses in hypoxia, who are located nationwide. Some of the nurses are bilingual, all keep their passports up-to-date and will accompany travelers on any mode of transportation. This four-year-old service will coordinate travel details to provide the smoothest arrangements, but it is not a travel agency and cannot book your trip. You pay a professional fee for the time a nurse is with you, plus trip costs. Guardian Angels is at 21015 Victor St., Torrance, CA 90503, 213-541-1444.

I use oxygen twelve hours a day. How do I get it away from home?

Ask your local supplier. He may be able to arrange delivery at your destination, or give you the name of a supplier there. You can also check medical equipment rentals in the telephone Yellow Pages.

How soon can a post-stroke victim travel?

Every stroke victim is different. Most stroke victims are retrained in ambulation and self-care, and that in itself gives an individual a source from which he can gain this information: the staff at the rehabilitation center who work with him in such things as transfers, locomotion, and self-care. A stroke is a disability of the kind that leaves an individual with certain restricted capacities. If you know your capacities and they are sufficient for you to get around in your hometown—go to theaters and restaurants and do sightseeing—then they are sufficient to get around anywhere else. That is the best general rule. Start with some small trips—half-day or full-day trips—as tests before you start off on a long journey (although on cruise ships and airlines, you have many people around to help you). But if you are ambulatory, there is no problem getting to the bathroom, no problem getting on a plane, and the like. If you need a wheelchair, then you need assistance and should travel with a competent traveling companion. A competent traveling companion is someone who is used to you, who knows what you need and what you can do, and is not overprotective. These things you learn during your rehabilitation period from the rehab person who has been closest to you.

Is it safe for someone suffering from multiple sclerosis (MS) to travel?

Generally speaking, it is safe for someone with MS to travel. This is a condition with many possible manifestations, however. Some have a tendency to have "exacerbations," or periodic progressions of the disease. Since this is an unstable period, it is best to postpone travel until the episode, which may last for a varying period of weeks or months, has remitted. It is much safer to travel during remissions, which often last a long time. During such periods, one's continued ability to perform at a known level is more certain. If you must travel and the exacerbation is very slowly progressive in nature, the day-to-day change may be so minor that your level of performance will not change much over a period of a few weeks. This kind of judgment should be made in conjunction with a physician knowledgeable in the vagaries of multiple sclerosis.

If you are able to walk in a stable fashion, you can travel alone. If you can walk only with assistance or if you cannot walk but must use a wheelchair, a competent travel companion is strongly advisable. In either case, you may fatigue easily and therefore should rest frequently and for more than just a few minutes. Your own sense of fatigue should determine when rest is necessary. It is not that fatigue worsens the disease, but a tired individual is an unhappy individual incapable of enjoying the trip. Hot climates as well as hot baths tend to heighten the unwelcome manifestations of the condition and to increase fatigue. Therefore, several hours of bed rest should be taken at the end of a trip or excursion. Even though the trip may involve sitting for several hours, it is not the same as resting. Ablebodied individuals also suffer from travel fatigue. In addition, the spasticity which is a manifestation of multiple sclerosis results in an uncomfortable stiffness if there are sustained periods of sitting, whether in an airplane, train, bus, or automobile. An ablebodied individual may get up, stretch, and walk about from time to time, something which it may not be possible for the individual with multiple sclerosis to do.

Avoid hot weather. A person with multiple sclerosis should be perceptive enough to know at what time of the year he does best. Generally, the spring and autumn are best for traveling. Nevertheless, you should find out the temperature ranges of your destination and match them to the ranges of comfort at your home base. In addition, the status of the air-conditioning of the methods of transportation and of hotels should be ascertained beforehand. (You might ask the hotel where you plan to stay if the air conditioning is centrally controlled, or if you can adjust the temperature in your room.) There is nothing like being well prepared with a target temperature of 72° F (22° C), although temporary variations are permissible.

Since multiple sclerosis is often accompanied by disorders of elimination, the potential traveler should also see the questions and answers dealing with the care of bladder and bowel contained in this section.

Is it possible for a kidney patient requiring dialysis to travel?

This is a question that only your doctor can answer. It is worth noting, however, that by prearrangement low-sodium meals are available on many airlines, ship lines, and trains and in hotel dining rooms.

Two directories of hospitals with dialysis units that can be used in trip planning by traveling kidney patients are:

Dialysis World-Wide for the Traveling Patient, available from the National Association of Patients on Hemodialysis and Transplantation, 505 Northern Blvd., Great Neck, NY 11021, 516-482-2720. Listed are units at U.S. hospitals, including the Virgin Islands, as well as units at VA hospitals and hospitals abroad. One feature of the directory is a section of fifty-two phrases (e.g., "My Heparin dosage is ___ cc per hour/or for duration" or "I generally dialize at ___ mm positive/negative pressure") in French, German, Spanish, and Italian.

The List of Transient Dialysis Centers, published by the Seattle Artificial Kidney Supply Company, and available from the National Kidney Foundation, 116 E. 27th St., New York, NY 10016. Again, this list is nationwide and worldwide.

At least two travel agencies are experienced in arranging independent or group tours for persons requiring dialysis. They are Wings on Wheels, which has arranged itineraries around hospital dialysis schedules and for individuals who have their own machines and are accompanied by private nurses; and Varan Travels, a local, retail travel agency in New Jersey (see index for addresses).

Is it necessary to refrigerate insulin?

No, providing you do not keep it out in extremely hot weather for an extremely long time. Then, like anything else, it would deteriorate. It should keep a month or more without refrigeration.

It might be noted here that the Diabetes Travel Service (DTS) answers many specific travel questions that concern diabetics (such as food conversions when you visit foreign countries, or how to say "Sugar or orange juice" and other phrases in foreign languages). DTS also organizes tours and cruises for members and publishes a monthly newspaper of pertinent travel information and tips (e.g., "Don't wait until the last minute to order [hotel] room service. Allow 30–40 minutes for delivery, particularly during peak periods"). Individual membership is $15 a year, $50 for travel agents. DTS is at 349 E. 52nd St., New York, NY 10022, 212-751-1076. Available to members is a booklet, *Vacationing with Diabetes—Not from Diabetes* by Stanley Mirsky, M.D., F.A.C.P., assistant clinical professor of metabolic diseases at the Mount Sinai School of Medicine.

What if someone needs home nursing at his destination?

Do basically what you would do at home. Ask the doctor who is treating you for suggestions; look in the telephone Yellow Pages under "Nurses" for such companies as Homemakers Upjohn; call an association or foundation identified with your disability and ask for recommendations. Also note that some of the state information or the accessibility guides to various cities and states, described under the state listings in Part III, Section 3, include home nursing services.

What if my catheter becomes displaced while I am traveling?

Unless you are trained in self-catheterization or you are traveling with an attendant who knows what to do, see a doctor. Until you can get there, however, you can soil yourself. Men should take along several packets of external collecting devices that they can attach temporarily to the penis. A woman should have available diapers and waterproof panties for "padding up." Practice doing this before leaving on the trip.

What if my prosthetic device or wheelchair needs repairs?

There are prosthetics firms all over the country, or you might want to know how to make minor repairs beforehand. Take with you the small tools that you need, such as a screwdriver, a small hammer, Allen wrench, and some spare buckles to replace any that loosen and get lost. You can obtain them from the firm that supplied your device. In any emergency you might find that the mechanical department of a hotel could do some welding or brazing or find parts or do minor repairs. It's worth asking.

For a wheelchair, take along a spoke wrench and extra spokes. Wheelchair service firms are located nationwide, or ask the hotel mechanical department.

What happens if I need a doctor in a strange place?

If you foresee a need, get the names and phone numbers of doctors before the need arises. Ask your own doctor for names of specialists at your destination. Take your doctor's phone number along; you can always call him, although there is nothing like being prepared. Most hotels have house doctors, or you might call the local county medical society or ask an association or foundation associated with your disability for referrals.

If you will be traveling outside the United States, you can join the International Association for Medical Assistance to Travellers (IAMAT), which supplies a directory of English-speaking doctors in 450 cities in 120 countries, including the Caribbean islands and Mexico, who provide twenty-four-hour service at nominal fees (example: $20 for a house or hotel call or $25 for night, weekend, and holiday calls). IAMAT is at 350 Fifth Ave., Suite 5620, New York, NY 10001. IAMAT membership is free, but a donation is requested.

A similar referral service, INTERMEDIC, offers a directory of physicians in more than 170 foreign cities (in eighty-nine countries) that are most often visited by American travelers. Membership is $6 a year ($10 for a family) from INTERMEDIC, 777 Third Ave., New York, NY 10017, 212-486-8974.

A reference that might be used in conjunction with a directory, such as IAMAT's (to assure a nominal fee), is *Traveler's Guide to U.S. Certified Doctors Abroad* by Marquis Who's Who (London, 1976,

George Prior Associates), compiled with the cooperation of the American Board of Medical Specialties. Physicians are listed according to their specialty—from allergists and rehabilitation specialists to urologists—and country. A vita tells where each doctor studied and trained.

If prone to illness, have your doctor make up a medical history to carry with you. Also see the discussion of Medic Alert in the introduction to this Question and Answer section.

Note that IAMAT can also provide an immunization chart for persons planning foreign travel. For the most current immunization information check with your local, state, or U.S. department of health, as well as with a government office of the country or countries you will be visiting. Or ask your travel agent.

Can I travel with a thirty-pound respirator?

Probably. If you will be flying, check with the airline, which may be able to set up a respirator to use during the flight. You cannot use your own.

If traveling by car, you can plug it into the cigarette lighter if you have an attachment and save your batteries.

If traveling by ship, ask the ship line what its voltage is and whether or not you can use "electrical appliances" in your stateroom.

SHIP

What if I become ill on a cruise?

Go to the hospital. Aside from freighters carrying no more than twelve passengers, the passenger ships all have doctors and hospitals that range from standard to the impressive facilities aboard *QE2*. The patient will have to pay on board for any medical services received. Health insurance such as Blue Cross is usually not accepted as payment for medical expenses incurred aboard ship. They must be paid by the individual. One may be reimbursed for such expenses by his health insurance company. See the question on health insurance in this section.

Is seasickness cause for concern?

Probably not. Modern cruise ships have stabilizers that prevent extreme tossing. And ship doctors now give an effective injection, such as promethazine hydrochloride, at the onset of seasickness, which seems to "cure" it and lasts for the duration of the voyage.

TRAIN

Because of a heart condition, my doctor has advised me not to fly. Would it be safe to make a cross-country trip by train?

Yes, if your doctor says so. Have him determine the highest altitude you can safely sustain. Then check the altitudes of the various cross-country train routes. It is quite possible that modern jet aircraft will maintain cabin altitude lower than those encountered on a train or auto trip across mountain ranges. The duration at the higher altitude may also be much shorter in pressurized aircraft.

Can a person on a stretcher travel by Amtrak?

Yes, in many cases. Amtrak requires ten days notice. The stretcher-borne passenger must book a suitable bedroom on the train and will be loaded through the window. Private arrangements must be made for the boarding, since Amtrak personnel will not lift or carry stretchers. Amtrak can arrange for a qualified medical attendant to accompany the traveler, at the traveler's expense.

Also see Trains in Part II, Section 3.

AUTOMOBILE

I am planning a car trip out West, but the route must be smooth, as I am neurologically sensitive to jarring.

Have one of the professional route-planning services (see the section on Cars in Part II, Section 1) map out your route. Specify that you want the smoothest highways. The services can help you avoid highway construction. You might also wish to sit on a foam-filled cushion.

AIR

Must a nonambulatory passenger who cannot get to the lavatory dehydrate before a flight and drink nothing during the flight?

Probably, although the duration of the flight is certainly a factor.

As a rule, this passenger should dehydrate for a minimum of six to eight hours. For some persons, however, that can carry dangers due to the nature of their condition. If you have a neurogenic bladder, for example, there is a need for a large water exchange in the bladder. Therefore, if you do dehydrate, when you get to your destination you must immediately force fluids in large amounts in order to wash the tract out quickly. Do *not* dehydrate if you have any kind of urinary infection. A nonambulatory passenger who is traveling with a companion may carry a urinal (or equivalent) to use in flight, which the companion can take to the lavatory in a little satchel or flight bag.

I have heard that doctors can prescribe a pill for nonambulatory travelers that prevents urination for the duration of a flight. What is the pill and should I take it?

Anti-diuretic pills are usually hormones. The pills must retain sodium to retain the water. I think that's interfering with human metabolism too much. There are also drugs, such as probanthine, which tend to reduce bladder contractions and are sometimes used to prevent urination for the duration of a flight. Excessive use of this drug can lead to abnormal retention of urine and should not be used except upon the advice of a physician. If you want to prevent urination for the duration of the flight, you have to know your own capacity. It is obvious that if you limit your fluid intake before the flight, and make sure that your bladder is completely empty just before the flight, you can then estimate the time before you have to void again. It is possible to dry yourself out enough to go through a six-hour flight, which is probably just about the maximum length of any flight within the United States. (And even if you have an eleven-hour flight from New York to Hawaii, you have a break in San Francisco, where you can use the airport restroom.) I think it is not safe to monkey around with the body's metabolism with a pill to prevent urination.

How does a nonambulatory man traveling alone, who is incontinent and uses a leg bag, manage during a flight of several hours?

Theoretically he should manage quite well if he has made sure that the bladder is empty at the onset and that he is completely dehydrated. There are large-size disposable leg bags that are sufficient for flights of almost any length. They can be discreetly detached (and replaced) under a blanket, sealed, placed in an air-sickness bag (found in the pocket of every seat) and given to the flight attendant to dispose of.

How can a nonambulatory person with poor bowel control fly?

Forty-eight hours before your flight, stop eating high fiber foods, such as salads or brans, in order to reduce the bulk. Make sure the bowel is empty before going on the trip. Some people may have to do so by enema. If you are overly concerned, there is nothing better to completely allay the activity of the bowel, which may be caused by anxiety, than a Lomotil pill. This is also good for any person whose bowels tend to be loose. Any nonambulatory individual who is afraid he will have a problem in this department might use Lomotil to reduce anxiety. In any case, it should be used only by prescription of your doctor.

Do you have any suggestions for nonambulatory air travelers who have had a colostomy?

Be sure to have a colostomy bag of sufficient size. It should *not* be changed during the flight.

Should I take a tranquilizer before flying?

If you suffer extreme anxiety while flying (not necessarily from fear of flying but from all the pressure that comes from finding the proper seat, getting yourself settled down, and so forth), there's no reason you shouldn't take a tranquilizer, as prescribed by your own doctor. Do not take tranquilizers in excessive amounts. One moderate-size tablet is sufficient for a whole trip. Do not drink alcoholic beverages if you have taken a tranquilizer.

Is it all right to drink alcohol while flying?

Generally speaking, *one* drink probably will not hurt you if you are in the habit of drinking. But do exercise moderation, because in an aircraft pressurized at 5,000 feet or so, one drink has the effect of two on the ground. If you are on any medication, check with your own physician to make sure that alcohol in combination with that medicine will not produce counter effects. Persons suffering from pulmonary conditions such as emphysema, chronic bronchitis, and asthma or prone to motion sickness are well advised not to drink during flights.

How can I prevent air sickness?

By and large, air travel tends to be very smooth, so the best thing to do—unless you have had previous experience with it—is not to anticipate it, and not bother. If you have had air sickness in the past, get a remedy from your own physician.

There are also some tips that might help: Choose a nonwindow seat in the center of the airplane just behind the left wing, since an airplane generally turns to that side in aerial traffic. (Note, however, that while seats over the wings are most stable, the airlines probably will not seat nonambulatory passengers there, since an emergency evacuation from that position would be via the more difficult emergency exit over a wing.) Eat a light meal *before* boarding and do not drink alcohol before or during the flight.

How do I adjust insulin to jet lag?

You should work out your timing and take it up with your physician, who will tell you precisely what to do. For example, a person flying from Hawaii to New York will experience a six-hour time difference. When it is 1 A.M. in Hawaii it is 7 A.M in New York. Thus, this traveler would not need a full normal dose of insulin his first morning in New York. Be sure to give the physician your specific itinerary.

I develop swelling during prolonged sitting in a car, or train, but especially on a plane. Any suggestions?

Have yourself fitted with a pair of good, one-way stretch elastic stockings or Supp-Hose. Do not wear constricting bands such as garters or elastic bands on pantyhose. If possible, walk up and down the aisle every hour. Use a footrest or small case or pillow under feet to avoid pressure of the seat against the back of your knees, which impedes return flow of blood from the feet. Flex and extend your feet periodically to pump the blood and if you can walk, do so every hour.

How can someone wearing a brace be more comfortable during a flight?

Loosen the pelvic band of the brace once you are settled in your seat (the same applies to cars and trains), just as you would loosen a belt or any constricting garment. Aside from digging in and causing discomfort, a tight brace can also cause gastrointestinal problems during a flight.

Does a synthetic hip (or other joint) register on the airport's security magnetometer?

The newer jobs have more plastic and less metal than those used in earlier operations and probably will not. But if you are traveling for the first time since your operation—or you know that yours does register—you might carry a letter from your surgeon stating that he performed such an operation. You can show this at the security check point. Or you can just spend an extra minute every time you fly and let the security staff scan you with a hand-held magnetometer.

Do the security magnetometers or electronic airline equipment, such as the ovens, affect a cardiac pacemaker?

According to Dr. C. C. Gullett, director of TWA medical services, cardiac pacemakers are not affected by the security magnetometer, nor by the airline's electronic equipment used in the United States. Some types of pacemakers are sensitive to the radiation field generated by electrical devices such as ignition systems of cars, lawnmowers, and some microwave ovens used in some sandwich vending shops that do not meet safe standards or are not properly maintained. Keeping some distance from such devices while in operation will normally avoid problems.

Should a person with an obstructive pulmonary disease fly?

That depends on the severity of the condition, whether it be emphysema, chronic bronchitis, asthma, or other. If your doctor says that you can function at the 5,000 to 8,000 feet above sea level, which the airplane is pressurized at, you should book a seat in the nonsmoking section of the plane at the same time you make your reservation. Carry a doctor's letter stating that a seat in nonsmoking is necessary.

A booklet, *Travel for the patient with chronic obstructive pulmonary disease*, contains thirty-six pages of health tips that concern this particular disorder. Among the topics covered are nerves, fatigue, jet lag, and altitude. The booklet is available for $1.25 from Rehabilitation Research & Training Center, George Washington University Medical Center, Ross Hall, Room 714, 2300 Eye Street, N.W., Washington, DC 20037.

If supplemental oxygen is needed, arrange in advance through airline reservation office (see the following question). The standard supplemental oxygen used on many commercial airplanes is four liters per minute. Frequently, in advanced obstructive lung disease, only one to two liters per minute supplemental oxygen is required to avoid suppression of the respiratory reflex mechanism.

How does a person who uses oxygen manage during a flight?

No personal oxygen supply is allowed in the cabin of the plane, but some airlines will supply oxygen for your use on board, provided they have advance notice of twenty-four to seventy-two hours, depending on the airline. Your personal physician would have to arrange this through the airline's medical department, and the airline would require a medical certificate to permit you to fly. You pay at the rate of about $40 *per flight coupon* to use oxygen provided by the airline. That is, every time you change planes, you pay an additional $40. Persons needing oxygen will probably be required to travel with an assistant capable of administering it.

Passenger-owned oxygen may be shipped as *cargo* (not baggage), provided it meets Federal Regulations (ask the airline) regarding approved containers, packing, marking, labeling, and quantity.

If you suffer from shortness of breath, be sure to request in advance that the airline have its wheelchair available to you for use in the terminal upon departure and arrival.

If prone to venous disease (thrombosis or phlebitis) how does one fly?

At every opportunity, when the aisle is free, walk up and down. In fact, *every* passenger should do this. Nobody should sit for a prolonged period of time, and even persons who normally do not have this condition may suffer from "passenger phlebitis" on a long flight. Every hour you should get up and walk briskly. You might do isometrics in your seat. This will develop the muscle pumps that keep the legs drained for persons suffering from thrombosis or phlebitis.

Lufthansa, the German airline, has published a booklet *Fitness in the Chair*, describing isometric exercise you can do while sitting. On Lufthansa's long-haul flights, a passenger can tune in on his headphones for special music to flex by. Here are samples from the booklet:

1. Tighten a muscle or group of muscles with about one-third of your maximum strength. Repeat six times in rhythm. Systematically do the thighs (left, right), buttocks (left, right), back, shoulders.

2. Clasp hands together, placing the palm against the slightly pulled-in abdomen. Tense stomach muscles, using two-thirds of your strength. Press hands firmly against tightened stomach muscles. Count to seven. Relax.

3. Grasp the left hand with the right, as if you wanted to shake hands with yourself. Squeeze with both hands, using two-thirds of your strength. Count to seven. Relax.

Now the question is how to get more legroom. It is obvious that legroom is normally constrictive in coach class and that first class may have somewhat more legroom. But wherever you are, the legroom is limited. Get a letter from your physician stating that you require a bulkhead seat. (The latter is also advisable for a person with a stiff knee or hip, artificial limb, or the like.) Bulkhead seats do not always have more legroom, however, and not all bulkhead seats recline.

Fitness in the Chair is available from Lufthansa German Airlines, Lufthansa Building, 1640 Hempstead Turnpike, East Meadow, NY 11554, 516-794-2020. By the way, the *chair* in the title is one that's behind a desk, but many tips might benefit anyone who sits all day in a wheelchair.

Can a stretcher-borne person fly?

Not all regular scheduled airlines (or aircraft) are set up to handle such passengers, but some do. There are also air ambulance services. See a full discussion of them in the Airline section in Part II of this book.

When is flying inadvisable?

Your doctor should consult the airline's doctor* where there are

* Among the airlines with full-time medical departments staffed by a doctor or doctors are American, Eastern, United, Pan Am, and TWA. National's medical department is staffed by a nurse. Western uses Air Medic as its consultant. The special services desk of an airline will refer you or your doctor to its medical department or consultant when necessary.

conditions and circumstances that would make flying inadvisable. These include: after a recent operation; with severe chronic heart, lung, or respiratory conditions; with an active ulcer; if a cast has been installed for less than twenty-four to forty-eight hours; if a jaw is wired; if requiring intravenous (IV) fluid during flight; if an infant less than seven days old; if suffering from sickle-cell disease or severe anemia; during treatment or after an eye operation; during the last month or two of pregnancy except with a physician's certificate issued within seventy-two hours of the flight stating the estimated date of birth (at press time, this is being contested by some feminist leaders).

The following conditions require careful consideration, and if persons suffering them are transported, they may need special handling, according to *Medical Criteria for Passenger Flying:* mediastinal tumors; extremely large unsupported hernias; intestinal obstruction; cranial diseases involving increased pressure; disturbance of the cerebrospinal circulation; tumor of the brain or fracture of the skull; injuries to the spinal cord; recent cerebrovascular accidents; and angioneurotic edema with a record of laryngeal involvement. Also persons who have sustained multiple fractures and persons wearing body casts.

Also note that the following persons will not be accepted by regular airlines: persons with contagious diseases; or persons with certain degrees of retardation or certain mental conditions, unless accompanied. The Federal Aviation Administration (FAA) has developed guidance material on the handling of certain mental patients. It is contained in Advisory Circular AC No. 120-34, 6/29/77, and is available from the U.S. Department of Transportation, FAA, Washington, DC 20591.

An Air Transport Association sponsored meeting on the carriage of handicapped persons (April 27, 1978) developed this list for recommendation to ATA members of types of passengers for whom advance notification might be required: nonambulatory; aero-stretcher; oxygen-assisted; respirator-assisted; infant (under seven days); deaf or blind with or without dogs; deaf-and-blind, with or without dogs; pregnant, ninth month; mentally handicapped, with escort; unable-to-be seated (nonstretcher); reclined-seat-required; nonstatic disease; requiring assistance; intravenous feeding required; jaw wired.

Single copies of *Medical Criteria for Passenger Flying,* prepared jointly by the American Medical Association (AMA) and the Aerospace Medical Association, are available. The booklet is somewhat out of date. It was published in 1961 and does not, for example, list operational factors for recent aircraft such as the DC-10 and Boeing 747, while it does give such information as the rate of climb and descent, the cabin pressure, and the like for the 707 and the DC-8 and other older aircraft. It also lists as restricted certain physical conditions that no longer apply. The book is of special interest to physicians, giving guiding principles for air travel which help determine "Is the patient able to travel or to be moved by *any* means?" Send requests to the AMA at 535 N. Dearborn St., Chicago, IL 60610, 312-751-6000.

Who needs a medical certificate to fly?

Airlines provide a form to be filled out by an examining physician before persons suffering from some of the more severe medical conditions can fly. Note again that anyone who prebooks oxygen for use during a flight must have a certificate. In some cases, an unaccompanied passenger, who is unable to visit the lavatory on his own or attend to other personal needs, may be asked for a doctor's certificate stating that the passenger can manage for the duration of his flight.

With U.S. airlines, however, medical certificates are generally related to health considerations only, not to mobility problems.

And while this book is primarily concerned with travel in the United States, it should be mentioned that many foreign airlines require anyone who has what even appears to be any kind of disability or mobility problem to have a medical certificate and, in many cases, an on-the-spot physical exam by an airport physician. They may also require you to hire an ambulance at your expense to board and deplane you.

3

LET'S PLAN A TRIP—RECAP

Allow enough time to plan thoroughly. This usually ranges from a few weeks, to a few months in the event you will visit a popular tourist destination at a peak holiday or vacation period.

Think about whom you want to travel with. Will you travel alone, or with friends or family? Independently, or on a group tour? Mainstream or go on an organized tour for handicapped travelers?

Decide where you would like to go (try to narrow it down to two or three possibilities) or the type of vacation you would enjoy. Roughly budget your time and money.

Consult a travel agent or contact the individual suppliers (airlines, ship lines, hotels, and the like) you will work with for preliminary information.

Gather as much information as possible on the place or places you are considering. Compare facilities, attractions, and costs. Which will it be?

Have your agent book your trip, or do it yourself, getting written confirmation from hotels, sightseeing companies, and the like where it seems advisable.

Working with the tourist literature you have collected, determine an accurate budget for your trip, and set up an itinerary.

About two weeks prior to departure, decide on your wardrobe and suitcases and shop for anything you will need. Make a list of every thing you plan to take and check it off the day you pack.

Have a doctor's checkup if it is in order.

The final week before departure:

- Buy enough medicine to last for the duration of the trip.
- Take out special trip insurance through your travel agent or an insurance company.
- Buy traveler's checks and withdraw from the bank the cash you wish to take.
- Pick up your tickets and confirmations or have your travel agent send them over.
- Give your friends or family an address and phone number where you can be reached (and take their numbers). If you are touring, leave a copy of your day-by-day itinerary.

The day before departure:

- Pack. Put tickets, traveler's checks, medicine and things you will need en route in your pocket, purse or hand luggage.
- Get a good night's sleep.

The day of departure:

- Secure your house or apartment against break-ins. (A day or two before you should arrange to stop milk and paper deliveries. Ask your local police department for other suggestions so there are no tip-offs that your house is unoccupied.)
- Allow yourself sufficient time to get to the airport, pier or train station, taking into account rush hour or weekend traffic and an early arrival if you will be preboarded.
- Check in.
- Use the restroom if you will be confined to your seat.
- Go to your boarding gate.

You're off.

APPENDIX

International References

TRANSLATOR

Contact Rehabilitation International USA (RIUSA), 20 W. 40th St., New York, NY 10018, attention of Ed Rust, for information on availability of multilingual translator of terms and phrases used by disabled persons (e.g., "Is there a ramp?"). Translator pamphlet is being prepared by an Englishman in several languages, including English, French, German, and Spanish.

HOME VISITS

By writing to RIUSA (above), you can have your name put on a watch list for an international home visit exchange program now being developed in conjunction with Mobility International, which encompasses travel/rehab organizations from sixty-two nations.

MOBILITY INTERNATIONAL

An international organization which has links with most European, Asian, and North American countries for the promotion of travel and exchange for the handicapped (see item immediately above). Mobility International has an international library as well as lists of contacts for persons wishing to visit other countries. Specific inquiries are welcome. Mobility International, Central Bureau for Educational Visits and Exchanges, 43 Dorset St., London W1H 3FN, England (telephone 01 486 5101, cable Edvisex London, Telex 21386 CBE-VEX G).

PEOPLE-TO-PEOPLE

Contact People-to-People, 1028 Connecticut Ave., N.W., #610, Washington, DC 20036, 202-785-0755, for exchange programs for the handicapped with contacts in thirty countries.

Note: Whenever there is a charge for one of the books listed below send the payment in international postage coupons that can be bought at a post office. The price conversions in U.S. dollars below are offered here as an approximation of what the books and booklets will cost. Because of the fluctuation of the U.S. dollar abroad, it is advisable to work out the actual cost based on the rate of exchange at the time you order. Banks, travel agencies, and some newspapers are sources of the latest exchange rates. The publications are often shipped by surface mail and take a month or longer to arrive. While some books are available in a foreign language only, they are often easy to use because of codes.

AFRICA, EAST

Lindblad Travel, specialists in adventure trips, is introducing (probably in the last quarter of 1978) a variation of its East African Wing Safari to the game parks for persons with limited mobility. Lindblad Travel, 133 E. 55th St., New York, NY 10022, 212-751-2300.

AUSTRALIA

Sydney for the Handicapped, Australian Council for Rehabilitation of Disabled, Cleaveland House, corner Bedford & Buckingham Sts., Surry Hills, New South Wales, 2010, telephone 69-5358. *A*

Guide to Perth for the Handicapped, W.A. Committee on Access for the Disabled, c/o Royal Perth (Rehab) Committee on Access for the Disabled, c/o Royal Perth (Rehab) Hospital, Shenton Park, W.A. 6008, telephone 81 2333, ext. 264. *Melbourne for the Handicapped,* Victorian Association of Occupational Therapists, 24 Golf Rd., Melbourne, 3167, Australia.

AUSTRIA

Mobility Tours, c/o Egnatia Tours, Piaristengasse 60, A—1082 Wien, P.O.B. 19, telephone (0222) 43 97 32, Telex 01 2301 egnat, organizes tours of Vienna for handicapped tourists.

BELGIUM

Bâtiments Accessibles aux handicapes en chaise roulante (*Buildings Accessible to the Handicapped in Wheelchairs*), French, F50 ($1.50), Welfare de la Croix-Rouge de Belgique, 93, chaussee de Vleurgat, 1050, Brussels, Belgium. *Accueil des Handicapes* (*Welcome Handicapped*), a guide to train travel in Belgium. French. From address above. *Belgium Hotels,* Belgian National Tourist Office, 720 Fifth Ave., New York, NY 10019, 212-582-1750, an overall hotel guide showing wheelchair symbols. Additional information on travel for the handicapped in Belgium available from Belgian Clearing House, J. M. Lorand, Grand Rue 231, B-6000, Charleroi, Belgium.

BRITISH ISLES

Guide for the Disabled for England, Scotland, and Ireland, Publications Division, The Automobile Association, Fanum House, Basingstoke, Hants, RG21 2EA, England, 75p ($1.50). *Holidays for the Physically Handicapped,* The Royal Association for Disability and Rehabilitation, 25 Mortimer St., London WIN 8AB, England, telephone 01 637 5400, more than 600 pages listing holiday plans and specially equipped holiday homes for disabled tourists. Includes a classified section; about £2.63 ($5.00) with postage. Also *Oxford for the Disabled* at 35p ($0.70). General information for the handicapped, Saga Senior Citizens Holidays Ltd., 119 Sandgate Rd., Folkestone,

Kent CT20 2BN, England, telephone 0303 57300, Telex 96213, also arranges holidays in Margate, Folkestone, Deal, Dover, Colchester, Torquay and the Devonshire countryside. British Airports Authority, 2 Buckingham Gate, London SW1 E6JL, England, telephone 01 834 6621, publishes leaflets containing maps and guides under separate titles, *Who looks after who at . . . ?* for Heathrow, Gatwick, and Stansted (London), as well as Prestwick, Edinburgh, Aberdeen, and Glasgow (Scotland). *Care in the Air*, Civil Aviation Authority, Greville House, 37 Gratton Rd., Cheltenham, Glos. GL50 2BN, England. Advice for handicapped passengers.

England—London for the Disabled by Freda Bruce Lockhart, British Travel Bookshop, 680 Fifth Ave., New York, NY 10019, $1.90. *Access to Public Conveniences*, 30p, plus 50p postage ($1.55), and guide to London's Underground stations, 19p, plus 19p postage ($0.75), both available from The Royal Association for Disability and Rehabilitation, address above.

Ireland—Guide to Dublin for the Disabled, National Rehabilitation Board, 24–25 Clyde Rd., Dublin 4, Ireland.

Scotland—Disabled Visitors and *Elderly Visitors*, accommodations and facilities, Scottish Tourist Board, 25 Ravelston Terrace, Edinburgh, EH4 3EU, Scotland.

Wales—Disabled Visitors Guide, Wales Tourist Board, P.O. Box 151, W.D.O., Cardiff CE5 1XS, England, 25p, plus postage ($1.00).

Jersey—Access in Jersey, 68B Castlebar Rd., Ealing, London W5, England (a $5 donation suggested).

CANADA

The Fourteenth World Congress of Rehabilitation International, a network of rehabilitation agencies in more than sixty countries, will be held in Winnipeg, Manitoba, June 22 to 27, 1980. The conference site will be the Winnipeg Convention Center, which was chosen because of its accessibility. For information contact C. H. Flintoft, co-chairman, Winnipeg Committee, P.O. Box 1980, Winnipeg R3C 3R3, Manitoba, Canada. The official travel agent for the conference is P. Lawson Travel.

Manitoba Vacation Guide 1977–78, Manitoba Government Travel, 200 Vaughan St., Winnipeg R3C 1T5, Manitoba, Canada, lists accessible accommodations and has a map of the province. *A Guide to Kingston for the Handicapped*, Zonta Club of Kingston, 8 Birch Ave., Kingston, Ontario, Canada. *Le Québec en Chaise Roulante* (*Quebec in a Wheelchair*), in French and English, a travel guide to the province of Quebec for the handicapped and *Accessibility Guide for Sherbrooke and Vicinity*, $2 surface mail or $3 airmail, both available from Guide du Québec, 1725 rue Dunant, Sherbrooke, Quebec, Canada, attention of Henriette Germain. A list of "Accessible Places for Wheelchairs" for Toronto and Ontario, Canadian Paraplegic Association, 520 Sutherland Dr., Toronto M4G 3V9, Ontario, Canada. *Transportation in Canada: A Guide for the Disadvantaged*, Transport Canada, from Research and Development Center, 1000 Sherbrooke St. W., P.O. Box 549, Pl. de l'Aviation, Montreal H3A 2R3, Quebec, Canada, is a useful handbook with excellent airport maps, French and English.

The Day Care Rehab Programme, Chedoke Continuing Care Centre, Sanatorium Rd., M.P.O. Box 590, Hamilton L8N 3L6, Ontario, Canada, 416-388-0240, will answer specific questions on vacation accessibility in Canada.

DENMARK

Handicapped Visitors Are Welcome in Denmark, National Association of Handicapped in Denmark, Landsforeningen AF Vanføre, Hans Knudsens Plads 1, 2100 Copenhagen Ø, Denmark, telephone 01 29 35 350. Danish National Tourist Office, 75 Rockefeller Plaza, New York, NY 10019, 212-582-2802, periodically releases information on vacation possibilities for the handicapped.

FRANCE

Travel Anyway, a guidebook for France for the physically handicapped. French and English, listed according to region, with a classified section. 380 pages. From Comité National Français de Liaison pour la Readaptation des Handicapes, 38, Bd. Raspail, 75007 Paris, France, telephone 222 33 96; 49F30 includes postage ($10.00). *Michelin Guide* (Red) to France uses a symbol to connote accessible hotels. Available at leading bookstores. *Assistance to disabled persons*, for Orly Airport and Charles de Gaulle Airport. English. Both available from Headquarters, 291, Bd. Raspail, 75675 Paris, France, CEDEX 14 (telephone 326 10 00). *Access in Paris*, 80 pages, and *Loire Guide*. English. 68B Castlebar Rd., Ealing, London W5, England (a contribution of $4 [surface mail] or $6 [air mail] each is suggested). *Guide des Vacances pour Handicapes* (*Vacation Guide for the Handicapped*), F30 ($6), and *Guide des Sports* (*Sports Guide*), 17F75 ($3.60), CIDJ, 101, Quai Branly, 75 740 Paris, France, CEDEX 15, telephone 566 40 20, Telex CIDJ 250 907 F.

GERMANY, WEST

Ferienführer—"Hilfe für Behinderte" (*Travel Guide—"Aids for the Handicapped"*), general tourist information for the country. German, Dutch, French and English. From BAG, Hilfe für Behinderte e.V., Kirchfeldstrasse 149, Düsseldorf, Federal Republic of Germany. *Campingführer für Behinderte* (*Camping Guide for the Handicapped*), Postfach 1521, 65oo Mainz. A list of guidebooks to German places, including some of the smaller towns, is available from: Deutsche Vereinigung für die Rehabilitation Behinderter e.V., 6900 Heidelberg 1, Friedrich-Ebert-Anlage 9, Federal Republic of Germany. Landeshauptstadt Düsseldorf, Jugendamt, Stadtverwaltung Amt 51—Postfach 1120, 4000 Düsseldorf 1, Federal Republic of Germany, will answer specific questions on accessibility. At press time a travel guide for the handicapped to Düsseldorf is being prepared. *Informationen für Behinderte* (*Information for the Handicapped*) includes a section on barrier free hotels, museums, cabarets, etc., plus vacation possibilities in Berlin. German. From Der Senator für Gesundheit und Umweltschutz, An der Urania 12–14, 1000 Berlin 30. *Behinderten—Wegweiser* and *Erganzung 1* (*Tips for the Handicapped* and *Supplement 1*), Kontaktstelle für Körperbehinderte und Langzeitkranke, Eschersheimer Landstrasse 567, 6000 Frankfurt Am Main 50, Federal Republic of Germany (tel 5802-257). German. Includes travel guides to the city. Supplement contains a medical listing of doctors, drugstores, etc. *München—Stadtführer für Behinderte* (*Munich—City Guide for the Handicapped*) VdK, Landesverband Bayern e.V., 8000 München 34, Federal Republic of Germany.

ISRAEL

Jerusalem—A Guide for the Handicapped. Hebrew only. School of Occupational Therapy, Mount Scopus, Jerusalem, Israel, telephone 287530.

ITALY

Have Wheels: Will Travel, a guide for the handicapped to Rome. Educational Solutions Inc., 80 Fifth Ave., New York, NY 10011. $8.06 including postage, handling, and taxes.

JAPAN

Contact Japan Charity Plate Association, Han El Building, 2-2 1 Chome Shinjuka, Shinjuka-Ku, Tokyo, Japan; or Takeo Noda, Management Consulting Center for Employment of Handicapped, Tokyo Yo Fuku Kaikan Building, 13 Hachiman-Cho, Shinjuku-Ku, Tokyo 162, Japan.

THE NETHERLANDS

Holidays for People with Physical or Sensory Disabilities, an excellent English-language guide which canvasses travel for the handicapped. Includes information on other European countries as well as the Netherlands. Ranges from Rhine River cruses to farmhouse vacations. Available from Nederlandse Vereniging voor Revalidatie, 136 Oudegracht, Utrecht, The Netherlands.

NORWAY-SWEDEN

The Norwegian and the Swedish National Tourist Offices, 75 Rockefeller Plaza, New York, NY 10019 (212-582-2802) offer periodic information on travel in Norway and Sweden including the following: Arevidden Hotel at Are, a hotel for the handicapped at Bjornange, Sweden (on Lake Aresjon); accessible hotels and boarding houses in Sweden; the Erling Stordahl "Culture Garden" for the blind and handicapped at Skjeberg, Norway. *Access in Norway*, a guidebook for the disabled, 68B Castlebar Rd., Ealing, London W1 ($5 contribution suggested). Klantours Scandinavia AB, Stureplan 19, S 111 45 Stockholm, Sweden (tel 08/20 30 93) conducts a fifteen-day escorted tour with North American departures for visits to Sweden, Finland, and Norway for the handicapped (information from Norwegian-Swedish National Tourist Offices, above). The following organizations can provide information for handicapped persons in Norway: Norges Vanforelag, Nils Hansensvei 2, Oslo 6, Norway; Vestlandske Vanforelag, Daniel Hansensgate 16, N-5000 Bergen, Norway; Trondelag Krets av Norges Vanforelag, Kongensgate 72, N-7000 Trondheim, Norway. Stockholms Socielförvaltning, Hemserviceavdelningen Handikappbyrån, Fack, 106 64 Stockholm, Sweden (tel 08/68 05 00 or locally 68 05 00), answers telephone inquiries from handicapped persons.

SWEDEN

See Norway-Sweden, above.

SWITZERLAND

Hotelführer für Behinderte (*Hotel Guide for the Handicapped*), Swiss National Tourist Office, 608 Fifth Ave., New York, NY 10020, 212-757-5944, a sixty-page guide in French, German, and English that is all-inclusive, with a listing of spas indicating "cures" for different maladies. Altitudes are noted. Additional information available from Schweizerischer, Invaliden-Verband, Zentralsitz in Olten, Swiss Association for the Handicapped, P.O. Box 357, Olten 46-1809, Switzerland, telephone 062 212242.

TUNISIA

Contacts: Croissant Rouge Tunisien, 19, rue d'Angleterre, Tunis, Tunisia, telephone 240 630; Union Nationale des Aveugles de Tunisie, 81, avenue de Londres, Tunis, Tunisia, telephone 252 005; Tunisian Association of the Assistance to the Deaf, 108 rue de Yougoslavie, Tunis, Tunisia.

INDEX